Jung and the Shadow of Anti-Semitism

On The Hudson
Jung
BOOK SERIES

The Jung on the Hudson Book Series was instituted by The New York Center for Jungian Studies in 1997. This ongoing series is designed to present books that will be of interest to individuals of all fields, as well as mental health professionals, who are interested in exploring the relevance of the psychology and ideas of C. G. Jung to their personal lives and professional activities.

For more information about the annual Jung on the Hudson seminars, this series, and the New York Center for Jungian Studies contact: Aryeh Maidenbaum, Ph.D., 27 North Chestnut St., Suite 3, New Paltz, NY 12561, telephone (845) 256-0191, fax (845) 256-0196.

For more information about becoming part of this series, contact: Nicolas-Hays, Inc., P. O. Box 1126, Berwick, ME 03901-1126, telephone: 207-698-1041, fax: 207-698-1042, e-mail: info@nicolashays.com.

Jung and the Shadow of Anti-Semitism

Aryeh Maidenbaum, editor

Nicolas-Hays, Inc.
Berwick, ME

First published in 2002 by Nicolas-Hays, Inc.
P. O. Box 1126
Berwick, ME 03901-1126
Distributed to the trade by Red Wheel/Weiser, LLC
P. O. Box 612
York Beach, ME 03910-0612
www.redwheelweiser.com

Library of Congress Cataloging-in-Publication Data

Jung and the shadow of anti-Semitism / Aryeh Maidenbaum, editor.
p. cm.
Includes bibliographical references.
ISBN 0-89254-040-0
1. Jung, C. G. (Carl Gustav), 1875-1961–Views on Jews. 2. Judaism and psychoanalysis–History. 3. Antisemitism–History–20th century. 4. Psychoanalysis–History. I. Maidenbaum, Aryeh.
BF109.J8 J86 2002
150.19'54'092--dc21 2002013023

TP

Cover design by Kathryn Sky-Peck
Type design by Phillip Augusta
Typeset in Minion
Printed in Canada

09 08 07 06 05 04 03 7 6 5 4 3 2 1

The paper used in this publication meets the minimum requirements of the American National Standard for Information Sciences—Permanence of Paper for Printed Library Materials Z39.48–1992 (R1997).

Contents

Credits

The editors thank the following publishers for permission to reprint material copyrighted or controlled by them:

Shambalah Publications for the following chapters reprinted from Aryeh Maidenbaum and Stephen A. Martin, eds., *Lingering Shadows: Jungians, Freudians, and Anti-Semitism* (Boston: Shambhala Publications, 1991), copyright © 1991 C. G. Jung Foundation for Analytical Psychology: "Jung and Anti-Semitism" by Paul Roazen; "The Nazis and C. G. Jung by Geoffrey Cocks"; "On the Relationship between Erich Neumann and C. G. Jung" by Micha Neumann; "Lingering Shadows: A Personal Perspective" by Aryeh Maidenbaum; "Scapegoating: The Double Cross," by Anne Belford Ulanov; "Reflections on Jung and the Collective Anti-Semitism" by Adolf Guggenbühl-Craig; "Jung, Anti-Semitism, and the Nazi Regime" by Marga Speicher; "Thoughts and Memories of C. G. Jung" by Werner H. Engel (copyright © 1991 Werner H. Engel); and the Appendices by Michael Vannoy Adams and Jay Sherry, here revised and updated.

Princeton University Press and Routledge for excerpts from the *Collected Works of C. G. Jung*, trans. R. F. C. Hull, Bollingen Series XX: vol. 7, *Two Essays on Analytical Psychology*, copyright 1953, 1966 by Princeton University Press; vol. 10, *Civilization in Transition*, copyright 1964, 1970 by Princeton University Press; vol. 18, *The Symbolic Life*, copyright 1950, 1953, 1955, 1958, 1959, 1963, 1968, 1969, 1970, 1973, 1976 by Princeton University Press; and for excerpts from *C. G. Jung Speaking: Interviews and Encounters*, ed. William McGuire and R. F. C. Hull, Bollingen Series XCVII, copyright 1977 by Princeton University Press. Reprinted by permission of Princeton University Press and Routledge.

Alfred A. Knopf, Inc., for excerpts from *Moses and Monotheism* by Sigmund Freud, translated by Katherine Jones, copyright 1939 by Alfred A. Knopf, Inc., and renewed 1967 by Ernst L. Freud and Anna Freud. Reprinted by permission of the publisher.

Pantheon Books, Inc., and HarperCollins Publishers for excerpts from *Memories, Dreams, Reflections* by C. G. Jung, recorded and edited by Aniela Jaffé, translated by Richard and Clara Winston, translation copyright 1961, 1962, 1963 by Random House, Inc. Reprinted by permission of Pantheon Books, a division of Random House, Inc., and of HarperCollins Publishers Limited.

The American Psychological Association for "Jung, Kabbalah and Judaism" by Sanford L. Drob, copyright © 1999 The Educational Publishing Foundation, reprinted with kind permission, first published in the *History of Psychology* 2, (1999), 102–118

The Allen Dulles letters in Chapter 4 come from Box Numbers 35, 39, 44, 50, 53, and 55, the Allen W. Dulles Papers, Seeley G. Mudd Manuscript Library, Princeton University. Published with permission of Princeton University Library.

Acknowledgments

First and foremost, I would like to dedicate this book to my wonderful, treasured children, Leah, Barak, Hepzibah, and Jordana, who have been with me on several continents while I pursued my studies and career. They are all a blessing and a gift to me. I would also like to thank my wife Diana Rubin for her encouragement and support. Notwithstanding having her own full career and psychotherapy practice, she has been a loving wife, mother to our child, partner and *femme inspiratrice* to me in my life, my varied and many projects, and work. Knowing my inner need to complete this book—work that took away from our family many a weekend and evening—her understanding and support for the importance of this topic for me never wavered. I could not have done this without her support, help and love.

Over the years, and thanks to my Jungian analysis, my life has been enriched immeasurably by my exposure to the psychology and ideas of Jung. Through my Jungian analysis and work, I have come to value and understand Judaism in a way I never could within the confines of the Orthodox Jewish world. The two most important individuals for me in this exploration have been Dr. Rivkah Schaerf Kluger and Dr. Rene Malamud. Although Rivkah passed away years ago, her spirit still inspires me and keeps me connected to my Jewish roots. Fortunately for me, Rene continues to provide me with friendship, support, and insight while also shedding light on many an archetypal aspect of Judaism I would not have understood on my own. I am grateful to have him—at first as analyst and then as dearest friend and mentor—in my life.

Several friends and colleagues merit particular thanks in helping me birth this book. Jay Sherry, a diligent psycho-historian and individual with a deep, long-standing commitment to understanding Jung's personal and professional psychology, was the first person I turned to when deciding whether to undertake a new edition of *Lingering Shadows*. His new, original chapter on Jung's earlier years, as well as his agreement to update the chronology and comments of Jung on this topic, were essential elements in insuring the book's contemporary relevance.

Additionally, within the context of the first edition of *Lingering Shadows*, the assistance of Robert Hinshaw, close friend and colleague, was crucial. Dr. Hinshaw helped arrange important interviews with several of the first generation of Jungians, especially Aniela Jaffé and Sigmund Hurwitz. These individuals, along with C. A. Meier and others we interviewed, represented a generation of people who knew Jung personally—a generation that, unfortunately, is all but gone now. Bob, who I first met soon after my arrival at the Jung Institute in Zurich in 1977, has always been an important friend and colleague for me. His knowledge and familiarity with the first generation Jungians, as well as the material we were dealing with, was indispensable. And, as always, his generosity in sharing his resources and contacts was a gift.

Another close friend and colleague whom I would like to thank is Dr. Stephen Martin. His friendship, insight, and creativity—which he has offered me for the past 25 years—have been important cornerstones for my work as a Jungian. Dr. Martin, co-editor of *Lingering Shadows: Jungians, Freudians and Anti-Semitism*, graciously deferred to me in this new publication. While his analytic practice, fatherhood, activities in the Philadelphia Association of Jungian Analysts and expertise and involvement as author and astute collector of the works of Paul Klee and Archibald Knox left him no time to co-edit this book with me, his encouragement from the sidelines was heartening. Indeed, his friendship and support for this work, one which clearly built on the contributions he also made to the original volume of *Lingering Shadows*, were of great importance to me.

Finally, last but far from least, one woman in particular who believed in the importance of this project, and enthusiastically encouraged me to insure that this topic always be in print, was Betty Lundsted—publisher of Nicolas-Hays. Without Betty's push, initial help, valuable contribution, and support for our Jung on the Hudson book series, this edition would never have come into being. Superb, unrelentingly honest, and enthusiastic editor and friend, Betty was always true to her belief that, come what may, this uncomfortable-as-it-was subject was relevant to any discussion on the life and work of Carl

Jung. Betty's untimely death before I was able to complete my task is a huge loss for me, personally, as well as for the world in general. While I feel extreme sadness that she could not witness the publication of this book, I feel fortunate that her work is being continued by Donald Weiser and Valerie Cooper—who I would like to thank for insuring that this book has come to light.

Preface

When I first wrote and spoke about the subject of Jung and anti-Semitism, I noted that the seed for this book was planted in Jerusalem, germinated in Zurich, and blossomed in New York. Some 25 years ago, while applying for a postdoctoral grant from the Hebrew University to study at the C. G. Jung Institute in Switzerland, I was unexpectedly confronted with what I have now come to understand is the shadowy specter of Jung's "Jewish connection." Basically, I was told that Jung was an anti-Semite at best and, in fact, quite possibly a Nazi sympathizer, if not an active party member.

At the time, I was in analysis with Rivkah Schaerf Kluger, who then lived in Haifa, Israel. Dr. Kluger, a widely-respected scholar and author, had herself been a student and analysand of Jung. Through her testimony, and the corroboration of other professors at the Hebrew University who had known Jung, I was able to rebut these accusations and convince both myself and university officials that the charges were unjust. I was ultimately granted the award and spent the next three years studying at the C. G. Jung Institute of Zurich.

Nevertheless, during my years of study and training, I began reading some of Jung's statements and became increasingly uncomfortable with my own ignorance of the topic. Moreover, Jung's public and private comments left me feeling that there was more to this than meets the eye. Realizing that the help I'd received personally from my Jungian analysis with Rivkah, combined with a passionate desire to train as a Jungian analyst, had propelled me to plow ahead as if caught in an archetypal force, I resolved to continue researching this topic until I felt satisfied I had all the facts straight. A fellow student and friend, Stephen Martin, shared my concern and curiosity, and we spent many an hour in Zurich discussing various aspects of Jung's work, his personal life history, and his attitudes toward and involvements with Jews during the 1930s and later. Helpful to us was the contact we had with individuals who had known Jung personally as well as the published and archival material available in Zurich.

Over the course of time, both Dr. Martin and I completed our studies, returned to the United States, established analytical practices, and became actively involved in the Jungian world—Dr. Martin in Philadelphia, and myself in New York. What struck us both was that the subject of Jung and anti-Semitism kept cropping up over and over. We found, for example, that many of our non-Jungian professional colleagues who knew little or nothing about Jung and his work cited as a reason for not teaching Jung's psychology in their respective Universities (thereby dismissing his unique contributions), the charge that he was a Nazi or an anti-Semite. Moreover, among the public at large, especially the academic world, many found their genuine interest in Jung's psychology and ideas threatened by accusations revolving around Jung's alleged anti-Semitism.

Over the years, we came to realize that while rebuttals have been written by Jungians themselves addressing this issue, there was no systematic effort to examine it in an objective, scholarly, and balanced manner. The literature on this topic ranged from idolatry to witch hunting, from those who felt Jung could do no wrong to others who blatantly condemned him without familiarizing themselves with the factual material.

Dr. Martin and I spent several years organizing and gathering material for the first international conference that was held on this subject. Sponsored by the C. G. Jung Foundation of New York, and co-sponsored by The Postgraduate Center for Mental Health and the Union of American Hebrew Congregations, it was the first public, Jungian-sponsored, forum to involve serious academicians as well as Jungian and non-Jungian analysts who objectively discussed the issue and its implications. Ultimately, a book—*Lingering Shadows: Jungians, Freudians and Anti-Semitism*—emerged, which included many of the presentations of the conference as well as encompassed all of Jung's pertinent statements on the topic that we could find.

At that time, I delivered a presentation of my own on this subject—a presentation that publicly revealed a secret document I had come across in my research. The revelation of this document, a quota on Jewish membership in the Analytical Psychology Club of Zurich, fostered a great deal of internal controversy in the Jungian world as the Club was known as an organization inspired by and closely connected to Jung. It was a paper I did not want to write, on a topic I did not want to deal with, about a man whose psychology and ideas have played a most important part of my life.

I was raised in a strong Orthodox Jewish background, and to this day Israel, Jewish history, culture, and tradition are a paramount aspect of the world I live in. Jung's psychology, in fact, helped me reconnect to my own Jewish roots and become a better Jew in the process. To have to deal with confronting this volatile and emotional issue of Jung and the shadow of anti-Semitism was not an easy task then, and indeed, still is a difficult topic for me to this day.

It was pleasing and gratifying, both personally and on behalf of the conference sponsors, that we were able to accomplish the task of having Jungians, Freudians and scholars alike examine this issue in a substantive manner. Additionally, as an added and unexpected bonus resulting from the interest generated by the New York conference, the International Association for Analytical Psychology (IAAP, the official, international, organization of Jungian analysts) added a special workshop on this topic at its August 1989 conference in Paris. It was the first time that this topic was aired by the international Jungian community—an important development that eventually led to the Analytical Psychology Club in Zurich apologizing for the imposition of a 10% quota on Jewish membership that was in existence until 1950. This was a long, involved, and sensitive process that Jungian analyst Dr. Jerome Bernstein (who was the person who should be credited for having the IAAP put this workshop in its program) describes in chapter 9 of this book.

Jung often pointed out that great lights have great shadows. Carl Gustav Jung, being one the most important figures in the development of the field of psychology, had both. Nevertheless, in the end, if one goes to the trouble of sifting out all the material at hand, one comes to realize that he was neither guilty of most of the accusations hurled at him nor wholly innocent of prejudice, especially so in the early stages of his career. When *Lingering Shadows* was first published, we trusted and hoped that this book would contribute to the important task at hand, that of lifting Jung's important message from the shadowy place to which it has been relegated and casting light on the many insights he has given us into the human psyche. Unfortunately, or perhaps fortunately, *Lingering Shadows* is no longer in print, which was one of the primary factors and impetus for me to compile and edit this new edition.

Years ago, I remember coming across Jung's comment that every generation should exceed the one that came before it as it is privileged to sit on the shoulders of the previous generation. It is my fondest hope that this edition will indeed serve that function as well in its examination of Jung and the shadow of anti-Semitism.

Aryeh Maidenbaum, Ph.D.

Introduction by Dr. Stephen A. Martin

In the more than 10 years since the original publication of *Lingering Shadows* there has been no lessening of the pertinence and persistence of the complicated question of anti-Semitism in relationship to C. G. Jung, the man, and Jung, the psychologist. In fact, in a world far more multi-cultural and conscious of and sensitive to issues of racial and psychological, political, and national differences, clarifying Jung's position and freeing his psychology of the unconscious to be a creative force in the individuation of our world seems essential. By revisiting this difficult issue in a far more mature and expanded fashion with new information, new research, and new and varied voices raises the debate far above cults of personality and illuminates a darkness we Jungians call "shadow" so that this new volume becomes a tool for greater consciousness and dialogue. To this end, I am proud to have my introduction included in it.

There has been an obvious collective shift in the debate about Jung and anti-Semitism over the last 20 years. On more than one occasion while I was doing my doctoral work in a major Eastern medical school in the 1970s, upon learning that I was a "Jungian," professors and students alike confronted me with a smug question that was really an accusation: "Wasn't Jung a Nazi?" Now, in 2002, I no longer hear such accusations. Instead, Jung and his psychology have entered the mainstream to the point where books by Jungian authors hug the tops of best seller lists, and he is being cited more and more in a range of literature from every academic, clinical, and popular avenue. In some respects, I myself feel smug in having trusted the inherent value of Jungian psychology and expected its versatility and relevance to grow, and with this growth a lessening of interest in slanderous accusation by both the informed professional and public world. Perhaps aiding this shift has been the ousting of orthodox psychoanalysis from its sacrosanct position as "the one true depth psychology" as other psychologies prove their greater theoretical and clinical value. Thus, psychoanalysis is no longer a major engine propelling this accusation that, as my introduction pointed out, began with Freud and his closest associates.

In the end, whatever the reasons for this shift, now is the time for seeing through the literal questions of "Was or wasn't Jung this or that," to move beyond accusation and defense and to enter a consciousness wide enough to recognize that every one of us carries the darkness we project onto others. If we can do that, as Jung tried to do then, like the black sun in the alchemical night, our darkness illuminates the path to deeper relationship to our own depths and to those of our human family.

The early years of this century were legend-making times. New ground was being broken in every field, and creative personalities were redefining reality at every turn. Nowhere was the power of this fruitful time more obvious than in the field of depth psychology. As an assistant under the guidance of Eugen Bleuler at Burgholzli, the cantonal psychiatric hospital in Zurich, Jung was one of the leaders of a growing Swiss cadre of professionals interested in psychoanalysis. He had read Freud's *Interpretation of Dreams* several times and had incorporated Freud's ideas about repression into his own research. Thus, by the time Jung first contacted Freud by sending him an inscribed copy of his *Studies in Word Association* around the end of 1905, he was well acquainted with Freud's work. The personal and professional relationship between the two men blossomed after this initial exchange, as is well documented.[1] Here I wish to focus on just a few aspects of their collaboration, for the purpose of navigating the treacherous waters of accusation and counteraccusation.

Freud was drawn to Jung because of the younger man's keen and inquiring mind and his understanding of psychoanalysis—and because he was *not* Jewish. On a number of occasions Freud commented that by enlisting Jung, the son of a Swiss Reformed pastor, psychoanalysis would escape the danger of becoming a "Jewish national affair."[2] Moreover, both men were drawn passionately into what appears to have been a father-son relationship that was characterized by massive projection and the potential for both creative partnership and destructive competition and enmity.[3]

Freud and Jung were collaborators of the closest kind. Exchanging hundreds of letters and many visits, they also shared the limelight internationally, traveling together to the United States in 1909 to advance the standing of psychoanalysis. Freud supported Jung's presidency of the International Psychoanalytical Association and the editorship of the *Jahrbücher für psychoanalytische und psycho pathologische Forschungen,* and he regularly looked forward to Jung's contributions to the growing field. Jung, for his part, viewed Freud with great esteem as "the first man of real importance" in the field of depth psychology.[4]

Despite this seeming compatibility, there was much that separated the two men from the start.[5] They disagreed on the value of the occult in psychological life: Freud saw occultism as regressive and dangerous, while Jung was strongly drawn to the psychological mysteries that it might contain. Of greater importance, however, was their difference over the role of sexuality in psychic functioning. At first cautiously then more openly, Jung expressed doubt about Freud's theory of the libido and his insistence on the primacy of the sexual drive. Jung envisioned libido as a more generic life urge that appears not only in sexuality but finds legitimate, primary expression in creative, intellectual, and spiritual activities as well.

On a more personal level, Jung had obvious difficulty acceding to Freud's paternal authority. Having been a rebellious son who at an early age saw through his own father's doubts about his religious beliefs, Jung had trouble acquiescing to his role as "adopted son" and "heir" to Freud and the expectations that he would follow in his mentor-father's footsteps.[6] Clearly both men were locked in a dialogue of projection; neither was to blame for the situation, nor was one more misguided than the other. As we have learned, complexes occur in an interpersonal field: when activated, they draw the individuals inexorably into this field, distorting perception and understanding with strong primitive emotions and all manner of unconscious material. Despite the psychological understanding of these two remarkable men, their respective needs and complexes contaminated the relationship and set the stage for its most painful demise.

The climax of the drama was precipitated by Jung's publication of *Wandlungen und Symbole der Libido* in 1912, a work that openly challenged Freud's theory of the child's incestuous desire for the parent of the opposite sex. Jung felt that such longings were symbolic expressions of psychic energy and not to be taken literally. In fact, the publication of this work merely tipped the scales of an already changing relationship between Freud and Jung. Skirmishes had been increasing around the issues of sexuality and of Freud's authority, particularly between the Vienna and Zurich camps of the psychoanalytic community. As

Jung's relationship with Freud grew more problematic, and Jung grew uncomfortable with the role of "crown prince" and heir,[7] the delicate balance of forces in the world of psychoanalysis began to fall apart, culminating in the final severance of their personal and professional connections in 1913.

It is out of this tumultuous ending of their relationship that the first published accusations of anti-Semitism were leveled at Jung. Although as early as 1908, Ernest Jones, a close colleague of Freud's and his biographer, seemed to have detected anti-Semitism in Jung, this feeling was held in check.[8] Undoubtedly, the very nature of Freud's reliance on Jung's being Christian (thus staving off the accusation that psychoanalysis was an exclusively Jewish science) constellated the potential for anti-Semitism by this very strategy directly and dramatically; but so long as a working relationship existed in the psychoanalytic community, there was no overt discord. However, by the time Jung withdrew from Freud and others in the psychoanalytic community, the accusation of anti-Semitism spread with alarming rapidity, like a malignancy that could no longer be policed by a healthy immune system. Whether it was Freud's reference to "the brutal sanctimonious Jung," in a letter to Karl Abraham in 1914[9] or his private accusations of Jung's anti-Semitism in a letter to James Putnam in 1915,[10] nowhere was his condemnation more fateful than when Freud wrote in his "Outline to a History of Psychoanalysis" (1914) that Jung was unable to remain faithful to psychoanalysis because of "certain racial prejudices."[11] Coming from the pen of the master himself in a seemingly official document, this damning, retributive, and, for Freud, clearly face-saving statement began a historical controversy that has simmered and frequently boiled over, with disastrous results, since that time.

Following the end of his relationship with Freud, Jung retreated for some time into a period of introversion, a time of personal and professional crisis and reevaluation that culminated in 1921 with the publication of *Psychological Types,* a work that Jung felt addressed the differences between himself, Freud, and Freud's other apostate son, Alfred Adler.[12] Freud was extremely prolific during that time as well, producing some of his most important theoretical papers. There seemed little of substance to fuel the issue of anti-Semitism between 1915 and the early 1920s. Jung, however, was clearly attempting to process and defend himself against the accusation of anti-Semitism, while at the same time differentiating himself from the "Jewish doctrines" of psychoanalysis. As early as 1917, he was drawing distinctions between a Jewish and a Germanic psychology. The Jewish psyche, he believed, though extremely sophisticated and rich, was not in touch with the "power of the chthonic depths,"[13] whereas the Germanic psyche was so deeply enmeshed in this primeval reality as to be almost "barbarian," a quality he described as both a "dangerous peculiarity" and a potentially "valuable . . . asset."[14] Some ten years later, in 1928, he challenged the lingering charge of anti-Semitism directly by stating that all races, although having a common collective point of origin, differentiate and develop specific essential characteristics and that none of these characteristics is generally valid for all the other groups. The perception and recognition of these differences, he said, did not equal anti-Semitism. Despite the logic of these arguments, one can sense between the lines of Jung's theorizing a continuing struggle with the legacy of his involvement in the psychoanalytic movement. It is likely that his comments arose out of more than theoretical issues—that in fact they were expressions of Jung's negative feelings toward Freud and evidence of the projections that persisted in Jung (and in Freud as well) as a result of their traumatic parting of the ways.

By the beginning of the 1930s, the stage was set for extraordinary developments with regard to the allegations of Jung's anti-Semitism. The success of Hitler and the Nazi party and the full-scale persecution of Jews and other "undesirables" in Germany were becoming horrific facts of life. Out of this overheating container erupted a critical turn of events in 1933. Responding to a "frenzied" call from his colleagues, Jung assumed the presidency of the General Medical Society for Psychotherapy from the German psychiatrist Ernst Kretschmer.[15] It is well substantiated that Jung purposefully and rapidly sought to reconstitute the Society as an international body by 1934 in an effort to stave off German demands to exclude certain colleagues, notably Jewish ones, from membership.[16] According to Geoffrey Cocks, Jung wanted to enable these excluded colleagues to join as "extraordinary members" beyond the veto power of the large and "newly aggressive" German society headed by Matthias Heinrich Göring, a cousin of the Nazi party leader Hermann Göring. At the same time, Jung became the nominal editor of the society's journal, the *Zentralblatt für Psychotherapie,* which had been published in Germany. It was in this publication, in late 1933, that a manifesto appeared by Matthias Göring—with the consent of Jung, who had thought that it was to be published only in a special German edition—which called for a rallying by professional colleagues to the racial colors of Nazi Germany.[17] To compound matters, appearing in this same issue of the journal was Jung's essay "On the State of Psychotherapy Today," in which he starkly reiterated the differences between German and Jewish psychologies that he had posited some years earlier. In addition, his article compared Jews unfavorably to "nomads" and women, and criticized Freud and Adler for stressing pathology while failing to appreciate the creative aspects of psychological life. This essay was ill-timed, easily misunderstood, and—coupled with Göring's piece—certain to put Jung in the worst possible light. And indeed, it became the principal theoretical document that Jung's accusers offered as a demonstration of his anti-Semitism.

Jung's writings of the 1930s and 1940s display a consistency of theme and thrust. He returns again and again to the supposition that there are definite, obvious differences in the psychologies of "races" and "nations" that must be acknowledged and understood. Jung also criticizes Freud's denial of his spiritual roots and the embeddedness of psychoanalysis in a "materialistic" and "rationalistic" framework. Jung takes pains to distinguish between "culture" and "cultural form," trying to make clear that although the Jews have an ancient culture, their lack of a homeland has worked against the evolution of a "cultural form." In Hitler, Jung saw a leader "possessed" by archetypal energies that symbolized the profound "inferiority complex" of the German people and the compensatory drive toward superiority at any cost, one who personified their collective shadow: that is, their unacknowledged and uncontrolled unconscious motivations and their blindly nationalistic longings. By way of a "mass psychosis," Jung felt, Hitler was able to subvert German consciousness to the negative and evil potential of these unconscious forces and lead it to inevitable catastrophe. His reflections on Germany and Hitler characterized Jung's frequent attempts to apply the principles of individual psychology to the understanding of nations, national character, and political action, thereby viewing Germany, for instance, as if it were a patient and he the doctor. He frequently bridled at the fact that his criticisms of Freud and psychoanalysis were immediately perceived as anti-Semitic. He would write often that he was no anti-Semite and that his sole aim was to explore and illuminate the complexities of the human psyche. Finally, in several instances, he admitted that he had been wrong to believe that the arousal of unconscious forces in Germany might bring about positive results in the form of a genuine psychocultural and spiritual transformation.

Historical realities are referred to again and again in this anthology, as if the writers hope that by restating the facts enough times, they can dispel the extraordinary misinterpretations generated by the activities and writings of Jung that I have touched upon. As soon after the war as 1946, Ernest Harms, in *Lingering Shadows*,[18] laid out the facts unequivocally but, oddly enough, to little avail. Aniela Jaffé, one of Jung's closest colleagues and a Jew to whom Jung gave personal, financial, and emotional help during the difficult war years,[19] restated them again in the late 1960s and 1970s, but failed to stem the distortions and misconstruals. As recently as 1982, James Kirsch, one of the best-known German Jewish analysts who worked and communicated with Jung during these critical years, presented the details again, this time in response to a diatribe against Jung in a Jewish publication. I hope that the publication of some of these papers, along with others of more recent and revealing scholarship, will promote a more balanced assessment of Jung in the light of documented evidence.

More problematic is the question of Jung's motivations, both conscious and unconscious, and the way they influence the allegation of his anti-Semitism. While some writers flatly deny this charge and others forthrightly affirm it, most feel that Jung temporarily lost his perspective, fell prey to unintegrated shadow feelings, and acted them out. The most obvious reason for Jung's lapse is, as I have indicated, his unresolved feelings about Freud, the father figure, mentor, and friend by whom Jung felt painfully disappointed and betrayed. Some have speculated that something more than astute theoretical observation lay behind Jung's sharp criticism of Freudian psychology for its tendency to impose itself on other "psychologies": out of his resistance to being personally "imposed upon" by Freud's expectations and demands, Jung may have unconsciously sought to do damage to his mentor. In reaction to these demands, or by way of compensation, Jung might have fallen into an unconscious identification with events in Germany, and perhaps even with the power of Hitler. Caught in this inflation and unconscious power drive, Jung may very well have taken the opportunity during the 1930s, when Freud and psychoanalysis were being hounded, to promote his own psychology and himself with such ambitious concerns as "diagnosing dictators," becoming a psychologist of nations, and attempting, with good but perhaps overstated intent, to help rescue the field of psychotherapy from the fires of totalitarianism.

Alongside his possible opportunism was Jung's fascination with the archetypal images of Wotan, the "inspired leader," and the alchemical figure of Mercurius. Jung was beguiled by the events in Germany and the way in which the forces of the irrational, the heroic, and the instinctive were taking over and leading a civilized people. It was as if his observations about the archetypal Germanic "blond beast" of 1918 were coming true, or as if his own observations of renewal from the depths of the unconscious at the hands of an inspired leader were being enacted and confirmed on a national scale.[20] How could this renewal from the depths not fascinate a psychological explorer of Jung's vision or, more personally, a man who himself sought guidance with regard to his desire for leadership in his profession and who must have identified with the archetypal image of the formerly misunderstood yet inspired leader? And how could he help getting caught in the duplicity of the situation? Here, as Jay Sherry points out, one thinks of Mercurius duplex, the presiding spirit of alchemy, a duplicitous archetypal permutation of Wotan who dupes those in whom he manifests by causing them to see only half of a very complex and dangerous state of affairs.

Whatever the reasons for Jung's attitudes and actions, he displayed, in the midst of a dangerous and frightening time, a regrettable lack of sensitivity toward the plight of the Jews and a lack of awareness of the political and personal consequences of his written and spoken words. There is no doubt that he wished to help friends, patients, and colleagues who were suffering from the madness infecting the European continent. But in dramatically human fashion, he proved himself vulnerable to the insidious effects of the very forces he was seeking to make sensible, and to the accumulated and unprocessed depths of his own past as a rebellious Swiss pastor's son and the fallen heir to a "Jewish science."

Perhaps Jung personally experienced some redemption for this lack and loss when, after a heart attack in 1944, he had a series of visions of a distinctly Jewish nature. In them, he saw himself attended to by an "old Jewish nurse" and nurtured on "ritually prepared kosher food," and was privileged to be present at the Kabbalistic marriage of Malchuth and Tifereth.[21] Also, in his forceful *Answer to Job* of 1952, in which he wrestles with the problem of a Jewish God who seems capricious and unresponsive to the undeserved suffering of his loyal servant, Job, and in his later studies of Kabbalah, Jung may have discovered what was missing in his encounter with Freud: connection to a Judaism that was connected to its original spiritual roots and that could truly "feed" him in a way that he was so painfully denied by the empty religiosity of his natural father. Perhaps in this profound near-death encounter with the imagery of the mystical tradition of Judaism, Jung experienced a healing, a bringing together of his Christian worldview with the hidden spring that fed Freud's, and to which he was undoubtedly deeply attracted from the start. It is sad that the two men did not accomplish the same conjunction on a personal level and thus lay to rest the divisiveness that has for so many years fueled the accusation of anti-Semitism.

In view of Jung's belief that a psychological system is a "subjective confession" of its founder, an important question raised by this anthology is whether shortsightedness or failing on the part of Jung invalidates the psychology that he created. When he was attacking psychoanalysis, Jung referred often to the idea that Freud's Jewishness rendered him unable to appreciate the "chthnoic" dimension of the Germanic psyche. Would it not be equally true to say that Jungian psychology would be comparably blinded or constrained? Were we to evaluate Jungian psychology as primarily a reflection of its creator in the context of the disturbing question of Jung's possible anti-Semitism, could it not be judged a psychology of elitism or racism? Or, insofar as Jung seemed fascinated by the unconscious power of the German psyche, could his psychology not be judged as one that is too susceptible to intoxication with the irrational at the terrible expense of the rational? The answer to this basic question, both for psychoanalysis and for Jungian psychology, must be an unequivocal "No." To hold a creation accountable for the flaws of its creator would leave us with little if any greatness or breadth in our culture. For the sake of comparison, it would invalidate the extraordinary vision of Van Gogh's art because of his mental illness, or the beauty of Ezra Pound's poetry because of his fascist beliefs. Jung himself must have recognized this when, as late as 1953, in a response to questions from the *New York Times,* he was prepared to credit "Freud's contributions to our knowledge of the psyche" as being of the "greatest importance" without any reference to his misgivings about Freud the man or how his psychology betrays his personal limitations.[22] Yet, at the same time, there is truth to the notion that the creator's personality informs and conditions what he observes, describes, and analyzes. As Goethe said, "we see what we know," so must Jung's complexes have affected the development of his psychology. Therefore, as some of the contributors to this book point out, Jungian psychology must be extremely sensitive to such tendencies to value the transpersonal over the quotidian and thus miss the "real" in favor of the "symbolic," or to "analyze" nations, peoples, races when trying to discern what is specific about how they have embodied aspects of the archetypal or universal and risk falling into dangerous stereotyping and possibly even more dangerous scapegoating.

To encounter and integrate the shadow is one of the great tasks of individuation. That does not mean the rejection of what is found but rather the painful acceptance of its role in the making of consciousness. It is painful for us as Jungians to look squarely at the questions raised in this anthology, to see displayed so blatantly how our standard bearer's own shadow distorted his judgment and perception. But as Jung's psychology is a psychology of consciousness, by confronting his personal flaws and opening ourselves and the system to the same hard, tireless scrutiny, we do the work of consciousness-making. In so doing, we go beyond personal vendettas of the past and the battlegrounds of intellectual giants, to arrive at the creative present, that moment in which we can, for ourselves and for the future, make history anew.

Notes

1. See William McGuire, ed. *The Freud/Jung Letters* (Princeton: Princeton University Press, 1974); Peter Gay, *Freud: A Life for Our Time* (New York: W. W. Norton, 1988); C. G. Jung, *Memories, Dreams, Reflections;* and Gerhard Wehr, *Jung: A Biography* (Boston and London: Shambhala, 1987).

2. Sigmund Freud and Karl Abraham, *A Psycho-Analytic Dialogue: The Letters of Sigmund Freud and Karl Abraham* 1907–1926, p. 34.

3. Alexander Irving, "The Freud/Jung Relationship: The Other Side of Oedipus and Countertransference," *American Psychologist,* Spring 1982, pp. 1009–1018; Gay, *Freud,* pp. 200–202.

4. Jung, *Memories, Dreams, Reflections,* p. 149.

5. Liliane Frey-Rohn, *From Freud to Jung: A Comparative Study of the Psychology of the Unconscious* (Boston and London: Shambhala, 1990).

6. Jung, *Memories, Dreams, Reflections,* pp. 52 *ff.*; Murray Stein, "The Significance of Jung's Father in His Destiny as a Therapist of Christianity," *Quadrant,* Spring 1985, pp. 23–33; cf. note 3.

7. Letters from Freud to Jung, April 16, 1909, and October 15, 1908. *Freud/Jung Letters,* pp. 172 and 218; Gay, *Freud,* p. 198.

8. Ernest Jones, quote in Ronald W. Clark, *Freud: The Man and the Cause* (New York: Random House, 1980), pp. 249–250.

9. Freud and Abraham, *A Psycho-Analytic Dialogue,* p. 186.

10. Gay, *Freud,* p. 333.

11. Sigmund Freud, "Outline to a History of Psychoanalysis," *Standard Edition,* 14, p. 43.

12. Jung, *Memories, Dreams, Reflections,* pp. 207–208; Henri Ellenberger, *The Discovery of the Unconscious* (New York: Basic Books, 1970), pp. 670–674.

13. C. G. Jung, "The Role of the Unconscious" (1918), *CW* 10, ¶ 19.

14. Ibid., ¶ 20.

15. C. G. Jung, "A Rejoinder to Dr. Bally" (1934) *CW* 10, ¶ 1016. It is worth noting that Kretschmer apparently did not resign this post because of his uncompromising rejection of Nazism, as is commonly believed. In fact, he continued his work quietly in Germany throughout the war years and as late as 1944 published an article on "the relevance of his theory of constitutional types to increasing war production," as noted by Geoffrey Cocks.

16. Geoffrey Cocks. *Psychotherapy in the Third Reich,* pp. 110, 127–128; Aniela Jaffé, "C. G. Jung and National Socialism," in *From the Life and Work of C. G. Jung,* pp. 78–102.

17. Cocks, *Psychotherapy in the Third Reich,* pp. 131–132; C. A. Meier, personal communication.

18. Ernest Harms, "Carl Gustav Jung—Defender of Freud and the Jews," in Aryeh Maidenbaum and Stephen Martin, eds., *Lingering Shadows: Jungians, Freudians, and Anti-Semitism* (Boston: Shambhala, 1991), pp. 17–49.

19. Aniela Jaffé, personal communication.

20. Jung, "The Role of the Unconscious," (1918) *CW* 10, ¶ 17.

21. Jung, *Memories, Dreams, Reflections,* pp. 293–294.

22. C. G. Jung, "Answers to Questions on Freud" (1953), *CW* 18, ¶ 1069.

Part I

Historical Overview

CHAPTER 1

Paul Roazen

Jung and Anti-Semitism

Paul Roazen is Professor of Social and Political Science at York University in Toronto. He is the author of six books on the history of psychoanalysis, including *Freud: Political and Social Thought* (1986), *Freud and His Followers* (1986), and *Encountering Freud: The Politics and Histories of Psychoanalysis* (1990), as well as the editor of several volumes, such as *Sigmund Freud* (1987).

Roazen observes in this paper that Jung has not received the recognition he deserves for his contributions to 20th-century thought. As a historian, a non-Jungian, and a Jew, he concludes that Jung's political views have been responsible for a general resistance to his ideas, and insists that Jung must be held accountable for his statements.

The subject of Jung and anti-Semitism is not one that I approach with any eagerness. Since I am myself a Jew, although an inadequately practicing one, I am bound to have a special concern with the fate of the Jewish people in this most terrible of centuries.

On the other hand, I am also a student of the history of psychoanalysis, and I am convinced that Jung's stature in the story of the development of depth psychology has been badly misunderstood. Perhaps one anecdote can serve to illustrate the historiographical problem I believe we face. Once, during the course of a few luncheon discussions I had a few years ago with Paul Ricoeur in Toronto, we got onto the subject of his book *Freud and Philosophy.* Since Ricoeur was both modest and self-critical about how he thought he had failed to achieve his objective in this book, I raised the subject of Jung. It seemed to me, and I told Ricoeur, that if he wanted to accomplish the philosophic purposes he had in mind, he would have been better advised to pick Jung as a central thinker instead of Freud. For Jung's view of the unconscious, rather than Freud's, seemed to me much closer to Ricoeur's thinking. The mention of Jung's name, however, posed a special perplexity to Ricoeur. For one could not in Paris, according to Ricoeur, read Jung; he was "on the Index" of forbidden books among French intellectuals.

Ricoeur is himself a Protestant, and one of his sons is a practicing psychoanalyst in France. I found Ricoeur sophisticated about the struggles within psychoanalysis in Paris, where so much is being published these days in connection with Freud, and yet Ricoeur seemed wholly unfamiliar with Jung's writings. And there was I, who had written on Freud, suggesting to Ricoeur the overlooked significance of Jung.

And yet as an intellectual historian I think it is impossible to divorce Jung's psychology from his politics. When I teach the writings of Dostoevsky and Nietzsche at my university, a standard question I ask is whether, and to what degree, their psychologies are interconnected with their politics. Just as Freud himself admired Dostoevsky, without at all going along with his particular set of political beliefs, so it is possible, I think, to say of Jung that he made a great and lasting contribution to psychology, without ignoring the nature of his collaboration with the Nazis.

I should spell out more concretely why I consider Jung to be so important in the history of ideas. First of all, I do not think that Freud ever had a better critic than Jung. It is often said that Freud himself saw some of his own worst failings, and there is a good deal of truth in that proposition; yet Freud usually managed to handle all the possible objections to his own system of thought so masterfully that readers have been inclined to go along with his dismissal of the possible flaws in his psychology.

Jung, however, was to my knowledge the first to insist that authoritarianism was implicit in Freud's therapeutic technique. Jung was also, doubtless in part because of his personal contact with Freud, the earliest to suggest that all analysts in the future be obliged to undergo training analyses. I should say that I am not by any means sure that this was such a good idea; the concept of a training analysis has had some unfortunate side consequences, in infantilizing candidates, for example, and ensuring their indoctrination into a particular teacher's way of doing things. It is of course for others than myself, since I have never been a clinician, to weigh the pros and cons of the institution of a training analysis.

I do believe, however, based on my own historical research, that not enough attention has been given to the whole vexed question of psychoanalytic education. Supervised psychoanalyses were invented precisely as a device to check the power that a senior training analyst is bound to have. But one finds so much sectarianism in psychoanalysis, right up until today, that it does not seem to me that previous devices have succeeded in being as effective as they should be. The literature keeps reinventing the wheel; one finds people from different schools of thought unaware of what others have been up to.

Two vignettes can illustrate what I have in mind. Once, during an interview with Jolande Jacobi in Switzerland in 1966, I raised the concept, then fashionable in orthodox psychoanalysis, of "regression in the service of the ego." Although Dr. Jacobi had known Ernst Kris personally in Vienna, and immediately understood the purport of what I described as his notion, she had not been familiar with it; she agreed with me that it bore striking similarities to Jung's own approach.

To give another example, I recall Anthony Storr telling me after he had stayed in Chicago once that the Freudian analysts there seemed to have picked up some of Jung's ideas about how to proceed with short-term psychotherapy. The Chicago Psychoanalytic Institute was founded by Franz Alexander, and although I am confident that Dr. Alexander was not directly influenced by Jung, he had worked out ideas on his own in the 1940s that bore many analogies to those Jung had had a generation earlier. Ideological enemies of Franz Alexander, like the orthodox Kurt Eissler, would no doubt be delighted to hear of Jungian parallels in Alexander's work, but I am raising the analogy in connection with intellectual history rather than as an aspect of the partisan politics of sectarian squabbling.

Different schools of psychoanalysis are like ships passing in the night. Although it might seem that the two examples I have just given are instances of people who have grown up within Jung's framework not being aware enough of Freudian contributions, I am certain that the general neglect is much more the other way around. In my experience those who have been trained as Freudians are far less likely ever to have read Jung than Jungians are apt to be familiar with Freud.

Perhaps the most striking instance of this in my own research came in the course of an interview I once conducted with René Spitz in Switzerland. "You won't believe," he told me, what Jung once "claimed": Jung had told Dr. Spitz that he had invented the idea of a training analysis.

Spitz considered this preposterous, and as far as I know Freudians today still agree with him. Yet some years ago I came across a passage in Freud's writings where he specifically credits "the Zurich school," meaning Jung, with that suggestion.

Since I have indicated some of my reservations about the drawbacks that I think have been associated with training analyses, I should immediately list some of the more unquestionably positive contributions that I think Jung was able to make. He understood, fifty years before it occurred to orthodox analysts, that clinically infantile material could be used as a defense. The idea that a preoccupation with the childhood past could become an evasion was only later dubbed by Max Schur as "resistance from below." Jung also knew that dreams were not just expressions of wishes and that they had to do with the dreamer's own self, not only with others in our life. Jung looked on the unconscious more constructively, and with less suspicion, than Freud did, and therefore Jung was likely, at least according to his theory, to take a more positive attitude toward the presence of symptoms.

In reality, of course, despite the difference in age between the two men, Jung and Freud shared much in common. If one reads some of Jung's social philosophy, it sounds strikingly like that of Freud himself, even though both men wrote their own works long after their association was over. And in Freud's *Moses and Monotheism,* for example, he commits himself to many views on the nature of symbols that sound to me very like Jung's. Although I do not have the space to document this point here, I am pretty sure that in their concrete clinical practices both Jung and Freud, despite their falling out, continued to share more things in common than one might expect.

But I am afraid that in the course of indicating my respect for Jung's stature within intellectual history, I have drifted too far from the subject at hand: anti-Semitism. It is obviously a very good sign that Jungians are able publicly to face up to this problem. Yet I myself am put in a great deal of inner conflict in addressing this topic.

Anti-Semitism is a vast subject, extending throughout Western thought, and the variety of prejudices about Jews constitutes a matter on which I cannot hope to be expert. With Jung, however, we are dealing with a specific problem that arises uniquely in connection with mid-20th-century intellectuals. Henry Adams, for example, died too early for anyone to get terribly excited about the specifics of what he thought about Jews. It would be ahistorical to consider his views in the light of later events. Anti-Semitism is a deeply rooted part of Western culture and has touched many otherwise admirable thinkers. Hannah Arendt once wrote that the rise of the Nazis had finally put an end to comments about Jews that once were considered culturally allowable; for as soon as it became possible to see that anti-Semitism could lead to gas chambers, then no respectable person could permit cracks about Jews that once might have been thought acceptably run-of-the-mill.

Other eminent figures in the middle of our century, besides Jung, have been caught in the same bind of having expressed morally compromising points about Jews that have a special status because of their timing. I take it mainly as a matter of authority that Martin Heidegger was a great philosopher; he is perhaps the most extreme example of the betrayal of an intellectual's ethics that comes to mind, since he actually joined the Nazi party; although he did not generalize about Jews, he allowed himself at least one negative reference to an individual academic as a Jew that struck other Nazis as so poisonous that it backfired. Ezra Pound's poetry is, I am told, a great work of world literature; yet Pound gave hundreds of perfectly dreadful broadcasts in behalf of Mussolini's regime, programs that sometimes were rebroadcast from Berlin. And then again, it has recently been discovered how Paul de Man, the eminent literary critic, wrote anti-Semitic newspaper articles in his youth during the German occupation of Belgium in World War II.

Of all these men, Jung is the only one I feel expert enough about to defend, in terms of the great contribution he made to psychology. If, however, I were French, and my family had endured World War II, I might well be in Ricoeur's position of not ever having read Jung. The closer one is to the Holocaust, the harder it becomes to take some distance toward the political views with which Jung was associated. I am, however, among the lucky ones, born on this continent; but the accident of geography and history does not spare me the obligation of thinking about the ethical implications that Jung's political commitments entail.

I should be more explicit. It is not correct to compartmentalize psychology and politics. At the same time we should not go to the other extreme and weigh everything on the scale of political judgment; it is the totalitarian regimes that have made all of reality subservient to politics. And yet, without overdoing the implications of what Jung wrote and did in the 1930s, it is indeed relevant to an overall appreciation of his standing.

The details of the controversy about Jung and anti-Semitism are already well known. Nevertheless, though I admire Robertson Davies's novels very much, I once read a book review of his in the New York Times in which he blankly repudiated the idea that Jung was an anti-Semite. Curiously enough, to me at least, it was Freud himself who first leveled this charge against Jung, in the course of Freud's polemic *On the History of the Psychoanalytic Movement.* As I recall from having studied the Freud-Jung correspondence, I detected no signs of such prejudice on Jung's part coming up in their exchanges. But I have no doubt that on Freud's side his enthusiasm about Jung as a disciple stemmed in part from Freud's own special kind of anti-Semitism, his concern that psychoanalysis not become exclusively a Jewish affair and that the movement be led by a Gentile. The bitterness of Freud's disappointment in Jung, and Freud's disillusionment with himself as a leader, can be found in the themes that were preoccupying Freud in *Moses and Monotheism.*

It is not easy for me to cite chapter and verse of what Jung wrote about Jews. In 1934 he argued:

> The Jew, who is something of a nomad, has never yet created a cultural form of his own and as far as we can see never will, since all his instincts and talents require a more or less civilized nation to act as host for their development. . . . The "Aryan" unconscious has a higher potential than the Jewish; that is both the advantage and the disadvantage of a youthfulness not yet fully weaned from barbarism. In my opinion it has been a grave error in medical psychology up to now to apply Jewish categories—which are not even binding on all Jews—indiscriminately to German and Slavic Christendom. Because of this the most precious secret of the Germanic peoples—their creative and intuitive depth of soul—has been explained as a mass of banal infantilism, while my own warning voice has for decades been suspected of anti-Semitism. This suspicion emanated from Freud. He did not understand the Germanic psyche any more than did his Germanic followers. Has the formidable phenomenon of National Socialism, on which the whole world gazes with astonished eyes, taught them better? . . . That is why I say that the Germanic unconscious contains tensions and potentialities which medical psychology must consider in its evaluation of the unconscious.[1]

I have no doubt that much of what Jung had to say has some validity to it; I think that the truth of the matter is that Freud's psychology is characteristically a Jewish one, and that this accounts for some of its strengths as well as for the defects in it that are in need of correction.[2] But the point is, and here I am speaking as a political scientist, the worst of what Jung wrote came in the early days of the rise to power of the Nazis in Germany. Worse still, Jung traveled there to deliver his message; he undertook to make political choices, for which he must historically be held responsible. It was a time when, it will be recalled, Jewish psychotherapists were being forced to flee abroad or were suffering in Germany.

Jung seems to have been politically naive, even stupid; but I must say that what often looks like stupidity can mask prejudice and conviction. In Jung's case it is not as if others in the field did not try to point out to him at the time where he was going wrong. Wilhelm Reich was among those who denounced Jung, as did Gustav Bally of Zurich, eliciting Jung's 1934 "Rejoinder to Dr. Bally." It was Erich Fromm, a man of the left, who advised me to consult with Dr. Bally in Zurich about Jung's politics. (Unfortunately Bally died too soon for me to have been able to see him.)

Jung always claimed that he had undertaken to accept the leadership of the German Medical Society for Psychotherapy in June 1933 in order to protect the profession, and the Jews who practiced it, from needlessly suffering during the ravages of the Nazi regime. I have no doubt that Jung helped many Jewish refugees from Germany to reestablish themselves abroad. But when, in 1935, the Dutch members of Jung's reconstituted international society refused on political grounds to act as hosts for a congress, Jung wrote to them that they were compromising the neutrality of science.

It is simply not the case, however, that when one is talking about the Nazis it is possible to sustain such an appeal to neutral science. The Dutch were, I think, morally right in refusing to collaborate with Jung's call. Those of us intellectuals who during the Vietnam war felt passionately that the war was immoral found ourselves experiencing utter frustration for years; it is not easy to point to more than a few mild acts of protest on our part. I do not claim to be some kind of political hero. But I do not think it is necessary to gloss over what Jung did. I cannot avoid calling a spade a spade.

After World War II it might have been possible for Jung to have better made amends for what had happened. According to the Index of the papers of the British Foreign Office, in 1946 a "booklet" existed that bore the title "The Case of Dr. Carl G. Jung—Pseudo-Scientist Nazi Auxiliary" by Maurice Leon, which outlined "Dr. Jung's connection with Nazis and Nazi Plans." Evidently there were Foreign Office minutes on a "proposed trial as war criminal." I have not succeeded in obtaining this documentation, which as I recall was still covered by a rule restricting access to state papers. Even if this particular file turns out to be wholly innocuous, still it is striking to me that as far as I know Jung never adequately acknowledged the immorality of any of his conduct. It might have been logically possible for him to have owned up to having made an error in judgment; but he stuck to his guns and made a consistent argument in his own defense.

Politically we are not talking about small potatoes. It is not as if we were evaluating why a particular political leader failed to resign, for example, from a government doing business with Hitler; appeasement does differ from being a fellow traveler. We are not even discussing the question of going along with a government that pursues a course of which we disapprove, or even would prefer to dissociate ourselves from.

In my opinion the rise of the Nazis is the most significant political event of the 20th century. It is appalling to find Jung in June 1933 remarking approvingly: "as Hitler said recently. . . ." In the same interview on Radio Berlin he referred to "the aimless conversation of parliamentary deliberations" that "drone on...."[3] And, as Edward Glover long ago pointed out, in 1936 Jung said: "The SS men are being transformed into a caste of knights ruling sixty million natives."[4] I have not attempted, nor could I bear to do so, a comprehensive review of all of Jung's political commentary.

Hitler did not seize power by force, but was duly elected to office; and the regime he displaced was a democratic one. One of the most distressing aspects of the whole matter is that a people willingly chose Hitler, knowing his program beforehand. Those of us who like to believe in democratic processes, and the enlightenment we associate with higher education, have to face up to the fact that Nazism existed in such a highly cultured community. Freud himself, when warned of the danger of Hitlerism in Germany, was in some sense sound to have dismissed the dread prospect on the grounds that "the nation of Goethe could never go to the bad."

No one could have appreciated the full horrors of the Nazis. But intellectual historians do rightly wonder about what elements in Western culture may have fed the long-term sources of Hitlerism. Can it be that an emphasis on the legitimacy of the irrational in psychology does also, when introduced to the world of politics, encourage Nazi-like movements? It would not be too speculative, I think, to suppose that some of Jung's ideas had enough echo in what he heard from Germany from 1933 on for him to think that his work might successfully fit in there. But to the extent that his actions were opportunistically motivated, he is not going to come off well on this particular score.

Many of you already know about the story of the children at an international school in Paris who were once asked to write essays on the elephant. The English boy wrote about hunting elephants in Africa. The

German boy wrote "The Sorrows of a Young Elephant." The French child wrote "On the Love Habits of the Elephant." And the Jewish boy called his contribution: "The Elephant and the Jewish Question."

The issue of anti-Semitism, however, does seem to me especially pertinent to Jung's thought as a whole. I know I could have chosen to address myself more evasively to the subject of the "Lingering Shadows" conference held in spring of 1989 at the New School for Social Research in New York. But I originally accepted the invitation to speak on the issue of Jung and anti-Semitism. It took me ages before I could sit down and write what little I had to say; I pondered the matter for months, each time putting the matter to the back of my mind, and more than once I cried out in anguish to myself: "What am I going to say!" I do not believe in pussyfooting, and yet I hope it is clear that I have not approached the topic in an embattled mood. I trust that what I have said will not, under the circumstances, seem offensive. But I have tried my best to address myself to the problem.

Each of us makes choices, and these decisions become deeds. We in North America know little of the tormenting moral problems that have wracked less fortunate societies. Hitlerism is the worst form of evil I can think of; and therefore, because of Jung's politics and their links to the Nazis, his genuinely great contributions to psychology can only be fully appreciated and evaluated once they are understood in terms of their association with his social views, and yet somehow ultimately detached from the politics of Hitler's regime. Just as it is possible, I think, to divorce Dostoevsky's psychology from his politics, so I hope Jung's psychology will endure in spite of his brand of anti-Semitism.

Notes

1. Quoted in Paul Roazen, *Freud and His Followers,* (Albany: State University of New York Press, 1985), pp. 291–92.

2. See Rosen, *Freud and His Followers*, especially pp. 22 *ff.*

3. *C. G. Jung Speaking,* W. McGuire and R. F. C. Hull, eds. (Princeton: Princeton University Press, 1977), pp. 77–78.

4. *C. G. Jung Speaking*, p. 103.

CHAPTER 2

Geoffrey Cocks

The Nazis and C. G. Jung

Geoffrey Cocks is Professor of History at Albion College in Michigan. He is the author of *Psychotherapy in the Third Reich: The Göring Institute* (1985) and coeditor of *Psycho/History: Readings in the Method of Psychology, Psychoanalysis and History* (1987) and *German Professions: 1800–1950* (1990).

While it is tempting to view history as a by-product of the ideas and actions of powerful and charismatic individuals, Cocks argues here that the historical context of Jung's attitudes must be fully understood before judgment is passed on his words and deeds. Jung's theories, he asserts, were somewhat amenable to certain tenets of the Nazi movement, including its anti-Semitism, and were thus not accorded the same discriminatory treatment as those of Freud. Although Jung was probably not displeased to have received this recognition, in no way did he seek it. Jung sought to use the influence accruing from this popularity to protect the psychotherapy movement in Germany and even to protect its Jewish practitioners. But, in the final analysis, Jung's involvement with psychotherapists in Germany between 1933 and 1940 also raises important questions of cultural prejudice as well as the social roles and moral duties of intellectuals and professionals.

In this essay I shall explore some of the historical context for Carl Jung's words and actions regarding Jews between 1933 and 1940. More specifically, my primary aim is to concentrate on events in Nazi Germany in order to complement the usual emphasis on Jung himself. This is why I have titled my paper "The Nazis and C. G. Jung." The word order of the proper nouns is meant to carry the action from the Nazis to Jung. This is not, as will shortly become evident, an attempt to whitewash Jung or portray him as passive or victimized. It is to show both the compromising and extenuating complexities of this fateful era.

There is a tendency among psychoanalysts, and nonhistorians generally, to focus on individuals, especially on the great in history. This was especially true in a time, the first half of the 20th century, when the world was seemingly dominated by larger-than-life figures, both benevolent and malevolent. Clearly, the significance of individuals, such as Freud or Jung—or Hitler—should not be underestimated, but too often forays into recent history by psychoanalysts in particular have slighted proper historical method and exhibited both an ahistorical concern with the anecdotal and, even more troublingly, the prejudgments that come with partisanship.

The latter problem is especially acute when it comes to debates between Jungians and Freudians, camps divided by deep philosophical differences, differences that became manifest in Europe during the period between the two world wars. Anti-Semitism of course bulked large in European life in those years and thus unavoidably played a role in the intramural clashes within the psychoanalytic movement. These general philosophical differences and the specific tradition of anti-Semitism also naturally played a part in the reception and use of Jung and Jungian psychology in Germany between 1933 and 1940.

First, I would like to offer a brief survey of Jung's involvement in German affairs during these years and the contemporary and subsequent reactions to it. I do this in order to highlight what I think are the major shortcomings on both sides of the debate about Jung's words and actions during the fascist era. This will also give me the opportunity to present some of my own views on this question.

On June 21, 1933, Jung took over the presidency of the General Medical Society for Psychotherapy from German psychiatrist Ernst Kretschmer. Kretschmer, no friend of the Nazis and an opponent of any psychotherapy or psychoanalysis independent of medical control, had resigned the office he had held since 1930 on April 6. On September 15, a German society was founded under the leadership of psychotherapist Matthias Heinrich Göring as part of what was to become an international society headed by Jung that was formally constituted in May of 1934. Jung had been vice-president of the old society, founded in 1926, since 1930. Thus it is not accurate to say, as Nathaniel Lehrman did in the spring of 1988 in a letter to the *New York Times*, that Jung and Göring presided jointly over the same organization. In the attempt to understand Jung's motives, historical accuracy is vital. That the intentions and attitudes of all concerned were overdetermined is exemplified by Kretschmer himself, who, contrary to the common implication of an uncomplicated rejection of the regime, went on to work quietly in Hitler's Germany, publishing as late as 1944 an article in the popular press on the relevance of his theory of constitutional types to increasing war production.[1]

As president of the International Society, Jung also became editor of the society's journal, the *Zentralblatt für Psychotherapie*, which was published in Germany by Hirzel Verlag of Leipzig. The journal, like the international society as a whole, was dominated by the large and newly aggressive German group that had formed the bulk and center of the old society. It was in this journal that Jung published his observations on the distinctions between German and Jewish psychology alongside calls by Göring to the Nazi colors. While Jung's words here betrayed habits of mind that I shall explore critically in a moment, Jung's opponents have often reduced these pronouncements to proof of unalloyed anti-Semitism and wholehearted collaboration with the Nazis. Such a view, however, ignores Jung's increasing disaffection toward the Nazis and his desire to protect psychotherapists in Germany from dangerous Nazi equations with so-called "Jewish" psychoanalysis. Any dissection of Jung's motives and actions, therefore, cannot be based simply on a recitation of his words in the *Zentralblatt*, as has most recently been attempted by Jeffrey Masson. By 1940, in any case, Jung had resigned as president of an international society rendered moribund by war and had likewise left the editorship of the journal to a now estranged Göring and his collaborators.

While Jung's critics must be more attentive to historical detail and to multiple and evolving motives on Jung's part, his defenders must be more candid about the disturbing ambiguities in his thought, especially with regard to Jews. As Paul Roazen has rightly observed, "just as Jung shared sexist prejudices toward women, it would not be surprising for him to have uncritically adopted many traditional stereotypes about Jews."[2] There have been two interrelated ways in which insufficiently critical admirers of Jung have attempted to render harmless his expressions of such views in connection with the Third Reich. The first is to quote Jung's postwar reflections on Nazism and to trace the growth of his doubts, beginning with his "Wotan" essay of 1936. The second, and less noted, means of rendering Jung's statements less ambiguous and questionable is through their alteration in translation.

For example, in his 1934 *Zentralblatt* essay, Jung twice uses the adjective *arisch* in discussing "Aryan" psychology. In the translation by R. F. C. Hull in the Bollingen Series of Jung's *Collected Works*, the German adjective *arisch* is capitalized and placed in quotation marks.[3] In the original, however, the word appears in the lower case and without quotation marks. The translator might argue that current usage demands the quotation marks or that they indicate what Jung really meant or would have said later on, but proper historical inquiry demands fidelity to the primary source. At the time, to be sure, the word "Aryan" was used often and without quotation marks. The word occurs regularly, for example, in Freud's correspondence, as Peter Gay has shown in his recent biography.[4] Of course, the important matter is what the word meant to its user, and in the case of Jung's *Collected Works* it seems likely that the editorial decision was designed to cosmeticize and thus alter the historical picture. The same is true of the translation of a footnote to a speech given by Jung in Vienna in November 1932 that was published in 1934 as part of a book titled *Wirklichkeit der Seele.* The note is to the following text:

> [T]he great liberating ideas of world history have sprung from leading personalities and never from the inert mass. . . . The huzzahs of the Italian nation go forth to the personality of the Duce, and the dirges of other nations lament the absence of strong 1eaders.[5]

The note itself in the original German reads: "*Seitdem dieser Satz geschrieben wurde, hat auch Deutschland semen Führer gefunden.*"[6] The translation reads, incorrectly: "After this was written, Germany also turned to a Führer." The latter verb construction implies a neutrality or even a disparagement on Jung's part and a resignation or desperation on the part of the Germans not expressed by the original language. The translation should read: "Since this sentence was written, Germany too has found its leader." The Jungian cultural specificity of the possessive pronoun is missing in the Hull translation, as is the positive connotation of discovery in "has found" that corresponds to the endorsement of strong leaders found in the text, a theme to which Jung returned in a 1933 interview on Radio Berlin with German disciple Adolf von Weizsäcker.[7]

Jung, however, did not involve himself unilaterally in the domestic affairs of Nazi Germany. He was in fact sought out by psychotherapists there who felt that his association and endorsement would add luster to their bid for professional autonomy from the dominant nosological psychiatry and dissociate them from Freud in the eyes of the Nazi regime. The German Jungians in particular were eager to promote Jung for generally defensive as well as specifically partisan purposes. This was precisely the theme, for example, of an article concerning the work of a Jungian member of the so-called Göring Institute, Gustav Schmaltz, that appeared in the major Cologne newspaper in 1937.[8] So though Jung could hardly have been averse to the advancement of his school of thought at the expense of that of Freud, he was involved in a project that he could rightly claim served the survival of psychotherapy in general. Should he have anticipated the extent to which psychotherapy could contribute to the repressive aims of National Socialism? Since Jung in any event had little influence on the operations of the Göring Institute, that is a question I shall not pursue here. Rather, I will concentrate on the specific reception and use of Jungian psychology in Nazi Germany.

Jung's abiding emphasis on the unique collective experiences and memories of the world's cultures, nations, and races provided inspiration for various individuals and groups in Nazi Germany. While Freud and his theories were officially disapproved and thus, when used, were cloaked in Aesopian language, Jung's ideas were often evaluated positively in Nazi literature. One article in the journal *Rasse* in 1939 equated Jung's notion of the collective unconscious with the Nazi concept of heredity and race.[9] And this article was listed in the official Nazi party bibliography. This is not to say that in fact Jung's ideas and those of the Nazis were identical, only that such identifications could be and were effected. And while, as Robert Proctor has noted in his recent book on medicine in Nazi Germany, Jung never went on from differentiation to denigration in his cultural relativism, Nazi "racial anthropologists" and physicians sought to elucidate the pernicious peculiarities of "Jewish" science and culture.[10]

Göring and others had originally hoped to use Jung and his followers at the institute in Berlin, individuals such as G. R. Heyer, Wolfgang Kranefeldt, and Olga von König-Fachsenfeld, as a major resource for the construction of a non-Freudian "German psychotherapy." Although this fascistic spirit pervaded the institute, neither a "German psychotherapy" nor Jung's theories by themselves in fact played a predominant role in the psychotherapists' activities. The various practical demands assumed by the psychotherapists in applying and advertising their therapeutic expertise in the realms of German society, industry, and the military took precedence over the more abstract and less pragmatic characteristics of Jungian psychology. Still, such Jungian themes continued to be applied to the events and rigors of the time. In 1943, for example, the *Zentralblatt* published an article extolling the asserted healing power of the symbols of mother earth and father heaven from the ancient German religion of nature, powers supposedly helpful in strengthening the "feminine" sphere of the home as a refuge for the returning soldier.[11]

The regime itself displayed little scientific interest in Jung or his followers. It did, however, monitor their activities even outside of Germany. This is clear from the files of the former Reich Education Ministry held by the Zentrales Staatsarchiv in Potsdam, Germany. From 1935 to 1939, various government agencies gathered information on the annual Eranos conferences at Ascona in Switzerland. In 1936 the Ministry refused to grant Germans permission to attend. The next year Göring arranged to have Eranos secretary Olga Fröbe-Kapteyn visit the Ministry to smooth the way for German participation. This intervention proved successful, but by 1938 the Nazi Auslands-Organisation was objecting that there were lots of Jews at the meetings, that some of the topics were "politically conflictual," and that in general the whole organization seemed "mysterious." To resolve such doubts, a Ministry official asked Göring to have a report prepared on that year's meeting. On August 23, 1938, Olga von König-Fachsenfeld duly reported that she had heard nothing political at the conference, that the Swiss in particular seemed to have gone out of their way not to criticize Germany, and that while there were a number of Jews in attendance, none was on the program. Permission was given for Germans to participate in 1939, and in December of that year the German consulate in Locarno commented that while the participants at the meeting were certainly "different," the conferences did not seem to serve the interests of foreign powers, Jews, or Masons and that therefore Germans should be allowed to attend. The only restriction was to be that they could not address sessions where Jews were present.[12]

By 1939 Jung, his ideas, and his followers were not an important issue for the Nazis. By that time as well, Jung and Göring were at odds over German domination of the international society, and Jung was now casting a critical eye over the Nazi phenomenon. The significance of Jung's attitudes, actions, and experiences during these years, I think, lies less in the question of any overt prejudices on his part than in the various suprapersonal dynamics his words and deeds engaged. Anti-Semitism was endemic in European society but particularly in the German lands where strong nationalism was aggravated by the proximity of the Slavic world and by the migration of

Ostjuden into Germany and Austria. The traditional elites in Germany, for example, remained closed to Jews. As historian Fritz Stern has put it in describing the homogeneity of the officer corps, "In Germany there was no Dreyfus Affair because there was no Dreyfus."[13] The medical profession was particularly anti-Semitic owing to the pervasiveness of Social Darwinist, eugenic, and racist theorizing and, after 1918, as a result of economic pressures that increased jealousy and resentment of the many prominent and successful Jewish physicians in Berlin and other large cities. Thus the Nazis could appeal to doctors and other professionals on the basis of an interlocking grid of nationalism, self-interest, and anti-Semitism.

European anti-Semitism was not usually racist in the Nazi sense; rather the interwar fascist movement capitalized on a more general cultural movement against materialism that often caricatured Jews as lacking "spirituality." Historian George Mosse has shown how pervasive this caricature was, citing as one example the late-19th-century Swiss historian Jacob Burckhardt, who, while not close to the nascent *völkisch* movement, fulminated against the decline of aesthetics and civilization as evidenced by the machinations, among others, of venal Jews.[14] Jung never expressed himself in this way, but did share the widespread concern about the deterioration of spiritual values that, among other things, led him to see in the mass movements of the 1920s and 1930s elements of what he called liberation. This philosophical stance cultivated degrees of anti-Semitism inherited from the culture, the intensity of which varied with time and event. It must be said that Jung broke from these notions in a way that suggests a dialectic of prejudice and tolerance within him that was ultimately resolved in favor of the latter. This is not to agree, however, with the argument of Wolfgang Giegerich that all along Jung was purposefully engaging the shadow of racial prejudice in order to extirpate it.[15] Such a judgment naively ignores the plurality of motives and conditions present in any human action, a number of which we have explored in the case at hand. Such a rationalization also turns a blind eye to the negative effects of Jung's lack of vigorous early criticism of Hitler and the possible legitimacy for the regime created in the minds of many or some through Jung's association with it, whatever protective professional capacity he effected or intended.

Jung's philosophical outlook also proved to be problematic in a more general way. Although the Nazis exploited modern technical and material resources, including medicine and psychotherapy, they also built their power on yearnings for the mysterious and the transcendent. In so doing, they revealed the perils of fascination among intellectual luminaries who, more than anyone, must maintain a critical, rational, and ethical distance from destructive enthusiasms, recognizing the crucial difference between saying "This is amazing" and saying "This is wrong."

Notes

1. Ernst Kretschmer, "Konstitution und Leistung," *Westfdlische Landeszeitung*, August 20, 1944; microcopy $T_7$8, roll 190, frames 1866–67, National Archives, Washington, DC.

2. Paul Roazen, *Freud and His Followers* (Albany: New York University Press, 1985), p. 292.

3. C. G. Jung, "The State of Psychotherapy Today," *CW* 10, pp. 165–166.

4. Peter Gay, *Freud: A Life for Our Times* (New York: Norton, 1988), pp. 205–239.

5. C. G. Jung, "The Development of Personality," *CW* 17, pp. 167–168.

6. C. G. Jung, "Vom Werden der Persönlichkeit," in idem, *Wirklichkeit der Seele* (Zurich: Rascher Verlag, 1934), p. 18 *ff*.

7. *C. G. Jung Speaking*, W. McGuire and R. F. C. Hull, eds. (Princeton: Princeton University Press, 1977), p. 65.

8. "Die Sprache des Unbewussten," *Kölnische Zeitung*, October 9, 1937; REM 2954; Zentrales Staatsarchiv, Potsdam. See also Paul Feldkeller, "Geist der Psychotherapie," *Deutsche Allgemeine Zeitung*, October 5, 1937; REM 2954.

9. Alfred A. Krauskopf, "Tiefenpsychologische Beiträge zur Rassenseelenforschung," *Rasse* 5 (1939): 362–368.

10. Robert Proctor, *Racial Hygiene* (Cambridge: Harvard University Press, 1988), pp. 162–163.

11. Frederik Adama van Scheltema, "Mutter Erde und Vater Himmel in der germanischen Naturreligion," *Zentralblatt für Psychotherapie* 14 (1943): 257–277.

12. REM 2797; Zentrales Staatsarchiv.

13. Fritz Stern, "The Burden of Success: Reflections on German Jewry," in idem, *Dreams and Delusions* (New York: Knopf, 1987), p. 108.

14. George Mosse, *Germans and Jews* (New York: Fertig, 1970), pp. 57–60.

15. Wolfgang Giegerich, "Postscript to Cocks," *Spring* 10 (1979): 228–231.

CHAPTER 3

Jay Sherry

Jung, Anti-Semitism and the Weimar Years (1918-1933)

Jay Sherry received a master's degree in psychology from the New School for Social Research, studied at the Jung Institute in Zurich and is actively interested in the interdisciplinary field of psychohistory. His research and expertise on the issue of Jung and Anti-Semitism led to his unique contributions to Lingering Shadows: Jungians, Freudians and Anti-Semitism. He is currently finishing a book about Jung's Swiss-German background and his relationship to the European avant-garde.

C. G. Jung's attitudes toward Jews and National Socialism have been the subject of debate since the 1930s. Much of it has focused on what he said and did in the aftermath of Hitler's assumption of the German chancellorship on January 30, 1933. In June he assumed the presidency of the General Medical Society for Psychotherapy, an organization that brought together most non-psychoanalytic therapists in Germany, as well as members from other European countries. In the December 1933 issue of the Society's journal, he made his most controversial remark when he said that it was important to openly discuss the differences that actually existed between Germanic and Jewish psychology (see "Significant Words and Events" in Appendix A). He developed what he meant by this in more detail in "The State of Psychotherapy Today," his contribution to the January 1934 issue of the journal. This article ignited the controversy that still reverberates today. Jung never quite understood what all the fuss was about. Responding to his first major critic, Jung wrote in the *Neue Zuricher Zeitung,* "why raise the Jewish problem today of all days and in Germany of all places? Pardon me, I raised it long ago, as anybody knows who is acquainted with the literature. I did not speak about it only since the revolution; I have been officially campaigning for criticism of subjective psychological premises as a necessary reform in psychology ever since 1913. This has nothing to do with the form of the German state."[1]

Jung had a point here: to truly understand what he was saying in 1933 and afterward, one needs to know what he said about Jewish psychology in the years after his break with Freud. I will introduce the intellectual network that Jung cultivated after his break with Freud and the influence that these individuals had on the development of his ideas. This facet of his career has generally been neglected due to the view that after his declaration of intellectual independence from Freud, Jung went his own way except for fruitful collaborations with such men as the sinologist Richard Wilhelm, the classicist Karl Kerenyi, and the physicist Wolfgang Pauli. In fact, I will be discussing a group of intellectuals in Weimar Germany who he found congenial, and who played a crucial role in promoting Jung through their organizations and publications.

Although the war years (1914–1918) were a period of isolation and introversion for Jung, a number of his important works appeared in English translation. This promoted his reputation in Britain and the United States and attracted new clients and opportunities. From 1919 to the mid-1920s, Jung was primarily involved with this Anglo-American circle. His trip to the American Southwest (1924) was a result of his long-standing relationship with the McCormick family of Chicago, while his travel to British East Africa (1925) was planned by his leading English follower H. G. Baynes. It was also through this circle that Jung was invited to speak at several international education conferences: at Territet, Switzerland (1923), London (1924), and Heidelberg (1925).

From this circle of analysands and followers developed the first generation of Jungian analysts. Since there was no formal Jungian training institute until 1948, the primary method of training, besides personal analysis with Jung, was participation in a series of seminars that Jung first began to hold in the UK in the 1920s. The first two were held in Cornwall: at Sennen Cove in 1920 and at Polzeath in 1923. Attendance grew from a dozen to over one hundred at Swange in 1925. Records exist for the last two in the form of notes taken by Esther Harding (supplemented by notes taken at Polzeath by Kristine Mann).

The notes reveal that Jung was in the process of articulating such core elements of his psychological system as the archetypes of the collective unconscious and psychological types. One of most significant elements of Jung's exposition is the contrast of his psychological approach with that of his former mentor Sigmund Freud. This had begun in his article "The Psychology of Unconscious Processes" (1917), in which he characterized the theories of Freud and Adler as reductive with their one-sided emphasis on Eros and the Will to Power, respectively. In these unpublished seminars, Jung was to make another important distinction. He concluded that the analysis of dreams of Jewish and Germanic individuals indicated a different level of psychic development in each group: Jewish dreams evoked the world of antique civilization, whereas Germanic dreams brought up material from a primitive level unknown to Jews. In analysis, Jews had to discover their sexuality, which Freud had correctly diagnosed. Persons of Germanic stock, on the other hand, were already aware of it and wanted to know what to do with it. In the 1925 seminar, Jung further elaborated upon this when he commented that Jews welcomed any trace of instinct since theirs were petrified like a nearly-extinct volcano.[2]

These private observations were clearly of importance to Jung at this time because they are corroborated by two individuals with whom Jung was intimate at this time, the British psychologist William McDougall and the German philosopher Hermann Keyserling. First McDougall who wrote, "each race and each people that has lived for many generations under or by a particular type of civilization has specialized its 'collective unconscious,' differentiated and developed the 'archetypes' into forms peculiar to itself. . . . He [Jung] claims even that sometimes a single rich dream has enabled him to discover the fact, say, of Jewish or Mediterranean blood in a patient who shows none of the outward physical marks of such descent. . . . He points out that the famous theory of Freud, which he himself at one time accepted, is a theory of the development and working of the mind which was evolved by a Jew who has studied chiefly Jewish patients; and it seems to appeal strongly to Jews; many, perhaps the majority, of those physicians who accept it as a new gospel, a new revelation, are Jews. It looks as though this theory, which to me and to most men of my sort seems so strange, bizarre, and fantastic, may be approximately true of the Jewish race."[3] In his 1928 book *Europe*, Keyserling wrote "C. G. Jung has shown, by a comparison of the dreams of Jews with those of Christians, that at the same level of the subconscious where the Germanic type is still a lake-dweller, the Jew is an Alexandrian."[4]

Jung's first public discussion of this distinction had been in his 1918 article "Über das Unbewußte," which appeared in English as "On the Role of the Unconscious" only with the publication of volume 10 of his *Collected Works* in 1964 in a translation that took liberties with the original German text. Referring to Freud in paragraph 19, the English reads "we still have a genuine barbarian in us who is not to be trifled with. . . ." The same phrase in German reads *wir Germanen*, "we Germans." Hull, the translator, has deleted Jung's identification of himself as a German, which explains a more serious discrepancy between the texts earlier, in paragraph 16. The English reads "As civilized human beings, we in Western Europe have a history reaching back perhaps 2,500 years" (*Wir haben als Kulturmenschen em Alter von etwas Funfzehnhundert* [1500] *Jahren*). To his original German-language readers, the "we" was a plainly marked reference to themselves as Germans and the "1500" would refer back to the time when the German tribes were converted to Christianity. In the English version, the "we" gets broadened to include Western Europeans, which necessitates recalibrating the time span to include the ancient Greeks. Jung's entire argument is structured in terms of the cultural stereotypes current at the time, most importantly the distinction between Aryans and Jews. Scholars have emphasized the major shift in how Jews were identified, from early in the 19th century as a religious community to their designation as a distinct race after the popularization of Darwin's theory of evolution.[5] Jung accepted this and some of the basic characterizations derived from it. One was the contrast between the "rooted ness" of the Aryan people and the "rootlessness" of Jews (". . . where has he his own earth underfoot?" ¶ 18). As we shall see later, this concern for the relationship between a people and their soil was to become a major theoretical preoccupation for Jung during the 1920s.

Jung continued his discussion in terms familiar to his German-speaking audience. "The Jew already had the culture of the ancient world and on top of that has taken over the culture of the *nations amongst whom he dwells* [Wirstsvolk]" (¶ 18, my italics). The English translation glosses over a nuance that is highly significant in the original German. *Wirtsvolk* is better translated as "host people," and had become commonplace in discussions about the relationship of Jews to the larger, national communities around them. Given this linguistic premise, there were two possible words to describe Jews. For Jung and the majority of people of the time, they would be considered as "guests." Others, influenced by the medical rhetoric of the burgeoning racial hygiene movement of the time had begun to view them as "parasites." In either case, they were "aliens" separated from their Aryan neighbors.

One of Jung's intentions in writing this article was to articulate his compensation theory of the psyche as a complement to Freud's repression theory. For Jung, compensation was one of the basic features of psychic functioning. Analogous to the body's homeostatic system, it balances the one-sidedness of conscious awareness with such unconscious material as symptoms or dreams. Since Jews have insufficient contact with the earth and the world of instincts, he found it understandable that Freud and Adler would reduce everything to their material beginnings. This became Jung's basic critique of Freud and would gain popularity with those uncomfortable with Freudian psychology. "The fact is, our unconscious is not to be got at with over-ingenious and grotesque interpretations. The psychotherapist with a Jewish background [more accurately, "The Jewish-oriented psychotherapist"] awakens in the Germanic psyche not those wistful and whimsical residues from the time of David, but the barbarian of yesterday, a being for whom matters suddenly become serious in the most unpleasant way" (¶ 19).

In this article Jung expressed views on Jews that relied heavily upon contemporary cultural stereotypes, which he continued to hold into the 1930s. A careful reading of what he wrote here also reveals an important linguistic strategy that he repeated elsewhere in his writings In ¶ 19 he writes first about "the specific Jewish need to reduce. . . " and then, in referring to Freud and Adler, to "these specifically Jewish doctrines." This was Jung's first use of the adjective "specific," which he would later employ as a standard qualification of Jewish thought. He used it in a manner that exuded certainty and aimed to close discussion rather than invite reflection.

Jung's postwar visits to England involved more than the promoting of his psychological approach through private seminars. By this time, he was recognized as one of Europe's leading psychiatrists and still considered by many to be a leading proponent of psychoanalysis. In July, 1919 he delivered papers to a variety of professional organizations, among them the Society for Psychical Research and the Psychiatry Section of the Royal Society of Medicine. It was then that Jung became friendly with William McDougall, a friendship that included Jung's analyzing McDougall's dreams. McDougall (1871–1938) was a leading psychologist of the time: after medical training he did anthropological field work in Borneo, later taught at Oxford, and published his landmark *An Introduction to Social Psychology* (1908). The two had several things in common: an interest in parapsychology (McDougall finished his career at Duke University where he supported the work of Joseph Rhine on ESP) and a shared antipathy to the scientific materialism dominant at the time. After seeing Jung in the summer of 1920, McDougall came to the United States to assume a professorship at Harvard.

In that year he delivered the Lowell Lectures, which appeared in 1921 as *Is America Safe for Democracy?* His main theme was the superiority of the Nordic race and the threat posed by the massive immigration of Italians, Jews, and Slavs to the United States. Such views made him "perhaps the most indefatigable of the race theorizers among the psychologists of the time."[6] Such racialist preoccupation with the "Nordic race" had begun with the 1916 publication of Madison Grant's *The Passing of the Great Race* and was popularized after the war by Lothrop Stoddard (who rated a reference in *The Great Gatsbv*). The anxieties of Anglo-Saxon Americans that had been stirred up found several outlets. The first was the rebirth of the Ku Klux Klan, which gained strength in the Midwest as well as the Deep South. The second was the growing support for legislation to limit immigration which resulted in the Immigration Act of 1924. It established a quota system that clearly favored immigrants from Northern and Western Europe and drastically curtailed those from Southern and Eastern Europe.

Since his first visit in 1909, Jung had been fascinated by the psychological consequences of America's racial mix. In January, 1925 Esther Harding wrote in her notebook "[Dr. Jung] spoke on racial psychology and said many interesting things about the ancestors, how they seem to be in the land. As evidence, he spoke about the morphological changes in the skulls of people here in the U.S.A. and in Australia."[7] Several years later Jung wrote an article entitled "Your Negroid and Indian Behavior" for the American "magazine of controversy" *Forum* (April, 1930; vol. 83, no. 4). While making some perceptive comments about the unconscious influence of the Negro upon white behavior and the role of the Indian as an American cultural ideal, Jung generally framed his argument in contemporary racial stereotypes. He writes about the threat to whites of "going black." "The inferior man exercises a tremendous pull upon civilized beings who are forced to live with him, because he fascinates the inferior layers of our psyche. . . . To our unconscious mind contact with primitives recalls not only our childhood, but also our prehistory; and with the Germanic races this means a harking back of only about twelve hundred years. The barbarous man in us is still wonderfully strong and he easily yields to the lure of his youthful memories. Therefore he needs very definite defenses. The Latin peoples, being older, don't need to be so much on their guard, hence their attitude toward the Negro is different from that of the Nordics" (p. 196).

The version of this article found in the *Collected Works*, "The Complications of American Psychology" (*CW* 10, pp. 502–514) deletes the reference to "Nordics" and so tones down the extent to which Jung had adopted the racialist vocabulary of the time. This deletion is most likely the result of an editorial decision to avoid the use of a word that had acquired a distinctly sinister connotation by 1945. Its appearance might have provided more ammunition to the postwar critics who were accusing Jung of Nazi sympathies.

While Jung was busy promoting his psychology in the Anglo-American world, Germany was experiencing the traumatic aftermath of its defeat in 1918. In quick succession, the replacement of the monarchy with a parliamentary democracy and the Treaty of Versailles shook the country. By 1923, Germany had lived through armed confrontations between the government and forces from both the Left and Right, hyperinflation, and the French occupation of the Saar. The appointment of Gustav Stresemann of the German People's Party first to the chancellorship and then to the foreign ministry led to economic and political stabilization. His renegotiation of reparations payments was followed by a prosperity fueled by the infusion of foreign capital. The Locarno Pact of 1925 normalized Germany's relations with its neighbors while admission to the League of Nations signaled its end of its pariah status. The political scene experienced a respite and the vibrant cultural life that characterized the Weimar Republic was in full swing.

Early in the 1920s, a German literary figure, Oscar A. H. Schmitz, discovered Jungian psychology, cultivated Jung's friendship, and became his most energetic promoter in Germany. The brother-in-law of the Expressionist artist Alfred Kubin, Schmitz attended Jung's 1925 and 1928 English-language seminars in Zurich.[8] He wrote numerous articles popularizing Jung, some for newspapers but the majority appeared in *Der Zeitschrift für Menschenkunde*, a cultural journal founded in 1925. Its list of contributors included such luminaries of the time as Alfred Adler, Thomas Mann, Emil Ludwig, and Stefan Zweig. More active contributors included a group of individuals whose social and intellectual connections to Jung in the subsequent years have received relatively little attention. The most important was Ludwig Klages, who, among other things, was Germany's leading graphologist; his journal, in fact, appeared as the second half of each issue of the *Zeitschrift*.

One of Jung's most important intellectual relationships during this period was with Count Hermann Keyserling, who had opened his School of Wisdom at Darmstadt in 1919 under the patronage of the Grandduke of Hesse. They were introduced by Schmitz there in the early 1920s, where Jung also made the acquaintance of the sinologist Richard Wilhelm.

Keyserling (1880-1946) was a Baltic German who settled in Germany where he married a granddaughter of Bismarck. *His Travel Diary of a Philosopher* (1919) became an international bestseller and helped make him one of the most popular philosophers of the time. His eclectic mix of Eastern spirituality, Jungian-flavored psychology, and observations on the "psychology of nations" proved phenomenally successful. His School of Wisdom sponsored a series of courses and annual conferences from 1920 to 1930 when it closed its doors due to financial difficulties brought on by the Depression. In conjunction with these activities it published a newsletter, books, and a journal *Der Leuchter* ("The Candelabra") with the Reichl Verlag of Darmstadt.

A broad cross-section of contemporary intellectuals became involved with Keyserling and his School. His 1925 *Book of Marriage* counted among its contributors the following: Leo Frobenius (German ethnologist), Rabindranath Tagore (Bengali poet and winner of the Nobel Prize for Literature), Beatrice Hinkle (American translator of Jung"s *Wandlunaen und Symbole der Libido*), Thomas Mann, Havelock Ellis, and Leo Baeck (the chief rabbi of Berlin).

Herman Hesse evokes the atmosphere of these years in his allegorical novel *The Journey to the East,* where he writes "It can be noted here that since the travel diary of Count Keyserling, several books have appeared in which the authors, partly unconsciously, but also partly deliberately, have given the impression that they are brothers of the League and have taken part in the Journey to the East. . . . They discovered no new territory, whereas at certain stages of our Journey to the East, although the commonplace aids of modern travel such as railways, steamers, telegraph, automobiles, airplanes, etc., were renounced, we penetrated into the heroic and magical. It was shortly after the World War, and the belief of the conquered nations were in an extraordinary state of unreality. There was a readiness to believe in things beyond reality even though only a few barriers were actually overcome and few advances made into the realm of a future psychiatry."[9]

Keyserling envisioned his School as the training ground for a spiritual elite that would help create a new European culture. Richard Noll's assertion that "he was unabashedly a volkisch German in his metaphysical outlook" is inaccurate.[10] Noll rightly identifies the racialist vocabulary evident in Keyserling's writings but fails to understand that this constitutes only one element in his philosophy. By labeling Keyserling "volkisch," Noll blurs important distinctions that must be maintained in order to have an accurate picture of the circles that Jung moved in after he broke with Freud. It is better to see Keyserling as an example of what I would call the "conservative avant-garde" that has its origins in the 1890s with such developments as the Symbolist movement in art and literature, the Occult Revival, cultural pessimism, and *lebens-philosophie* (the continental movement inspired by the life and work of Friedrich Nietzsche). Since the turn of the century, Henri Bergson had been *lebens-philosophie's* most internationally prominent exponent.[11]

Early in his career, Keyserling had made the personal acquaintance of Houston Chamberlain, whose *Foundations of the Nineteenth Century* gave pseudo-scientific respectability to a racialist interpretation of European history. It proved phenomenally successful in Germany where it was embraced by Kaiser Wilhelm and large segments of the German middle class.[12] Keyserling was also influenced by Gustave Le Bon, another personal acquaintance, who is now best known for his pioneering work of social psychology, *The Crowd* (1895). Le Bon also wrote frequently on the "psychology of nations," writings that reveal his anti-Semitic sentiments.[13]

All these influences are evident in two books Keyserling wrote in the late 1920s: *Europe* and *America Set Free*. Ethnic psychology is one of his main topics and there are, among others, many references to "Nordics" and their influence on history and the contemporary scene. His involvement with Jung is clearly evident in these works where he often uses such Jungian concepts as personality types and the collective unconscious to explain himself. Keyserling influenced Jung as well. One of the most obvious examples of this influence involves Keyserling's comment in *Europe* that "the old Roman type originally had a substratum of Nordic blood, like the Lombards of today" (p. 156). He had originally picked this idea up from Chamberlain (*Foundations*, p. 539) and passed it on to Jung who later quoted it almost verbatim in the *Zarathustra Seminars* where he says, "Fascism in Italy is old Wotan again; it is all Germanic blood down there with no trace of the Romans; they are Langobards, and they all have that Germanic spirit" (p. 814). In 1929 Keyserling published *The Recovery of Truth* in which appears an observation cited earlier, "Jung thinks that Freud's presuppositions often apply to Jews and much more rarely to the Nordic type. He holds the characteristics of the unconscious to be dependent on the history of the races, on their age and destinities; according to him, the Nordic's unconscious is on the whole barbaric and primitive, and correspondingly, unerotic, whereas the Jew with his far-reaching historic past is, within that same strata, a differentiated Alexandrian."[14] The only change was the substitution of the newly popular word "Nordic" for the more general "Germanic."

In April, 1927, the School of Wisdom held its most important conference. The theme was "Man and Earth" and attracted a group of speakers that included Jung, Wilhelm, Frobenius, the psychologist Hans Prinzhorn, and the philosopher Max Scheler. Appreciation for the landscape had been one of the chief characteristics of German Romantic painting. (Besides being one of Jung's acknowledged forerunners in psychology, Carl Gustav Carus [1789–1869] was also a talented landscape painter who authored an important series of essays on the subject.) In the late 19th century, interest in landscape shifted with the growth of German nationalism and the efforts of writers to define the relationship of the German people to their land. This became the domain of *volkisch* writers who glorified the pagan virtues of their barbarian ancestors at the expense of the Judaic-Christian heritage of European civilization. One core metaphor in this way of thinking was "rootedness," the degree to which a people were psychically connected to their native land. Another current of interest in "the earth" stemmed from the mass of information collected by anthropologists in the newly acquired colonies of the European powers. Any definition of Man now needed to include what had been learned about the beliefs and social institutions of "primitives."

Jung had read widely in all this literature and was, in addition, deeply influenced by the Taoist literature that he had been introduced to by Richard Wilhelm. This encounter did not just stimulate Jung intellectually, but had a profound personal effect on him after he began to consult the *I Ching* in the early 1920s. In later years, this would lead to major new theoretical formulations like his concept of synchronicity. At the time of the conference Jung was taken up with the relationship of the ideograms "Yin" and "Yang" to his archetypes of anima and shadow. Yin relates to the dark, feminine powers of the earth and something of this sensibility is conveyed in the title of Jung's lecture "Der Erdbedingtheit der Psyche" (literally translated, "The Earth-Conditioning of the Psyche"). The original appeared in the 1927 issue of *Der Leuchter* and later as "Mind and Earth" in *Contributions to Analytical Psychology* (1928). It was then divided into two articles, "The Structure of the Unconscious" (*CW* 8) and "Mind and Earth" (*CW* 10)

The earth/spirit dyad was one of the defining themes in Jung's relationship with Keyserling. Jung's reservations about the Count's spiritual pretensions led him to accentuate his interest in the "archaic" dimension of the psyche as manifested in his field trips to Africa and America (the "primitive" of the present) and his fascination with course of events in Germany (the "primitive" of the past reactivated). This all connects Jung to a group of intellectuals taken up with the role of the "tellluric" or "chthonic" forces in human history. This had its immediate roots in the writings of Jacob Bachofen (1815–1887), a native of Basel like Jung, whose research into early Roman history led him to postulate the existence of a period of matriarchy prior to the rise of patriarchy in human history. This sparked the interest of such diverse individuals as Friedrich Engels and Ludwig Klages, the graphologist and anti-Semitic renegade from the Circle around Stefan George, Germany's most important poet of the early 20th century.

Bachofen's theories gained wider exposure in the mid-1920s with the new edition of his 1859 book on grave symbols brought out by Klages and C. A. Bernoulli, one of his students, another Basel native who had written a book about Nietzsche.[15] Jung was certainly familiar with Bachofen's works but did not rely upon them for confirmation of his theories. His influence on Jungian psychology is most evident in Toni Wolff s work *The Structural Forms of the Feminine Psyche* which discussed the formative influence of such figures as the Amazon and the Hetaira, both of whom can be found in Bachofen.[16]

Most of Jung's long paper is an exposition of his theory of the collective unconscious and relies on his familiar mix of cultural and clinical examples (the solar phallus man makes a cameo appearance). At the point where the published article was subsequently divided, Jung described the archetypes as "essentially the chthonic portion of the mind—if we may use this expression—that portion through which the mind is linked to nature, or in which, at least, its relatedness to the earth and the universe seems most comprehensible. In these primordial images the effect of the earth and its laws upon the mind is clearest to us."[17] He then goes on to develop his thoughts on "night religion," *participation mystique,* and the anima.

Jung concludes by relating the theme of the earth-conditioning of the psyche to the wider world. He focuses on his findings from analytical work with Americans and his personal experiences in the United States. He summed up his highly original insights by saying that "the American presents a rare picture—a European with Negro manners and an Indian soul!"[18] Among the mannerisms that he identifies are the distinctly American styles of laughing, talking, and walking. The role of the Indian is less obvious but equally significant and functions as a hero-ideal which is manifested in the American passion for competitive sports.[19]

In trying to explain his working method Jung employed a word, *Menschenkenner*, that was comprehensible to his original German audience but has no exact equivalent in English, where it is translated as "student of human nature." The word evokes many associations, but is most directly related to one well-established school in German thought rooted in the scientific writings of Goethe. Goethe had reservations about the increasingly dominant scientific method promoted by the British empiricists. He wrote extensively on botany, developing a methodology that emphasized the observer's *anschauung*, or viewing into the phenomena. To truly understand anything he felt that a participating—not a detached—consciousness is required (this is the basis of Rudolf Steiner's life work). This approach championed intuition over rationality, and gained popularity with many German intellectuals who saw it as Germany's unique contribution to the world of science; it was a viewpoint espoused by Keyserling and his circle. It was marked by disdain for the experimental emphasis in contemporary psychology.

The example Jung gives to illustrate this approach is his anecdote about a stop he made in Buffalo during his 1910 trip to America where he stood outside a factory and watched the workers exit. He commented to his companion afterward how surprised he was at the high percentage of Indian blood in evidence. When his companion contradicted this, Jung concluded that what he saw, the "mysterious lndianization of the American people," must have been due to their contact with the American earth. In support of his observation Jung referred to the research done by the German-born, American anthropologist Franz Boas and published by the US Immigration Commission in 1909. This study noted significant changes in the bodily forms of descendants of immigrants and this included the skulls, which had been considered the most stable of anatomical features. This landmark field study concluded with the hypothesis that the changes were due to such environmental factors as intermarriage, family size, health, and nutrition. There is no mention of "lndianization," which Jung claims results in a "Yankee type" very similar to the "Indian type." In fact, the workers Jung was observing were not "Yankees" at all, but Slavic immigrants from Eastern Europe! The "Indian" features that Jung observed might well have been due to the Mongolian influence in portions of that population.

Jung is here pursuing a dubious line of reasoning, using scientific findings to support idiosyncratic conclusions at odds with those of the researcher. He put a premium on his own talent for *Menschebkenntnis*. Since this approach relies on feelings, it all too frequently became a rationalization for the cultural stereotypes of the day. This is evident in an example that Jung gave at the beginning of his discussion where he says, "At our elbows we can observe in the Jews of the various European countries noticeable differences..."[20] He goes on to list a number of different Jewish types, and further distinguishes among a variety of Russian Jews: Polish, North Russian, and Kossack. In his self-assurance, Jung does not realize that this is more problematic than he would like to think since there was no such thing as a "Kossack type" Jew. The Russan Orthodox Kossacks were notorious anti-Semites and responsible for numerous pogroms in the Ukraine. Even his opening remark plays to the prejudices of his audience by its association to rubbing elbows with Jews. All this should put us on guard when it comes to Jung's anecdotal anthropologizing.

Jung's new network provided a variety of different publishing opportunities. It is important to realize that Jung did not publish any original books between 1921 and 1944, those that did appear were either new editions of older works or were anthologies of articles that had been appearing in various journals. Through the efforts of Count Keyserling, the Reichl Verlag of Darmstadt rather than Rascher, Jung's regular publisher, brought out his 1928 work *The Relation between the Ego and the Unconscious*, a greatly expanded version of a work that first appeared in 1916 as *The Structure of the Unconscious*. The most significant addition for us appears in his discussion of the collective psyche. "[A collective attitude] means a ruthless disregard not only of individual differences but also of differences of a more general kind within the collective psyche itself, as for example differences of race."[21]

Jung elaborated on this statement in a footnote in which he identified the following races: Aryan, Semitic, Hamitic, and Mongolian. This is a clear indication that Jung had adopted racial categories current in the German-speaking world that were at variance with those generally accepted in the Anglo-American world. He went on to assert that with the beginning of racial differentiation, essential mental differences among the races developed. He concluded that the spirit of a foreign race cannot be transplanted into "our own" mentality without sensible injury. This troubling line of reasoning is made even more so by the first sentence of the footnote that is here translated accurately into English for the first time: "Thus it is a quite unpardonable mistake if we accept the conclusions of a Jewish psychology as generally valid!" The English versions in the original 1928 translation and in the *Collected Works* alter this in two very important ways: first, the exclamation point is replaced by a period and the "we" disappears. This manipulation blunts what was intended

Freud

by Jung to be an emotional wake-up call to his readers. In sum, he was cautioning them that to accept the conclusions of a Jewish psychology based on a mentality "essentially" different from their own was not only mistaken but injurious. As we have seen, Jung had for over ten years been articulating in public and in private his conviction that Freudian psychology must be understood in racial terms. Unfortunately he failed then and later to appreciate the emotional investment he had made in this position and dismissed the allegations of anti-Semitism by his critics as "cheap accusations."

It was at the School of Wisdom that Jung made the acquaintance of Prince Karl Anton Rohan, an Austrian aristocrat who had founded the Transnational Intellectual Union in 1922, announcing that "True culture demands not only the creative force of individual ingenuity, but also a social caste, trained by tradition for receiving and promoting the work of the creating mind, and helping to mold it. Therefore we desire to unite all such supporters of tradition as are willing to help in reforming . . . the problems of petrification and destruction."[22] Jung participated in the Kuturbund activities which Rohan organized in various European cities and it was through this that Jung met Jolande Jacobi, who was at that time the secretary of the main branch of the Kulturbund in Vienna. (She later moved to Zurich where she became a Jungian analyst, writer and cofounder of the Jung Institute.)

In 1925, Rohan started a journal, *Europaische Revue*, which became one of Germany's leading opinion-makers. It mixed articles on literature, current events, and economics from some of Europe's leading intellectuals, including Jung, who placed nine pieces in it between 1927 and 1934. Among them were "Women in Europe," "The Spiritual Problem of Modern Man," and "Basic Postulates of Analytical Psychology," whose original title was "The Unveiling of the Soul." Jung covered a great many different topics in these articles (for example, his first formulations about the "objective psyche") but what they do have in common is their rhetorical tone which can best be characterized as equal parts Nietzsche and Lao Tze. He was certainly flattering his audience when he wrote that unlike the pseudo-moderns "the really modern man is often found among those who call themselves old-fashioned."[23]

This contact led in turn to Jung's affiliation with the *Neue Schweizer Rundschau* and its editor Max Rychner. In 1929, "Women in Europe" appeared as a pamphlet from the journal's publishing company which also brought out short works by Max Scheler and Alfred Baumler, later to become one of the most outspoken of Nazi intellectuals. Involved as he was in publishing and lecturing, Jung later entertained the idea of starting his own journal with Jacobi's help. He went so far as to choose a title *Weltanschauung* and a list of possible contributors, but decided against it in light of the economic realities of such a venture during the economic depression of the time.[24] In 1936, the *Neue Schweizer Rundschau* published Jung's article "Wotan," his major analysis of the contemporary German scene. He interpreted events there through the prism of his archetypal theory, noting the widespread activation of the Wotan archetype in German culture and society. I will here confine myself to a consideration of the personal references Jung made in the article. Nietzsche dominates Jung's discussion, which is no surprise, since Jung was in the middle of his seminar on *Zarathustra*. Of more specific interest for us are his passing mention of Stefan George, Ludwig Klages, and Alfred Schuler. What must be understood is just how connected Jung was personally to these men.

Although not mentioned by name, the key figure in all this is Oscar Schmitz, who had been associated with the Stefan George circle before World War I, and who was a prominent figure on the Schwabing scene, Munich's bohemian quarter. He would have given Jung first-hand information about all these men and provided Jung with perceptive advice about the German cultural scene. It is very likely that it was Schmitz who introduced Jung to the 1919 novel *Kingdom Without Space* by Bruno Goetz which Jung would later declare to be a prophetic anticipation of coming events in Germany. The plot involved the impact that a group of mysterious boys had on the life of a small provincial town. In particular, Jung interpreted this allegorical work as an expression of the archetype of the puer aeternus that was also influencing the German Youth Movement.

With the deaths of Richard Wilhelm in 1930 and Schmitz in 1931 another phase of Jung's career came to an end. Wilhelm had introduced him to the wisdom of China, especially to the philosophy of Taoism and the I Ching. Schmitz's efforts to promote Jung's psychology in Germany had been successful: Jung was now lecturing there frequently and seeing his articles appear regularly in the *Europaische Revue*. This activity led to the formation of the first Jungian study groups in Germany and the inauguration of Jung's first German-language seminar in 1930, the topic being the visions of Christina Morgan that were being analyzed in a concurrent English-language seminar. The foundation of the Jungian movement in Germany was being laid.

Jung's most important disciple in Germany was a Munich doctor, Gustav Richard Heyer. He had been a peripheral figure in the Stefan George Circle and then a decorated war hero. His mentor at the

University of Munich was Friedrich Muller, the professor of internal medicine who had years before been Jung's professor at Basel. He had invited Jung to follow him to Munich and open a practice in internal medicine but without success. Heyer's interest shifted from medicine to psychotherapy and he became one of the leading organizers of the General Medical Society for Psychotherapy, founded in 1926 to promote the new profession. One of his co-founders was Carl Haberlin, a doctor working at a sanatorium in Bad Nauheim where many of the group's annual conferences were to be held. Haberlin had been early participant in Keyserling's School of Wisdom, lecturing on yoga at the School's 1923 conference. He was also a major proponent of Ludwig Klages' life-philosophy, writing many articles and books about it through the 1920s and 30s.

Most people picture Jung after his break with Freud as a solitary psychologist, the sage of Bolligen, surrounded by a small group of loyal followers. This image needs to be considerably revised, since Jung was very active throughout the 1920s promoting his work, especially in Germany. His affiliation with Keyserling was the key event in that it led to his meeting a congenial group of intellectuals through the School of Wisdom. Max Scheler, one of the decade's leading philosophers and a speaker at the School's 1927 conference, made the following comment in his lecture "[Ludwig Klages] is primarily responsible for providing the philosophical foundations for the pan-romantic conception of man which we now find among many thinkers in different scientific disciplines, for example Edgar Dacque, Leo Frobenius, C. G. Jung, H. Prinzhorn, Theodore Lessing, and to a certain extent, Oswald Spengler."[25] Although he is wrong in saying that Jung derived his ideas from Klages, Scheler does locate Jung accurately in his new, post-Freudian milieu. In spite of their many different interests and points of view, these thinkers all did share a common concern for the deeper dimensions of the human experience, exploring it with variations of the intuitive, symbolic epistemology pioneered by Goethe. We should remember that, in addition to the role of the personal equation in theory-making, there is an equally important "social equation" that establishes the intellectual context in which that theory is defined. That social equation is dominated by the network of intellectuals who debate the theory through such institutional forums as conferences and journals.

All this was leading Jung to greater involvement in the expanding psychotherapeutic movement in Germany. He joined the General Medical Society for Psychotherapy in 1928 and immediately became a regular presenter at its annual conference and contributor to its journal

Die Zentralblatt der Psychotherapie. Heyer soon became what can only be described as Jung's "crown prince," serving for Jung the function that Jung had himself once served for Freud. For example, Jung favored Heyer as the editor of his aborted magazine and his delegate in Germany after he had become the Society's president and Journal's editor in 1933. In the same year Heyer joined Jung as a charter member of the Eranos Conference where presenters from the moribund School of Wisdom found a new home.

Heyer introduced Jung to the Tubingen historian of religion Jacob Hauer, who got close to Heyer and Jung through his expertise in yoga, presenting on that topic at the Society's conference in 1931 and to the Psychology Club of Zurich in 1932. Shortly after Hitler's assumption of power in January, 1933, Hauer founded the *volkisch* German Faith Movement. The fact that Jung continued his friendship after this point was to have consequences as grave as his decision to accept the Society's presidency that same fateful year.

Notes

1. C. G. Jung, *Collected Works* 10, ¶ 1034.

2. 1923 and 1925 UK seminars are in the collection of the Kristine Mann Library, New York.

3. William McDougall, *Is America Safe for Democracy*? (New York: Scribners and Sons, 1921), pp. 125–127.

4. Herman Keyserling, *Europe* (New York: Harcourt, Brace, 1928), p. 333.

5. George Mosse, *The Crisis of German Ideology* (New York: Grosset and Dunlop, 1964), chapter. 7; Leon Poliakov, *The Aryan Myth* (New York: Barnes and Noble Books, 1996), chapters 10, 11.

6. Thomas Gosset, *Race* (New York: Oxford University Press, 1997), p. 377.

7. *C. G. Jung Speaking* (Princeton: Princeton University Press, 1977), p. 30.

8. C. G. Jung, *Analytical Psychology* (Princeton: Princeton University Press, 1989), edited and introduced by William McGuire, pp. xii–xiii.

9. Herman Hesse, *The Journey to the East* (New York: Noonday Press, 1969), p. 6.

10. Richard Noll, *The Jung Cult* (Princeton: Princeton University Press, 1994), p. 93. For more on Keyserling, see Walter Struve, *Elites Against Democracy* (Princeton: Princeton University Press, 1973), pp. 299–304; for a critique of Noll's scholarship, see Sonu Shamdasani, *Cult Fictions* (London and New York: Routledge, 1998).

11. For more on these various movements, see James Webb, *The Occult Establishment* (Glasgow: Richard Owen Publishing, 1981).

12. For more, see Geoffrey Field, *Evangelist of Race* (New York: Columbia University Press, 1981).

13. Leon Poliakov, *The Aryan Myth*, pp. 275, 285.

14. Herman Keyserling, *The Recovery of Truth* (New York, Harper and Brothers, 1929), p. 399.

15. For more, see *Myth, Religion, and Mother Right—Selected Writings of J. J. Bachofen* (Princeton: Princeton University Press, 1973), introduction by Joseph Campbell.

16. Toni Wolff, *Structural Forms of the Feminine Psyche* (privately printed for the Students' Association of the C. G. Jung Institute, Zurich, July, 1956).

17. C. G. Jung, *Contributions to Analytical Psychology* (New York: Harcourt, Brace, 1928), p. 118; *Collected Works* 10, ¶ 53.

18. Ibid., p. 139.

19. For a contemporary perspective on this dimension of Jung's thought, see Michael Vannoy Adams, *The Multicultural Imagination* (London and New York: Routledge, 1996).

20. C. G. Jung, *Contributions to Analytical Psychology*, p. 135.

21. *Collected Works* 7, ¶ 240.

22. Prince Karl Anton Rohan, "Manifesto of the Transnational Intellectual Union" in *Der Geistige Problem Europas von Heute* (Verlag der Wila, 1922).

23. *Collected Works* 10, ¶ 154.

24. Letter to Jolande Jacobi, December 23,1932 in *C. G. Jung Letters.* vol. 1 (Princeton: Princeton University Press, 1971), p. 113.

25. Max Scheler, *Man's Place in Nature* (Noonday Press, New York, 1971), p. 85.

CHAPTER 4

Joan Dulles Buresch-Talley

The C. G. Jung and Allen Dulles Correspondence

Joan Dulles Buresch-Talley received her B.A. from Harvard University and a Diploma in Analytical Psychology from the Society of Swiss Hospitals. She studied at the C. G. Jung Institute in Zurich and worked at the Klinik am Zurichberg. She was an extraordinary member of the Swiss Society for Analytical Psychology, past-president and Training Analyst for the Inter-regional Society of Jungian Analysts in North America and is a member and Training Analyst for the C. G. Jung Institute of Santa Fe, New Mexico.

In the autumn of 1942 my father, Allen W. Dulles, arrived in Switzerland to take up his post as mission chief of the Office of Strategic Services (OSS), the American intelligence agency. It was not long before he contacted Jung. He first met him in 1936 when Jung was in the United States for the celebration of the Harvard Tercentenary, and had had a long talk about the rise of Hitler and Mussolini and the European situation in general. This was the year Jung had written "Wotan," and my father had obviously been impressed with what he had to say. Now, with the United States in the war, psychological insight into enemy leaders took on heightened importance; psychological warfare was a top priority for Dulles. Out of this grew meetings between the two men. After the war, Jung, as we shall see, turned to my father for help

I myself arrived in Zurich very soon after the war ended in 1945. I found myself among people whose work with Jung and his ideas were central to their lives. Mary Bancroft, for instance, who had worked for my father, had analyzed with Jung, and had played a role in some of the Dulles/Jung exchanges. Also, my mother, always deeply interested in psychology, undertook an analysis with Jolande Jacobi in the course of which she had several sessions with Jung. At that time, I could never have imagined that 26 years later I myself would be a Jungian analyst

Allen Dulles, during his professional life, served under eight Presidents. In 1916 during the presidency of Woodrow Wilson he was First Secretary to the Minister to Austria and was part of the delegation representing the United States at the funeral of the Hapsburg Emperor Franz Joseph in Vienna in 1916. He retired nearly 40 years later under President John F. Kennedy, as the second and longest-serving director of the Central Intelligence Agency (CIA) to which post he had been appointed by Eisenhower in 1953. He was called out of retirement by President Johnson to sit on the Warren Commission, charged with investigating the assassination of President Kennedy. In his early years as Director of the CIA, his brother, John Foster Dulles, was Eisenhower's Secretary of State.

When Allen Dulles died in 1969, his papers were given to Princeton University, where they are housed in the Seely Mudd Library. It was only seven years ago that I went to Princeton to look at the collection. There I found a sequence of letters concerning Jung and one exchange between the two men.[1] There are eighteen letters in all, eleven of which are particularly pertinent, spanning twenty years, and all having to do with the accusations leveled against Jung concerning his attitudes toward the Nazis and the Jews. While my father's letters throw considerable historical light on the accusation that Jung was pro-Nazi, they do not address one way or the other the issue of anti-Semitism.

Belatedly, I had become conscious of the Lingering Shadows Conference, in 1989, the two day workshop on Jung and anti-Semitism in Paris and the book *Lingering Shadows: Jungians, Freudians and Anti-Semitism.* I was reminded of my own powerful experiences at the gatherings of Germans, Jews and others of us, once enemies, now colleagues, at both the Jerusalem (1983), where it had been unscheduled, and Berlin (1986) IAAP Conferences. Those gatherings were extraordinary. When I learned that a follow up volume to *Lingering Shadows* was in the making, it seemed the ideal place to publish these Princeton archival letters. As we know, a great many of Jung's personal papers have not been published nor have they been open to researchers; thus the historical record is seriously incomplete. I am glad to be able to contribute a small corrective to this situation.

Who, then, was Allen Dulles that Jung should wish to converse with him and later turn to him in distress? For this, I would like to quote from the introduction of a book that appeared in 1996, titled *From Hitler's Doorstep: The Wartime Intelligence Reports of Allen Dulles 1942–1945*:

> For thirty two months during World War II, the mission of the Office of Strategic Services (OSS) in Berne, Switzerland, was an American observation post at Hitler's doorstep. It transmitted thousands of messages to Washington, many of them bearing evidence of the personal involvement of Allen Dulles, mission chief. OSS Berne constituted a virtual Central Intelligence Agency in itself, with operations ranging from the gathering of battle order information, to running espionage networks in enemy territory, to orchestrating unconventional military operations. Dulles ventured far beyond the usual domain of intelligence, offering his own views on grand strategy and psychological warfare.
>
> The historical significance of the Berne episode is multifaceted. We see in action one of the important figures of twentieth-century American statecraft at the height of his powers. The messages also offer a new perspective on the history of World War II, providing rich detail and insight and a bridge between diplomacy and intelligence. The Berne Operations and the views of Dulles deserve a place in the final analysis of the political/military course and outcome of the conflict. With regard to the evolution of American intelligence, the Berne documents indicate the emergence of institutional cohesiveness and proficiency in trade craft. One stands at the moment of OSS transition from old-fashioned political intelligence-gathering to more sophisticated techniques of the modern era.[2] Three months after his arrival Dulles sent the following secret cable. (105 is David Bruce, head of OSS, London, Burns is Dulles) on February 3, 1943:
>
>> To 105 from Burns. . . I have been in touch with the prominent psychologist, Professor C. G. Jung. His opinions on the reactions of German leaders, especially Hitler in view of his psychopathic characteristics, should not be disregarded. It is Jung's belief that Hitler will (not) take recourse to any desperate measures up to the end, but he does not exclude the possibility of suicide in a desperate moment. Basing his statement on dependable information, Jung says that Hitler is living at East Prussia headquarters in underground quarters, and when

> even the highest officers wish to approach him, they must be disarmed and X-rayed before they are allowed to see him. When his staff eats with him, the Fuehrer does all the talking, the staff being forbidden to speak. The mental strain resulting from this association has broken several officers, according to Jung. Jung also thinks that the leaders of the Army are too disorganized and weakened to act against the Führer. You can inform Paul M. that I am certain that Mrs. Frobe Kapteyn and Jung are OK.[3]

In volume one of *C. G. Jung: Letters,* there is one to Allen Dulles dated February 1, 1945, three months before the end of WWII, in which Jung expresses his approval of Eisenhower's proclamations to the German people at the historic moment when Allied armies crossed the western border into Germany.[4] Mary Bancroft was at the time working for Dulles, specifically on German matters. She told me a story—which can also be found in her book *Autobiography of a Spy*—about this exchange of letters.[5] She said my father was interested in Jung's opinion of the effectiveness of U.S. propaganda. Jung had made the point that no one was going to risk their lives listening to the Allied radio only to be told what a terrible people they were. When Mary Bancroft told my father that Jung approved of Eisenhower's proclamation, Dulles suggested she ask Jung to write him a letter to that effect, which he would then forward to Eisenhower. Although the letter seems to me to be written in a typically Germanic style, Mary says that Jung asked her to write that letter and she did. Shortly, an answer came from General Bedell Smith, Eisenhower's Chief of Staff, saying how pleased Eisenhower was to have received Jung's letter and asking Dulles to inform Jung of this. Dulles then asked Mary to write appropriate letters to Jung and to Eisenhower for his signature. Mary ends the story by saying that she knew Jung would be amused to hear of her criss-cross role in this series of letters; she told him and indeed he was!

The war ended in May 1945, and so did the Jung/Dulles conversations; we do not know how frequent they were; we only know they were important to both sides. This is the way Dulles describes it in a letter to M. Esther Harding.

> [I]n the face of events as they developed toward the close of World War II. . . I was frequently in Zurich and often journeyed to Jung's house on the lake. I greatly profited from my conversations with Jung during these days.[6]

Two gifted men, close in age, at the height of their powers. They met, I fancy, on a common ground: Jung, the far-ranging, psycho-social theorist and Dulles the psycho-political internationalist. There was a war to be won, complex situations to be understood. That was their meeting place. And there was no question at all in Dulles's mind: Jung was unquestionably anti-Nazi.

Immediately after the war ended, however, there arose voices of accusation against Jung. For many different reasons, some justifiable, some much less so, Jung found himself at the center of controversy concerning his own views about Hitler, Hitler's rise to power especially, and Germany's attitudes towards the Jews. In the context of these accusations, Jung asked my father to be, in effect, a character witness for him. Included below are all the relevant letters held in the Allen Dulles archives at Princeton that have to do with Jung.

On February 25, 1950, C. G. Jung wrote to Allen Dulles, asking for his help in refuting the accusations that he was a Nazi. Unfortunately, we do not have a copy of this letter. My father replies on March 14th:

> Dear Dr. Jung,
>
> I have your letter of February 25, 1950 and 1 have sent it together with its enclosure, with regard to Dr. Bitter, to a very close friend of mine who has an important position with our High Commissioner to Germany, namely Mr. Shepard Stone, formerly of THE NEW YORK TIMES [*sic*].
>
> I have warmly endorsed your recommendation and hope to get a favorable reaction to it. As soon as I hear I will write you further.
>
> I look back to our days together in Switzerland during the war. I know how ridiculous are the charges which some people have made about you and I took great pleasure in writing a letter to Paul Mellon on the subject a few days ago.
>
> Faithfully yours,
> Allen Dulles[7]

Jung's response was sent on March 21, 1950:

> Dear Mr. Dulles,
>
> Thank you very much for your kind letter and most valuable help.

I am glad that you also have taken action in the case of that ridiculous accusation that I'm a Nazi. Well, you know what it is to be in the lime-light.

Gratefully yours,
C. G. Jung[8]

As he said he would, Dulles sent Jung's letter on to Shepard Stone, on March 14, 1950:

Dear Shep,

I enclose herewith a letter I received the other day from Dr. C. G. Jung of Zurich together with its enclosure, with respect to a certain Dr. Wilhelm Bitter.

During my work in Switzerland I saw a good deal of Dr. Jung and came to have a high regard for him. Certainly he was useful to me. Of course, you know of his reputation in the field of psychoanalysis, etc. To my mind he is one of the outstanding citizens of Switzerland and is prominently associated with the Universities of Zurich and Basel. The stories about Dr. Jung that have been circulated by malevolent people that he was pro-Nazi are, in my view, entirely unfounded and fall into the category of character assassination, of which we have too much these days.

I happen to know nothing about the case of Dr. Bitter but would appreciate it if you could have someone look into the matter. Personally I should be inclined to accept Jung's judgment about the man in the absence of striking proof to the contrary.[9]

Before receiving Jung's letter on March 25, 1950, Dulles had already written on the 17th of February to Paul Mellon of the Bollingen Foundation, with whom he had obviously discussed the matter of the accusations against Jung, probably elicited by the *Saturday Review of Literature* article mentioned in the letter. Once again, and perhaps in its clearest form, Dulles repeated that his experience of Jung was as anti-Nazi and anti-Fascist.

Dear Mr. Mellon,

When we met the other day I mentioned to you my surprise at the attacks which had been made on Dr. Karl [*sic*] Jung and I have told you that I would be quite willing to put down in writing what I had said to you orally.

I first met Dr. Jung in 1936 when he was here in connection with the Harvard Tercentenary. At that time I had a long talk with him about what was going on in Germany and Italy and I do not recall the slightest trace of anything which Jung said which indicated other than a deep anti-Nazi and anti-Fascist sentiment.

It was, however, in 1943 that I first came to know Dr. Jung well. At that time, I was the representative in Central Europe, with headquarters in Switzerland, of the Office of Strategic Services. In that capacity, I may add, it was a part of my job to be familiar with the backgrounds of the prominent personages in Switzerland who might have pro-Nazi or pro-Fascist leanings and who accordingly would be dangerous to me in my work. In the welter of rumors that came to me it was not always easy to judge truth from scandal-mongering. I may say, however, that to the best of my recollection it was never intimated to me from any quarter that Dr. Jung had any pro-Nazi or Fascist sympathies.

During my stay in Switzerland from time to time I had long conversations with Dr. Jung on political developments in the world and we discussed together the characteristics of the sinister leaders of Nazi Germany and Fascist Italy. His judgment on these leaders and on their likely reactions to passing events was of real help to me in gauging the political situation. His deep antipathy to what Nazism and Fascism stood for was clearly evidenced in these conversations and I personally do not credit the idle gossip, the twisted interpretation of casual remarks or phrases taken out of context which appear in certain articles I have seen in the Saturday Review of Literature and elsewhere regarding Dr. Jung.

There is grave danger in the public life of today of too easily accepting guilt by association, but these articles seem to me to go even beyond this by building up a fictitious association and then attempting to lay a charge of guilt on this strange base.

Faithfully yours,
A. W. Dulles[10]

This period in 1950 was by no means the first time that Allen Dulles had been approached to defend Jung. Geoffrey Parsons of the *New York Herald Tribune*, in a letter dated December 21, 1945 wrote to my father;

Dear Allen,

The Jewish campaign against Jung is in full cry. Its leaders have very little to go on. They keep repeating a few items out of their context. I don't want to go on giving them space. I would like very much, however, to give his enemies one more whack in our columns. I am wondering if you would be willing and feel free to have the last word on the other side?

What I have in mind is not a review of the evidence or any elaborate quotation from sources, but simply your own judgment as you stated it to me. Very possibly you do not feel free to take part in such a controversy. But if you do, I feel you could give an authoritative report. That would count weightily on the side of the angels. The mere statement that you had spent as many years as you did in Switzerland during the war, that in the course of your government service it was part of your responsibility to collect facts about such a figure as Jung, that your sources were both German and Swiss, and that on the basis of a thorough examination of the evidence you had no doubt whatever that Jung was consistently, before and during the war, anti-Nazi in thought and action, would constitute a real public service.

Incidentally, I find in the correspondence reaching me, a disputed fact. The supporters of Dr. Jung asserted that he was on the black list of the Nazis. Do you know whether that statement is correct? If it is, I suggest that you might include it in your statement.

I shall quite understand if you don't feel free to write such a "letter to the Editor." If you do, I shall be most grateful for anything that you send me.

Yours faithfully,
Geoffrey Parsons[11]

The exchange of letters follows:

January 2, 1946

Dear Geoffrey:

I spoke to you briefly at Ham's wedding about your letter with regard to Jung. As I told you, I liked the man, found him anti-Nazi and anti-Fascist in his ideas and approach to world problems. I am, however, ignorant of the positions he may have taken in writing and otherwise during the period prior to 1942 when I first got in touch with him and I hesitate to get into a controversy without knowing my facts. Accordingly, I have asked Clover, who is now in Zurich, to scout around and see what she can find on the subject. When I hear from her I shall get in touch with you.

As far as I recall there was no German blacklist which was available to the public. There was a booklet published early in the war by the Germans and circulated to their agents warning them against contact with a long list of people in neutral countries. I had a copy of that list but I do not recall whether Jung was on it. I am endeavoring to ascertain this fact.

Faithfully yours,[12]

January 22, 1946

Dear Geoffrey:

Referring to our correspondence with regard to Dr. Jung, I enclose a letter which I have just received from Clover.[13]

Some of this psychological jargon does not make much sense to me but the upshot of it seems to be general agreement in Switzerland as to Jung's proper attitude. I rather surmise, however, that some of his psychological writings might be twisted to mean almost anything to the uninitiated. Is the matter still a live issue here?

Please send back Clover's letter when you are through with it.

Faithfully yours,[14]

February 21, 1946

Dear Geoffrey:

With further reference to the matter of Dr. Jung, I enclose a copy of a letter which he wrote to a friend of mine in Zurich in connection with the attacks on him. I doubt whether you would be interested in the excerpt from the article on Jewish psychology which Jung enclosed in his letter and which is in German, but I will hold it available in case you should later wish to see it.

Faithfully yours,[15]

February 22, 1946

Dear Allen:

I am most grateful to you for securing that long and interesting letter from Clover, and also for the copy of the letter from Dr. Jung. I have decided for the time being to hold our horses. But I fear that the Jews will not rest until they have made further attacks. The leader of the anti-Jung-ites among our correspondents, Mr. Parelhoff, is still in touch with us. He asserted that he had been to Washington and secured a mass of evidence sufficient to blow Jung out of the water, and spoke vaguely of writing an article for some psychiatric journal. Nothing has appeared as yet. Perhaps in the end it may be necessary for you to write a definitive statement yourself. In the meantime I think we can wait till we see the whites of their eyes. The Jung letter is certainly persuasive, isn't it?

Yours faithfully,
Geoffrey[16]

It is clear that, as this exchange of letters developed, Allen Dulles knew he could not go into detail about all of Jung's views since he did not know his writings. However, his admiration for the man and his own experience with him in 1936 and in the war years more than justified his speaking out in his defense. One last pair of letters regarding Jung and my father is of some interest.

June 13, 1961

Dear Mr. Dulles,

The death of Professor Jung gives me the courage to write you these lines. It was you who in an evening party at Per Jacobssen's in 1942 gave me the impetus to be instrumental for the nomination of C. G. Jung as professor ordinary of the Basel University. For Jung it was a great satisfaction and for our university an everlasting honour. Behind all that it was your remark which was at the origin of that nomination. Basel has lost one of her greatest citizens. . . Jung was a great Swiss patriot and Switzerland looses with him a prophet. . . .

With my kindest regards, yours sincerely.
A. L. Vischer[17]

Dulles answers on July 25,1961:

Dear Mr. Vischer,

I received and read with the greatest interest your letter of the 13th of June about our mutual friend, Professor Jung. Both Mrs. Dulles, who knew Jung well and I have mourned his passing. He was a remarkable man and my own experiences have been enriched having known him.

Interestingly enough, I recall vividly the evening party to which you refer.

As I left the dinner, I said to myself that I had been rather brash in what I had said, but it came from the heart and I was really gratified when I heard later that this played some small role in Jung's nomination as Professor at Basel University.

Not only Switzerland but the world was the loser when he passed away.

Mrs. Dulles and I are in close touch with Mrs. Jacobi and if you see her, please pass on messages from us.

Faithfully yours,[18]

Jung, Jungians, and the World: A Personal Reflection

The fact that public allegations against Jung—the same ones addressed in the Dulles correspondence—continue through the decades to this very day, highlights Jung's silence at a defining moment in modern history. That silence cannot be overlooked. He himself never gave an accounting—a psychologically true accounting—of his own attitudes and feelings specifically about the plight of the Jews in Hitlerian Germany. Therefore, it has fallen upon us of the next and later generations of his students and practitioners to explore and open that silence. At the two-day "Jung and Anti-Semitism" workshop held during the 1989 IAAP Paris Congress, and earlier at the "Lingering Shadows Conference" in 1989 in New York City, and now in the two volumes inspired by that latter conference, we have come to realize that we must go beyond shadow theorizing. We must walk into Jung's life and make every effort to feel what was at work there, and remain open to what the record and individual experiences have to say, amid the judgments that follow. We are called upon individually to broaden the scope of review, and need to include ourselves in it in ways that were begun in the first volume of *Lingering Shadows.* It has been suggested that it is important to separate the work from the man. There are also times when it is equally important to keep the work and the man together. Jung's life, work, and shadow kept together are a storehouse of possibilities for our own self recognition.

The most influential part of my training was the five-plus years I worked at the Klinik am Zurichberg in Zurich,[19] the thirty-bed Jungian research hospital first envisioned by Dr. Frey-Wehrlin as he stood nearby as Jung was interred in his grave in Kusnacht. With help of many people including Dr C. A. Meier, the hospital, a place where Jung's insights into the psychoses could be implemented psychotherapeutically, opened its doors with Heinrich Fierz as Medical Director and Dr. C. T. Frey as Executive Director. Lodged in two private houses in a beautiful garden, it was as close to a home environment as any hospital could be. One of the houses had, in fact, been Marie-Louise von Franz's childhood home.

My years there were an initiation into living Jung, so great was the freedom to experiment, to learn on one's own, to absorb through oral transmission understandings of the conscious/unconscious interactions in the very ill. It was a rich mix of Jungian attitudes that Frey, Fierz, and Meier and others who had been close to Jung applied to the problems at hand and discussed theoretically. It was an incomparable place to study and learn.

Years later, I realized an even deeper importance to my training at the Klinik. Because I experience Jung as a man of extremes, someone who mines ore in dark places, declares paradoxes and dangers, and pushes us toward individuation—a goal of almost impossible dimensions—I found that the psyches of the profoundly disturbed gave me the best intimation of the journeys and challenges that Jung was saying the normal person might have to undertake in order to be fully alive. All around me in the clinic were the terrors of the encounter with the unconscious gone wrong; the terrible frozen stasis of the psyche identified with an archetype, and its opposite, the relentless inhuman energy of the psyche without a home base. These experiences that I had with very psychotic people demonstrated the need of the healthy mind not to lose its footing but also the need for that same healthy mind not to be aware that those dark extremes live in it and are enacted around us repeatedly, especially during times of war. Jung's work at Burgholzli, the state psychiatric hospital where he began his career, was surely central to his developing thought and for me the experience at the Klinik became the natural setting for Jung's ideas.

Beyond being a man of extremes, Jung was a Shape Changer. If I were the child in the fable, I would certainly not say of Jung "the emperor has no clothes." Rather, I would say "Forget the clothes. Can't you see that he is a Shape Changer, changing form over and over as he marches down the parade ground?" There is Jung the prophet, foretelling the German catastrophe, and Jung as mana figure offering cures for all the ills of the Western World. He is his own Siamese twin, the unconscious trickster figure. There is Jung the musician writing *Mysterium* as a never-ending composition of alchemical themes and variations, He is the diamond-cutter bringing forth facets of collective dreams and visions, as with Pauli and *The Vision Seminars*. He is the Ancient Mariner urgently grabbing hold of any passerby to tell of his fateful encounter with the unconscious that nearly killed him and could kill you and me, too, but we cannot afford to miss it. He is Jung the lonely seer who feels unheard and as messenger of the unconscious, little understood. And he is Jung the clear, wise, brilliant teacher. To differing degrees, we Jungian analysts are disciples, lovers, friends, and victims of these many forms and their penetrating insights.

There are aspects of Jung's psychology that are hard to bring into the world of private practice and normal, everyday, often affluent, life. The dramatic realities still jump off the pages of Jung's works, and while it is possible to see many of these things in our patients and ourselves, a reductive process is at work. Just as the water for a big city is brought to the city's edge in huge pipes and is then transferred into the size of pipe that brings the water in an orderly manner into our kitchens, so have we, in my opinion, done a similar process with Jung's ideas. We have narrowed the life force of Jung's teachings to meet the professional need to do therapy, lecture, teach, and make "therapeutic sense" to others. This is, indeed, a part of our work and appropriate to a large society. But equally there is the need to incarnate more of the complex fullness of Jung into our own individual attitudes in order to approach the crux of what the Jungian heritage is essentially about—who you are first, and therapy second. We sincerely imagine that we are "walking the talk" when, in fact, it is possible that we are instead largely accruing understanding. The shadow of understanding inexorably appears when understanding displaces lived life.

Was this in part what happened to Jung when he himself became enthralled with understanding the dynamics of the collective unconscious erupting in Germany to the detriment of the human dimension? Or, equally, I can imagine it went against his deepest ethical reality not to hold out hope until all hope was gone for the individuation of the German people. Was his allowing the Jews to be scapegoated one more time the terrible Faustian price he was willing to pay to satisfy his great desire to have his psychology valid for national life?

That Jung was tortured by his stance is clear from what he said in After the Catastrophe: "We are on the whole much more deeply involved in the recent events in Germany than we like to admit. . . . I confess that no article has given me so much trouble, from a moral as well as a human point of view. . . . I had not realized how much I myself was affected."[20] But almost as if this admission was too painful to continue, he shifts his diagnostic disdain on the "blood drenched madness of the Germans." It makes reading *After the Catastrophe* an unpleasant experience. Throughout his life, Jung enjoyed his eagle eye that could take in huge areas at a glance, but he often eschewed using the leopard feet needed to carry the body forward one step at a time, one feeling at a time, measuring out the distance in actuality, taking the time to develop feeling. Not long before his death, Franz Jung, in a conversation with Jerome Bernstein, told of his father's frustration throughout his life at not knowing how to build a bridge from his insights on collective matters to an application that could offer the possibility of a better outcome in the world.[21]

This must concern us, too. It isn't rash to say that too few of us are out there reading the book of life and reporting back. As Andrew Samuels wrote in *Lingering Shadows*, "Our private practice with a privileged clientele is not politically neutral. Our way of working has affected our way of thinking. We have to question our automatic preference for the inner world and our tendency to make 'inner and outer' into polar opposites rejecting multi-disciplinary work as unpsychological."[22] We have also, I believe, separated ourselves from a natural recognition of our and Jung's imperfections and so have not given sufficient attention to the criticisms that have confronted Jung and analytical psychology over the years.

The all-important role of mourning in renewal and de-idealization has been suggested in separate articles by Andrew Samuels and Arvid Erlenmeyer, et al.[23] In the latter piece, "There is a constant temptation to avoid the work of mourning, but a high probability of reproducing situations which threaten to be destructive to us."[24] For me personally, mourning within the context of *Lingering Shadows* requires that I identify and empathize with Jung's own loss and therefore our loss as Jungians, from his inability to put aside his arrogant opinions about the Jews, so that he could be personally affected and have had to address the inconceivable destruction of human life while it was happening. Even more painfully, I have been forced to identify and struggle to empathize with my own and my culture's failure to see the depth of our own unconsciousness with regard to the Jews.

Both Aniele Jaffé and Jolande Jacobi built mourning into their lives. Jacobi told me that she took time out at the end of work on Friday to spend time weeping for the sorrows of the world. If no event came to mind, she would go back over the saddest things she could think of because only actual affective participation in the tragic events of one's time can do justice to the actuality of one's embeddedness in the world. And similarly, Aniele Jaffé mourned with the knowledge and deep feeling that, given another draw of the cards, she could have been that criminal who had just that very day committed some heinous crime.

In concluding, I want to express my gratitude to those originators and organizers who, with courageous insistence, bore with all the ponderings and meetings that were necessary to bring to life the 1989 Lingering Shadows conference, the two-day Paris "Jung and Anti-Semitism Workshop," and the subsequent volumes and articles that their efforts sparked. It often takes 50 years for an individual or group to summon the reflective power to become subtle and persuasive critics of their own work and of their leader. This is an important time for those in the Jungian collective to make real for themselves all that which has been brought to the surface. And to assign a greater reality to many of our own unanswered doubts and questions.

Notes

1. The letters are located in the collection of Allen W. Dulles Papers archived in the Seeley Mudd Library at Princeton University, Princeton, New Jersey.

2. Neal H. Petersen, editor, *From Hitler's Doorstep: The Wartime Intelligence Reports of Allen Dulles 1942–1945* (University Park, Pennsylvania: The Pennsylvania State University Press, 1996), p. 1.

3. Ibid. pp. 36–37.

4. Gerhard Adler and Aniela Jaffé, eds., *C. G. Jung: Letters*, vol. 1 (Princeton: Princeton University Press, 1977).

5. Mary Bancroft, *Autobiography of a Spy* (New York, William Morrow and Company, 1983), pp. 73–74.

6. Quoted in a letter from Dennis Stillings to Allen W. Dulles dated June 22, 1967. Letter is in Box 50, in the Allen W. Dulles Papers collection in the Seeley Mudd Library at Princeton University.

7. Box 35, Allen W. Dulles Paper, Seeley Mudd Library, Princeton University.

8. Ibid.

9. Box 53, Allen W. Dulles Papers, Seeley Mudd Library, Princeton University.

10. Box 39, Allen W. Dulles Papers, Seeley Mudd Library, Princeton University.

11. Box 44, Allen W. Dulles Papers, Seeley Mudd Library, Princeton University.

12. Ibid.

13. Clover Dulles, wife of Allen Dulles. Whereabouts of letter unknown.

14. Box 44, Allen W. Dulles Papers, Seeley Mudd Library, Princeton University.

15. Ibid.

16. Ibid.

17. Box 55, Allen W. Dulles Papers, Seeley Mudd Library, Princeton University.

18. Ibid.

19. The Klinik am Zurichberg has changed hands and no longer holds the original philosophy of treatment that was in place when I trained there.

20. C. G. Jung, "After the Catastrophe", in *Collected Works,* vol. 10, ¶ 402 (Princeton: Princeton University Press, 1964).

21. Jerome Bernstein visited Franz Jung in August, 1989. He had sent him a copy of his recently published book *Power and Politics: The Psychology of Soviet American Partnership* and relates that in discussing the book, Franz Jung said he was astonished, for he could not have imagined his father's theories applied to the political context in such a direct and practical manner. He said his father would have been astonished, also. One of the great disappointments of Jung's life, especially in later years, was that he could not get principal political figures of his time to understand his concerns and to use his theories in an applied way on the world scene. He described to his son a dinner where Churchill and Allen Dulles were present. Churchill, who sat next to Jung, went sound asleep when Jung tried to engage him in a new approach to managing conflict and sustaining peace in the post-war world.

22. Andrew Samuels, "National Socialism, National Psychology, and Analytical Psychology," in Maidenbaum and Martin, eds., *Lingering Shadows,* pp. 206-207.

23. Ibid, p. 199.

24. Arvid Erlenmeyer, et al., "Destructiveness in the Tension between Myth and History," in *The Archetype of the Shadow in a Split World,* proceedings of the Tenth International Congress for Analytical Psychology, Berlin, 1986, p. 329.

Part II

Lingering Shadows: The New York Conference

CHAPTER 5

Jay Sherry

Instead of Heat, Light

The following article is Jay Sherry's comprehensive and insightful review of the 1989 Lingering Shadows Conference in New York. It originally appeared as "Instead of Heat, Light: Lingering Shadows: Jungians, Freudians, and Anti-Semitism—Conference Held at The New School, New York, March 28," in *The San Francisco Jung Institute Library Journal* 8, no. 4 (1989):28–42.

In the spring of 1989, an international conference of unusual significance was held in New York. Entitled "Lingering Shadows: Jungians, Freudians, and Anti-Semitism," it was co-sponsored by several organizations with widely differing perspectives on this topic: the C. G. Jung Foundation of New York, the Postgraduate Center for Mental Health, and the Union of American Hebrew Congregations. The conference itself was held at The New School for Social Research, which was a fitting location. The New School's Graduate Faculty was founded in 1933 as the University in Exile to provide a safe haven for intellectuals fleeing Hitler's Germans'. It was here that Jolande Jacobi faced down one of Jung's most fanatical postwar critics over the issue of his alleged anti-Semitism. The spring 1989 meeting was the first time in a public forum that this topic was discussed at length and in detail, permitting a direct confrontation with a controversy that has clouded Jung's reputation for over fifty years.

The conference format was as follows: introductions by Dr. Jeffrey Satinover, President of the C. G. Jung Foundation of New York, presentations by the speakers, reactions from two respondents each evening, and, finally, questions from the audience. The focus of the first night was on understanding what Jung actually said and did; the second night explored the broader phenomenon of prejudice and scapegoating; and the final night was more personal, including a report from Zurich and an up-close look at Jung's relationship with Erich Neumann. In this review of the conference I will first summarize the papers of each speaker with my own amplifications and personal remarks noted parenthetically; I will conclude with a few overall responses to the issues raised.

Paul Roazen, author of *Freud and His Followers* and other books on the history of depth psychology, expressed his reluctance to talk on this subject at all and spent the first half of his talk discussing Jung's generally unacknowledged contributions to psychoanalysis: the crucial importance of the training analysis, some techniques of short-term psychotherapy, the concept developed by Ernst Kris as "regression in service of the ego," and the use of infantile material as a defense (dubbed by Max Schur "resistance from below").

Roazen related learning from a discussion with the French intellectual Paul Ricoeur about the latter's *Freud and Philosophy,* that in spite of many similarities with Jung, Ricoeur was almost totally unfamiliar with Jung's work. When Roazen remarked on this, Ricoeur responded that in Paris one could not read Jung since he was on "the Index." The reason for the exclusion had to do with the theme of the conference—Jung's alleged anti-Semitism and possible Nazi collaboration. Postwar Paris, dominated by leftist intellectuals, would not tolerate a thinker who had so compromised his integrity. (This assumption about Jung became the basis for identifying him with a reactionary standpoint, in comparison to Freud, whose theories became associated with progressive thought through the efforts of Wilhelm Reich and the Frankfurt School of Social Psychology.) Since Jung was "not correct" politically, his whole work could be dismissed.

Roazen then located for the uninitiated the origin of the charges of Jung's anti-Semitism: they date from the 1914 publication of Freud's *On the History of the Psychoanalytic Movement.* (The damning passage that he did not quote is: "he [Jung] seemed ready to enter into a friendly relationship with me and for my sake give up certain racial prejudices which he had previously permitted himself.") In fact, there is no evidence of any prejudice on Jung's part during their collaboration. Freud's assertion may be seen as a projective identification inasmuch as his choice of Jung was determined by his effort to distance psychoanalysis from its

Jewish/Viennese origins. Roazen then quoted the passage in Jung's 1934 article "The State of Psychotherapy Today" *(Collected Works,* vol. 10, ¶ 353–354) in which Jung differentiates between Jewish and Aryan psychologies. (I would advise any reader interested in this topic to start by reading this article of Jung's.) Roazen then made two surprising assertions that he failed to explain or support: first, that much of this statement had validity and that Freud's psychology was a characteristically Jewish one. He then went on to ruminate about the relationship between what Jung wrote and did during the 1930s and the effect of this relationship on his theory of the psyche. In their mixture of directness and ambivalence, these remarks seemed to capture the nature of his talk.

Next up was Professor Geoffrey Cocks, author of *Psychotherapy in the Third Reich.* His talk was a historical review of Jung's relationship with Nazi Germany. Although brief, his accurate summary of events was important since so much misunderstanding stems from misinformation. (A recent example is the June Singer interview in *Gnosis* no. 10, Winter 1989, which confuses several key facts about Jung's activities during this period, creating a collaborationist image.) Jung became President of the General Medical Society for Psychotherapy in June, 1933, at the urging of his German colleagues and began to re-organize it as an international society, a change approved at the Bad Nauheim conference in May, 1934. An autonomous German society had been established the previous September and later took over the dissolved Berlin Psychoanalytic Institute, which it renamed as the Göring Institute after their leader, a cousin of the Reichsmarshal. Cocks made clear that Jung had nothing to do with the Institute. (The mistaken identification of Jung as head of the German Society has created the shadowy image of Jung as the "czar of Nazi psychiatry" in spite of the fact that the society was created to protect psychotherapy from control by psychiatry.)

Cocks cautioned Jung's critics to be more careful in their facts and his defenders to be more candid about what he said and did. He drew attention to the self-serving nature of some of Jung's postwar comments and to Jung's use of the word Aryan in the 1934 article. The word is in quotation marks in the English translation but is not in the original German text, indicating an editorial decision to alter its usage to create a, perhaps ironical, level of meaning other than the one Jung originally intended.

Looking at the broader cultural currents of the times, Cocks pointed out that Nazi ideology and Jung's psychological approach shared a common source in the German Romantic tradition, with its emphasis on the creative potential of the irrational. Both Jung and the Nazi propagandists decried modern materialism and longed for a spiritual rebirth, the Nazis through a mass political movement and Jung through individual self-reflection. (Although a German Romantic vocabulary resonated through both of these 20th-century developments they emerged in distinctly different ways: the Nazi ideology was based on a biological concept of blood; Jung's theory was based on his experience of the reality of the psyche.)

Jung's symbolic approach is grounded in typological distinctions that are cultural as well as individual. This cultural level was made clear by Andrew Samuels in the final paper, which was the evening's highlight. It opened and closed with his call for the audience to be both self-reflective and imaginally involved, admitting that, in spite of all our efforts, the shadows will linger anyway.

Samuels feels that pursuing the equation "collective unconscious = racial unconscious" is a mistake. He wants us to consider the twin ideograms of *nation* and *leadership* as pivotal in understanding Jung as a psychologist of nationhood. As far back as his 1918 article "Mind and Earth," Jung was imagining that nationhood was somehow created through the mysterious influence of a nation's soil on the bodies and psyches of its inhabitants. Samuels feels it was unfortunate that Jung emphasized the purely psychological interpretation of the nation at the expense of the complex historical, political, economic, and cultural forces that shape it. In effect, Jung constructed a typology of national characteristics, often speaking about French, English, and American psychologies. The most important of his typological schema for the history of his thought involved his distinction between Germanic and Jewish psychologies. Here Samuels clarified a point that has long concerned me. In discussing Jewish psychology, Jung never dearly distinguished the two possible uses of the term *psychology* as "mentality" or as "science." He viewed Freudian psychology as a "leveling psychology" which undermined the idea of national psychological differences ("in my opinion it has been a grave error in medical psychology up to now to apply Jewish categories—which are not even binding on all Jews—indiscriminately to German and Slavic Christendom"). Here Samuels saw a disconcerting parallel between Jung's view of the Jews and Hitler's: for Hitler, the Jews were internationalists who denationalize their host nations. Both men shared a persecutory obsession: for Hitler, it was a fear about the Jewish bacillus which was undermining the German nation; for Jung, it was a concern that a Jewish psychology was being imposed upon other groups and nations.

Samuels made another point: although Jung is generally viewed as apolitical, his interview on Radio Berlin in June, 1933, shows that Hitler's meteoric rise to power had impressed him and colored his thinking. After stating that every movement culminated in a leader ("Führer"), Jung gave Hitler as an example of a leader who listened to his own Voice. "The true leader is always one who has the courage to be himself." A textual analysis of the German language transcript shows how much Jung selected words and images that had a particular resonance for the contemporary German audience.

In his conclusion, Samuels urged Jungians to get on with the work of mourning Jung, of disidentifying with him so the achievements of the theory can be promoted and not the shortcomings of the man. In particular, he urged greater contacts with colleagues in the social sciences as well as using analytical psychology to explore the *experience* of group differences rather than advance formulaic definitions of these differences that often mask cultural stereotyping.

The two respondents offered a startling contrast to end the evening. The first was Hanna Kapit, a Professor of Psychiatry and a training analyst at the Postgraduate Center for Mental Health in New York. Her disjointed series of remarks seemed almost a caricature of critiques of Jung that have appeared over the years. She started off with an "analysis" of Jung's early life based on her reading of *Memories, Dreams, Reflections.* These early dreams and memories indicate, she said, a disturbed inner life: his cathedral fantasy and paternal difficulties contained problems that were repeated in his break with Freud. She then shifted her remarks to a consideration of the epistemological difference between psychoanalysis and Jung's approach. While psychoanalysis conforms to traditional parameters, she said, Jung was not interested in truth but only in "telling stories." She felt that Jung's conflicted personality resulted in dishonesty with Freud, his wife, and others. Her only reference to the issue of anti-Semitism came in her concluding remark, which was a rambling condemnation of Jung that without explanation linked him to the death of six million.

In contrast, the response of Michael Vannoy Adams, Associate Provost and Lecturer in Humanities at The New School, was alive with insights and flashes of wry humor. He first addressed the role of iconography in the Freud-Jung split, saying that although icons are okay, the differences that have split Freudians and Jungians have been more pathetic than tragic. The pathos of the split is symbolized in the relationship between Jung and Sabina Spielrein. Adams quoted one of her letters to Jung in which she discusses Siegfried, the symbolic Aryan-Semitic child that would be a result of their union, a union of Jung's and Freud's theories.

Adams then analyzed the conscious and unconscious components that go into the semantics of anti-Semitism. Taking Jung's statement "I am no anti-Semite," he considered what the moral implications of its unconscious opposite would be.

Adams concluded that the whole issue is an imaginative/imaginative question rather than a factual/historical one. Recalling a postwar photo of Jung with Rabbi Leo Baeck (to whom Jung had admitted "slipping up" for what he said in the 1930s), Adams asked the question, "What is that picture worth?"

The second session was opened by Arthur Williamson, Dean of Graduate Studies at California State University in Sacramento. His histrionic presentation was on the development of modern anti-Semitism. He claims this development had two phases. In the first, during the 16th and 17th centuries, England and Spain marked out different strategies for handling the Jews as a religious minority: for England, the path taken was political rights and civil toleration; for Spain, the path was racialized religion—intolerance, forced conversions, and laws of blood. (Throughout Europe, a controlling image for the biblically derived discourse of the time was the Beast of the Apocalypse and the feeling that one was living in "end times.")

The second phase in the development of modern anti-Semitism was the Age of Enlightenment, with its belief in the universal rights of man and the secular foundation of civil society. Williamson made the peculiar claim that anti-Semitism was not a reaction to the American and French Revolutions but rather was derived from them. His support for this assertion seemed to rest on a reference to Spinoza whose championship of universal reason led him to reject revelation and to imply that the Jews were obscurantists of his Enlightenment vision. After a few remarks about modern anti-Semitism (the word first appeared in Germany in the 1880s) Williamson concluded with the observation that modernism has been viewed as being derived from Jewish thinking, and so a rejection of modernism entails a rejection of the Jews.

Ann Ulanov's paper "Scapegoating: the Double Cross," which followed, was an insightful and moving one. Her evocative use of the word "cross" resonated through her talk. The double cross involves two crosses: one can be caught either in a complex of opposites in collision or in a betrayal. She gave a description of the Jewish rite of the two scapegoats: one was killed and its blood sprinkled around the temple precincts; the other bore the sins of the community and was driven into the desert. The fate of the two scapegoats might be seen as symbolic of the fate of the Jewish people: persecution and exile.

Ulanov explored the psychological dynamics of anti-Semitism, in particular the role of projection, where the "other" carries the feared bit of ourselves and so needs to be controlled. Such control involves a very basic psycho-social phenomenon: boundary setting. For Jung, this struggle was no mere intellectual exercise but was an experience that was both painful and blissful. One result of his struggle with the God-image was *Answer to Job.* There he makes clear that a deep encounter with the Self is always experienced by the ego as a wounding or defeat. Christians have tended to associate the Jews with this primordial, direct experience of the God-image; Jews are then persecuted out of the Christians' alternating desire and fear of the center.

Ulanov thinks Jung's strengths double-crossed him into complexes which stirred up his shadow and pitched him into the muck. He came up smelling and striking out at others. He failed to appreciate the subjective factor in his remarks about Jews and so violated his own analytical guidelines, applying categories to a whole group and failing to encounter the individual living persons involved. In his discussions of Jewish and German psychology, attack and defense are in greater evidence than therapeutic clarification. (One of the most notorious examples of this unconscious aggressivity was in a 1938 interview in which Jung says, "studying Germany as I would a patient, and Europe as I would a patient's family and neighbors, let her go into Russia. There is plenty of land there—one sixth of the surface of the earth. It wouldn't matter to Russia if somebody took a bite..." [William McGuire, ed., *C. G. Jung Speaking; Interviews and Encounters,* Princeton: Princeton University Press, 1977, p. 133].) I would note that this lack of feeling can also be seen in Jung's 1939 dream of Hitler where a sick cow appears *(Jung Speaking,* p. 181), indicating a problem with maternal empathy.

Jung's example reminds us of our own entanglements, according to Ulanov. How can we affirm our own way without condemning those who follow another way? She suggests that it is possible to recognize our boundaries, bring our opposites to awareness and so undergo spiritual transformation, rather than reinforcing our boundaries by expelling as "evil" what does not fit for us.

"The Analytical Psychology of C. G. Jung and the Zeitgeist in the First Half of Our Century" was the title of Dr. Hans Dieckmann's paper. He spoke with authority as one who had personally experienced both Jung's psychology and the Zeitgeist in Germany. I found it more valuable for individual insights than for its overall thesis. Dieckmann, who is now President of the International Association for Analytical Psychology, recalls that after the war he was treated as either a psychotic or as a criminal for being a Jungian! Leftists were equating Jungian psychology with elitism and fascism. Admitting that there is some truth to the charges of elitism and disdain for the masses, Dieckmann referred to Jung's response to a UNESCO inquiry in 1947 *(Collected Works,* vol. 18, ¶ 1388-1402). In discussing the efficacy of his analytical method, Jung wrote on that occasion that:

> [O]ne can apply this method with reasonable hope of success only to individuals endowed with a certain degree of intelligence and sound sense of morality. A marked lack of education, a low degree of intelligence and a moral defect are prohibitive. As 50 per cent of the population are below normal in one or other of these respects, the method could not have any effect on them even under ideal circumstances (¶ 1392).

Dieckmann himself refuted this claim, referring to his analytic work with patients of varving social and economic classes.

Admitting that Jung's correspondence shows that he was affected by anti-Semitism, he asked, as one would ask an analysand, "Where did it come from?" His own answer to this question came only after a psycho-historical survey that culminated in his analysis of how the 20th century's overthrow of kings led to the rise of dictators. He saw this regressive development as the result of the search for the Great Father who embodies the principle of order. Here Dieckmann cautioned against the danger of such collective solutions to the need for individuation by quoting a Chinese proverb: "A great man is a misery to his people." Dictators require enemies upon whom to project their paranoid fantasies. Dieckmann then answered the analytic question about where Jung's unconscious anti-Semitism came from with an interpretation: because Jung never overcame his earlier feelings about Freud, he identified for a while with the superiority expressed by Hitler. Dieckmann concluded by evoking in comparison to Jung's consciousness the image of a large lighthouse: it has a stronger beam to reach a wider horizon, but it is also darker at its base.

Edward Whitmont chose to focus his response that night on themes raised by Ulanov. He emphasized the universality of anti-Semitism in Europe and America and reiterated her interpretation of it as a religious problem. Materialism and literalism have been projected onto the Jews as God-killers, but it is the Jew who has become the *Agnus Dei* to take away the sins of the world. He warned against any false optimism about anti-Semitism, saying that it will persist until a genuine Christianity has developed which involves a persistent confrontation with the shadow and a withdrawal of projections.

Whitmont was followed by Dr. Mortimer Ostow, Professor of Psychiatry at the Jewish Theological Seminary of America. Most of what Ostow said stemmed from his participation in an ongoing psychoanalytic group studying anti-Semitism. Not surprisingly, anti-Semitic comments in analysis seem often to stem from a disappointment in a relationship with a Jew, such as Jung's disappointment with Freud. More recent research has focused on the anti-Semitic attitudes and actions of apocalyptic fundamentalist Christian groups. Many of these groups are dominated by regressive fantasies of a destructive and millenarian nature, quite similar to the Nazis. Such thinking can be connected psychoanalytically with the attempts of depressive personalities to regain balance: were the destructive fantasies to be turned inward, there would be the possibility of suicide, but turned outward, the aggression can be projected onto a "demon."

The final evening began on a personal note: Aryeh Maidenbaum, Executive Director of the C. G. Jung Foundation of New York confessed how difficult it had been for him as a Jew to deal with the issue of Jung's anti-Semitism. Introduced to Jung's thought by Dr. Kluger in Haifa, he had decided to pursue his studies in spite of some of the things he had heard about Jung. In Maidenbaum's opinion, Jung was neither a Nazi sympathizer nor an explicit anti-Semite. It is a matter of record that Jung had sponsored rules changes to accommodate Jewish members expelled from the German section of the International Society and that he did help Jewish refugees. We must, however, Maidenbaum told us, recognize the element of opportunism in Jung's acceptance of the Presidency of the General Medical Society for Psychotherapy. It was a means of gaining greater recognition for his theories, which he felt had been overshadowed by Freud's. What Maidenbaum found troubling was that Jung never issued an editorial rejoinder to the Göring manifesto and that he never published after the war a clear, unequivocal statement about his writings on Jewish psychology and his changes of heart.

The most unsettling information that Maidenbaum presented is a new fact that emerged from a series of interviews conducted in Zurich in preparation for the conference. It was confirmed that starting in December, 1944, the Analytical Psychology Club in Zurich instituted a rule that Jewish membership was not to exceed 10 per cent. This rule was in the form of an appendix to the club by-laws and never made public. One explanation referred to the wartime hysteria: members wanted to protect the Swiss character of the Club, fearing it might become dominated by Jewish refugees. Another was that it might protect Jung in the event of a Nazi invasion. This latter suggestion is not very convincing, since chances of an invasion at this late date were almost nil. Nor would it in any case explain why the rule was not rescinded until 1950, unless in both setting up and taking down the rule Jungians were characteristically slow to act. Further research would be necessary to determine Jung's culpability in this sad development. One story told on Jung's behalf concerned difficulties Aniela Jaffé was having in the Club, which led to Jung's threat to resign. Maidenbaum concluded by saying that although the existence of this rule was something of which no one could be proud, the honesty of those who would talk about it after all these years was admirable.

He was followed by the son of one of Jung's most important colleagues, Erich Neumann. Dr. Micah Neumann is a psychoanalyst and President of the Israel Psychiatric Association. He spoke about growing up in a household where the name Jung held a special place. When the rumors about Jung came up, his parents were embarrassed and said only that Jung had made mistakes. His father had worked with Jung in Zurich in 1933–1934 after leaving Germany and before going to Israel; at that time, he pleaded with Jung, to no avail, to make a clear statement of his position toward events in Germany.

Micah Neumann said that he had written about the Freud-Jung relationship and that his discovery of his father's correspondence with Jung after his mother's death in 1985 had given him an opportunity to explore yet another case of the father-son relationship.

He first reviewed Jung's 1934 article with its aggressive anti-Semitism and pro-nationalistic sentiments; he quoted the strong reactions to it expressed at the time by Jung's Jewish followers. How could the attitudes revealed in this article be reconciled with the fact that his father was working comfortably with Jung at this very time? Micah Neumann answered by saying that on a personal level, Jung was connected, but that he was unconnected on the collective level. This lack of relatedness stemmed from his relationship with Freud, where the father-son dynamics were compounded by religious differences.

He then surveyed the unpublished correspondence between his father and Jung. Neumann was looking for a spiritual mentor and wanted to engage Jung in his experiences as a Jew in Palestine. After the war, Jung supported Neumann who had been criticized for what he had written in *Depth Psychology and a New Ethic;* Neumann reciprocated by hailing *Answer to Job,* and in his last letter in February, 1959, expressed his admiration and identification with Jung's account of his life in *Memories,*

Dreams, Reflections. In Micah Neumann's judgment, Jung supported his father, whose Jewishness neither increased nor decreased his importance to Jung. In conclusion, he said that although there was no trace of anti-Semitism in that relationship, Jung was nevertheless anti-Semitic in the full sense of the word until after the war and that he never integrated this shadow experience into his life. The power of unexamined unconscious forces, he said, is something for us all to ponder.

Appropriately, one son of a first generation Jungian was followed by another—Dr. Thomas Kirsch, who described his experiences growing up in another Jungian home, where both parents, James and Hilda Kirsch, were Jungian analysts. His father took the same boat to Palestine that Neumann did but didn't feel at home and went on to England. Although Jung offered to sponsor him in Switzerland, he accepted a position in London and later emigrated to Los Angeles.

Thomas Kirsch also heard rumors of Jung's anti-Semitism, which his parents, though, feeling uncomfortable, would dismiss. He continued to wonder, what was it all about? He shared with the audience his own observations, Jung's attraction to the stirrings in the German psyche and his indifference to scientific-rational terminology. Kirsch commented on the importance of appreciating Jung's Swiss heritage, which involved a deep attachment to the land and surely contributed to his concern about the "rootless" Jews. Also, there was the fact that his first sustained relationship with Jews was with Freud and his circle and that this relationship ended in a painful rupture, whose enduring effects on Jung's psyche we can only surmise.

Addressing himself directly to Neumann's paper, Kirsch commented on several points and concluded with a provocative, rhetorical question apropos of his generational contemporary's interest in the Freud-Jung and Jung-Neumann relationships: what about the Neumann-Neumann relationship? Did he want his father to change his mind? How did his father feel about his becoming a psychoanalyst? He said that he could appreciate Micah Neumann's need to separate, since his own need to separate entailed moving from Los Angeles to San Francisco.

Philip Zabriskie followed and was the conference's final speaker. He described his comments as feeling-reactions to a controversy in which Jung exhibited a profound failure of feeling. He had asked himself a very unsettling question: does Jung's theory lead to racism? At first, the question seems preposterous: "of course not, otherwise we couldn't be Jungians." Still, Jung's lack of feeling did affect his psychology. We need to be very careful, Zabriskie said, with Jung's comments about the ethnic expression of the collective unconscious and the value of the irrational.

This psychology is, in part, a psychology of peoples, and, as such, can it avoid the pitfalls of stereotyping and negativity? Must we give it up? Zabriskie's answer is no, although we must recognize its misuse and be careful to use it as a vocabulary rather than a tool for control. (I am reminded of Samuels's call to put aside a pseudo-objective typological agenda and concentrate as analysts on the subjective *experience* of difference.) Does a positive valuation of the irrational link up with political irrationalism? Jung's critique of rationality and organized religion came out of his attempt to tap the transpersonal realm which reason tends to suppress. This attempt was at the root of his differences with Freud, who found superstitious what Jung considered profound. Zabriskie argued that Freud represented Jung's skeptical, irreligious shadow. Jung's 1934 article was, for the most part, a battle with that shadow, an effort to combat the Freudian approach to neurosis.

What defines a "Jungian," according to Zabriskie, is the concern for consciousness rather than rationality. This distinction is no guarantee of safety, but it does insist that genuine ego development will only occur by following the unconscious.

The questions from the audience at the end of each of these provocative sessions were far tamer than one would expect, especially from a conference about such a sensitive topic. Several times, questions and comments raised the possibility of reconciliation between Freudians and Jungians. Not surprisingly, nothing conclusive was arrived at, Micah Neumann saying that we are still at an early stage of such a process. This rather quiescent situation was upset in the conference's closing moments when Neumann made the off-hand, not really psychological, comment that Jung was anti-Semitic in the dictionary sense of the word and was challenged from the floor to explain himself. Unfortunately, this challenge was cut off by the moderator, who then adjourned the conference. It was a tricksterish moment that reminded me that the case is not closed.

Among the conference's achievements was the presentation of new data concerning the issue. Besides the already-mentioned Psychology Club membership rule was a startling revelation from Roazen that according to the Index of papers of the British Foreign Office, there exists a postwar booklet documenting the case of Jung's Nazi collaboration and his possible trial as a war criminal. This material is apparently still under restricted access. Cocks, too, recently came across new information while doing research in Germany. Records from the Nazi Education Ministry show that Nazi observers attended the Eranos conference in 1936; after they filed a report about its non-political nature, German participation was permitted. Although this event had nothing to do with Jung personally, it does show the politically-charged atmosphere that was invading even the precincts of the sacred at Eranos. A more active presence there was Wilhelm Hauer, a German Indologist, who spoke several times during this time. He was a Nazi and founded the German Faith Movement, which Jung wrote positively about in his 1936 article "Wotan." One wonders how much influence he had on Jung's thinking about the Jews and Germany.

This points up something mentioned by several speakers, mainly that Jung and the Nazis shared a common vocabulary derived from the German Romantic tradition with its emphasis on the folk soul and the transformative potential of the irrational side of the psyche. Both sought to revive the Romantic emphasis on the soul and shared a contemptuous rejection of the materialistic philosophy of the last half of the 19th century. The differences were equally important, however: the Nazis advocated a retreat *from* rationality while Jung sought to establish a psychology *beyond* rationality.

What was striking was that all the speakers admitted that the opinions Jung voiced did express anti-Semitic feelings; most referred to the crucial role of his relationship with Freud as the source of these unacknowledged feelings. Unfortunately, the effects of this relationship were more referred to than analyzed. I think it caused a deep resentment in Jung, a narcissistic rage, which blinded him to those who cautioned him about his remarks and left him feeling entitled to seek redress through public pronouncements of dubious scientific integrity.

Several speakers noted that Jung never made a formal postwar statement about his views. If we read his postwar writings as he tells us to read his other writings, that is, as "subjective confession," we will find that there he did express his feelings about the Jews and Hitler. (Harry Slochower has given us a challenging interpretation of Jung along these lines in his article "Freud as Yahweh in Jung's *Answer to Job*" in *American Imago* [vol. 38, no. 1, Spring, 1981].)

The closest Jung came to a public admission of regret was in the opening paragraphs of his article "After the Catastrophe." There he says:

> [the doctor's and psychologist's] relationship to the world involves them and all their affects, otherwise their relationship would he incomplete. That being so, I found myself faced with the task of steering my ship between Scylla and Charybdis, and—as is usual on such a voyage—stopping my ears to one side of my being and

> lashing the other to the mast. I must confess that no article has given me so much trouble, from a moral as well as a human point of view *(Collected Works,* vol. 10, ¶ 195).

More important than the conscious admission of difficulty is the unconscious slip within his classical allusion. Jung confused Odysseus's encounter with Scylla and Charybdis with the hero's preceding encounter with the sirens. Jung's slip can he taken as a complex indicator pointing to an area of unconscious vulnerability. Who are the sirens and why were they forgotten? They were the beautiful sea nymphs whose beguiling songs lured sailors to their deaths, negative anima figures whose voices gave them power. A series of associations from Jung's writings will lead us to the conclusion that Hitler is at the root of this slip. In his various analyses of the German dictator, Jung (1) repeatedly emphasized the power of his Voice (2) compared him to the Sybil or the Delphic oracle *(C. G. Jung Speaking,* p. 93) (3) characterized his unconscious as feminine *(Collected Works,* vol. 18, par. 578), and (4) observed that as a result of an anima possession he was destructive *(C .G. Jung Speaking,* p. 140). Jung stopped his ears to the friends and critics who tried to bring the anti-Semitic nature of some of his remarks to his attention. Like Odysseus, he thought he could listen to the siren/Hitler's Voice and not be affected.

It is not enough to say that Jung was simply stupid. Much of what he had to say, even about the Jews, had acuity. In spite of his often brilliant analyses, what was missing in his pre-war viewpoint? Like the majority of the people of the time, Jung failed on a feeling level to appreciate the depth of *evil* incarnate in Hitler and his movement. The medical and political neutrality that he claimed in the 1930s was unfortunately accompanied by a *moral* neutrality as well, which helps explain the ambiguous tone of his contemporary comments. We must remember that Odysseus did not survive the perils of Scylla and Charybdis by sailing a middle course; rather he deliberately chose to sail past Scylla and lose six men than risk the loss of the ship and all its crew. Although Jung claimed to have done the same, I think he showed less courage in the course he steered.

Besides the information and insights generated by the conference, one very important by-product of the conference was the preparation of a packet of chronologically-ordered quotations from Jung and others, which was made available to those attending. Copies of this packet, titled "Significant Words and Events" are in the libraries of the New York and San Francisco Jung Institutes; it is an invaluable resource to anyone interested in further exploring the primary documentation on the subject (see the updated version in Appendix A, p. 219).

Aryeh Maidenbaum, his co-director Stephen Martin and the Board of the Foundation are to be thanked for sponsoring this conference. It took courage and patience for these Jungian analysts to overcome a reluctance to face the issue; this frank discussion was a long time in coming. If Jungians are going to do more than pay lip service to "wholeness," then the discomforting fallibilities of their founder must continue to be faced squarely, casting more light on lingering shadows.

CHAPTER 6

Micha Neumann

On the Relationship Between Erich Neumann and C. G. Jung and the Question of Anti-Semitism

Micha Neumann, M.D., is a psychiatrist, Professor of Psychiatry at the Sackler School of Medicine of Tel Aviv University, and medical director of Shalvata Mental Health Center in Israel. His parents, Julie and Erich Neumann, were both enthusiastic followers of Jung. The fact of Jung's close relationship to Erich Neumann, who was both a Jew and a Zionist, stands in sharp contrast to the allegations of anti-Semitism and pro-Nazi sympathies that have been leveled against Jung.

In this paper, Dr. Neumann portrays the relationship between his father and Jung through reference to their extensive correspondence. He emphasizes that Erich Neumann exhorted Jung to become more aware of Jewish religion and culture, and regrets the fact that Jung never did this. It is clear, however, that Jung very much valued his relationship to Neumann and encouraged him in his work.

Dr. Neumann compares his father's relationship to Jung with that of Freud to Jung, and finds Jung to be the more compassionate and less ethnocentric mentor. While Jung's relationship to Neumann seems free of anti-Semitic prejudice, his writings and actions around the year 1934 definitely were not. Dr. Neumann suggests that Jung never came to terms with this aspect of his shadow.

Since the time of my childhood, Jung was a central and positive figure in our family. His photographs decorated my father's desk. His name, whenever mentioned by my parents, reflected respect, love, and friendship. I perceived his presence as that of a friend and teacher.

As I was growing up, the rumors that Jung was pro-Nazi and an anti-Semite disturbed me a great deal. When I finally asked my parents about these accusations, they became embarrassed and defensive. They said the accusations were unjust but admitted that Jung made mistakes and that he had been misunderstood.

I learned that my father had worked with Jung during 1933–1934 in Zurich. My parents left Germany for Palestine a short while after the Nazi takeover in Germany. Before their departure they witnessed brutal anti-Jewish demonstrations, propaganda, and persecution. My father told me that he tried to convince Jung of the terrible danger of the Nazi movement, of the brutality and inhumanity of the Nazis. He asked Jung to express himself openly and clearly against their ideologies and especially their anti-Semitic ideas and policies. He admitted that he failed to change Jung's attitude. My father warned him that if he kept quiet at such a bad time for the Jews, then it would always be remembered and he would never be forgiven. Jung, believing in the qualities of the German collective unconscious, insisted that something positive might still emerge from the situation.

My father pleaded with Jung to learn more about Judaism so that he could have a deeper understanding of Jewish roots, culture, and psychology. Jung was a far more willing student of Far Eastern culture than of Jewish culture, which was much nearer to his own. My father expected Jung to apply his great wisdom, creativity, and knowledge in order to be more closely involved with the present Jewish problem.

Even though Jung promised my father that he would study Judaism, he never really kept his promise. My parents, although understandably disappointed, regarded Jung's "oversight" as only an error, an aberration, a blind spot. This did not change a bit their very positive attitude toward Jung. "Even great men make mistakes," they said, and their love and admiration for Jung was not diminished. When I talked about these matters in my own analysis (a Freudian psychoanalysis), my analyst said, "Every anti-Semite has his own good Jews." He had no doubts about Jung's anti-Semitism.

The relationship between Freud and Jung and their painful breakup captured my interest, and in 1986 I published an article about this fascinating subject in the *Hebrew Journal of Psychotherapy.* I found myself intensely involved in the father-son relationship between Freud and Jung. I regarded the relationship between Jung and Erich Neumann also as a father-son relationship. I could not resist delving deeper into this matter and exploring it. For me, as a psychoanalyst and a Jew, Freud is the great-grandfather who was in a bitter conflict with Jung, my father's spiritual father. I decided to study these problems and reach my own conclusions.

After my mother's death in 1985, I found the correspondence between my father Erich Neumann and Jung. This same correspondence was the basis for an article I wrote about the Jung-Neumann relationship. And, coincidentally, it was just when I finished this paper that I received the invitation to speak on the delicate problem of Jung and anti-Semitism at the "Lingering Shadows" conference that took place in spring of 1989. You can imagine my excitement about this synchronicity.

When I read Jung's article "Zur gegenwärtigen Lage der Psychotherapie," published in the *Zentralblatt für Psychotherapie* at the beginning of 1934, I was quite shocked at his aggressive anti-Semitic expressions and pro-Germanic, pro-Aryan, pro-National Socialistic opinions and beliefs. To think that all this was written and published in German at the time when the Nazis were carrying out their evil anti-Semitic and anti-democratic plans in Germany made it even worse. This article aroused much criticism in the Jewish world, especially among Jung's Jewish disciples and colleagues. I studied Jung's correspondence from the year 1934 with these Jewish friends and found additional expressions that I could not avoid regarding as anti-Semitic. And finally, there was a letter from Jung to his former assistant in Berlin, Dr. Kranefeldt, a Nazi, dated February 9, 1934. This letter was full of contemptuous and sarcastic anti-Semitic remarks and expressions.

For me to realize that all these anti-Semitic ideas and terminologies were expressed at the same time that my father lived in Zurich and worked with Jung was shocking. Equally disturbing was the fact that, during that same period, while Jung held the Nazis in high regard and expressed such negative feelings against "the Jews," he also felt affection, respect, and even friendship toward my father.

Could my analyst have been right when he said, "Every anti-Semite has his good Jews whom he regards as exceptions, as different from the rest of the Jews"? How can it be explained that at the individual level Jung helped Jews and supported them, while at the collective level he was so completely indifferent and insensitive to their tragedy?

There must have been a *scotoma*, a blind spot, in Jung's psyche that was responsible for these outstanding discrepancies in his attitude and his behavior. The roots of this problem can be traced back to Jung's complicated, conflict-laden, and unanalyzed relationship with Freud. There were not only father projections on Freud but also strong elements of unconscious religious contents. He identified himself unconsciously with Nazi symbols, ideology, and anti-Semitism. He believed in the positive collective "Germanic soul," to which he felt he belonged. Is it not true that Jung's shadow remained repressed and cut off from his own consciousness?

In that same year, 1934, Jung declared his willingness to relate to the Jewish problem and to concentrate on the very special conditions in Palestine through his correspondence with my father, who had immigrated to Palestine. He even mentioned these promises and intentions in his letter to James Kirsch dated May 26, 1934. Through reading the correspondence between Jung and my father, I uncovered a different aspect of his attitude to his Jewish pupil Erich Neumann. Could this be the same anti-Semite who collaborated with the Nazis and believed in their future?

My father's first letter to Jung was written in the summer of 1934. It is a long and very interesting letter in which he tells Jung all about his first impressions and strong feelings as a new immigrant in Palestine and about his first encounter with the Jews there. The letter is very open, warm, and friendly. Neumann ends it by writing: "Dear Dr. Jung, as always it seems to me to be too cheap to thank you for all that I received from you. My ambition encourages me to give you as a gift of gratitude a creation of my own. I do not think it is difficult for me to say thank you, but it seems too little."

On August 12, 1934, Jung replied in a letter that has not been published:

> I do not think that the Jews suffered from a collective neurosis until the emancipation. The question is whether or not the emancipation influenced them in the direction of neurotization. The group, social, and national perception of the Jews until their emancipation was to some extent parallel to the spiritual and political situation of the Christians during the Middle Ages. With the liberation of the Christians from the authority of the church, archetypes awakened to life, and the Christian world is still busy assimilating them. In Germany this awakening brought manifestations of a new kind of paganism, which hearkens back to the distant past of the Germans and is a concession to the might of the ancient archaic pagan archetypes. Therefore, I believe that the Jews, who were emancipated from the authority of their religion, are threatened in a similar way from the awakening to life of their collective unconscious. One awakening archetype is no doubt connected to the land, hence the spiritual need of Zionism. To the extent that these awakening archetypes do not undergo digestion, assimilation, and integration, a neurotic situation can easily ensue. In the Western Christian world, neurotic restlessness is clear and apparent. . . .
>
> . . . I know that the Jewish problem is a serious subject that concerns you, while for me the psychic life of the individual and his

> mental situation are the most important issues. You can be assured that I will devote myself to your problem with all the means at my disposal. I feel it is especially important to discuss the complexity of modern culture and the spiritual situation in Europe with a Jew just like yourself. You know the situation in Europe well and yet think from a point of view that is different than mine, and you stand on your own archetypal ground. By the way, I was very intrigued by your dreams as a result of your encounter with Palestine. This is a real psychic blood transfusion.

Now comes an amazing passage:

> Jacob, in contrast to Esau, constitutes a symbolic attempt at collective individuation or, better, a stage in a collective development, as, for instance, historically Hitler is an attempt at collective individuation for the German, or mythologically, Jesus, Mithras, Attis, Osiris, etc. You are therefore quite right to look at the problem as a whole from the side of the collective unconscious and grasp Jacob as a symbolic exponent of the *Volkspsychologie.*

Further passages of this unpublished letter say:

> The non-Jews as "citizens of the world" cannot fall into an "outside" *(Aussen)* because they are already in the outside. Their number and the fact that they own the land are a counterbalance against the danger of the within. . . . Through his mere existence the Jew draws attention to these unpleasantnesses. Thus he falls into the shadow zone of the non-Jewish masses. They do not need self-defense (except in emergency situations) and only a small amount of intuition and therefore have a stronger perception for sensation and aesthetic perception (in order to enjoy their safe life).
>
> . . . In this way the Christians fall into the shadow of the Jews and are assured of their secret contempt, because they live in an immoral peace with all that the Jews may desire but is forbidden to them. . . . Only with the liberalization—i.e., the disintegration of Christianity with the enlightenment—did the Jew receive the counter-gift of the Danær (the Greeks), emancipation, and with it, the tradition, contradictory and God-alien joy of the world, which is always the fruit of living in physical safety.

The letter ends with the sentence: "What is the meaning of *Galuth* ["exile"]? A riddle."

In this letter, Jung impressed me as completely different from the Jung who expressed pro-Nazi and anti-Jewish prejudices. His observations about the influence of emancipation on the Jewish awakening archetypes is anything but anti-Semitic. His willingness to discuss Jewish problems and issues with Neumann is clear and friendly. No ambivalence or animosity against the Jews can be found.

The only striking passage in this letter is Jung's fantastic comparison between Jacob as a symbolic "stage in a collective [Jewish] development," and "Hitler as an attempt at collective individuation for the Germans." I believe that this most unfortunate passage from Jung's letter to Neumann is the reason for its exclusion from the published Jung letters. Yet it is interesting and astonishing to note that in August 1934 Jung still attributed to Hitler such significance as a collective individuation for the Germans.

The following passages are from a letter from Neumann to Jung dated May 19, 1935:

> I have stubbornly decided not to let you loose, and I want to warn you once again. I have a solid intention not to let you rest with the Jewish problem and, if necessary, I will regain the racial qualities of stubbornness and flexibility that I have lost. All this in order that you will lead me into the depth of these questions in such a manner that I will not be forced to see you in too narrow a light and too removed from Judaism. It seems that I have a confession to make, even though it is unpleasant for me to do so. Before I came to you in Zurich, I was a bit sad because I could not find a Jewish spiritual authority that I could accept as a teacher. Unfortunately I regarded it as typical of the present spiritual bankruptcy of Judaism and its inability to present me with a spiritual Jewish figure whom I could regard as a teacher.
>
> Only when at your side was that something which is prototypical of my situation revealed to me. It is written that the Jews have to go to "one of the righteous of the nations." Perhaps this is the reason they have none of their own. This Jewish situation and the beginning of mutual relationships and exchange of ideas between us are what make our correspondence so vital to me.

Neumann is still hoping that Jung, the teacher, will come closer to Judaism and lead him to the depth of the Jewish problem. He goes so far as to regard him as "one of the righteous of the nations," and this at the same time that Jung was under heavy attack for being pro-Nazi and anti-Semitic. This title, *michasidei umot ha-olam* ("one of the righteous of the nations of the world"), was given by the State of Israel after the Holocaust to those non-Jews who risked their lives and their families during World War II in order to save Jewish lives from a certain death.

In another letter to Jung, dated October 19, 1935, Neumann writes:

> . . . The work on Jewish contents is slow and difficult. Only slowly do I grasp in which points analytical psychology cannot be the sole ground on which I stand. This does not mean that I am not standing on this ground and that I cannot grasp its main meaning. What I comprehend today, more than before, is the fact that Jungian analytical psychology itself stands on its own ground, which is something so obvious that it is not conscious of it. Switzerland, Germany, the West, Christianity; this is no discovery, and yet it is for me. I have to learn to differentiate myself, and that is very difficult for me, especially when so much weight is just on the other side (the Western Christian). It certainly is easier to assimilate as "your Jews" are doing, but thus the assimilant Jews keep distant from their individuation, which must, in spite of everything, be based on our own archetypal collective foundations, which are different because we are Jews.
>
> I see a danger for me in analytical psychology. This is the danger of betrayal to my own Jewish foundations, for something that is more beautiful, wider, and more modern. Only a final realization of analytical psychology can prevent me from this danger. The temptation is regression instead of individuation (the golden calf instead of a "bad" Jehovah). Not in vain did you work so seriously on Christianity, but you lack knowledge and understanding of Judaism.
>
> . . . The obviousness of the fact that you are Swiss, a Christian, and a man of the West prevents you, and not only you, in a vital sense from understanding that we Jews are Jews. Do you not underestimate the significance of this difference in the analyses of your Jewish patients? It is true that you once expressed your disgust at the phenomenon of self-betrayal, but you never wrote about it and focused on the problem of Jewish identity. Do not regard this as insolence, but rather as a question. This matter is of extreme importance to me.
>
> . . . If you want to use the Jews as the yeast of European culture, they are really quite useful in this function, but in this way they remain *Kultur Juden*, psychologically without their own foundations, that is, without a potential for individuation. There must be a return to the land, as political Zionism demands, as

> well as a psychological return. In Europe the individuation of the Jews is impossible.

Here again Neumann deplores Jung's lack of knowledge and understanding of Jews, Judaism, and the problem of Jewish identity. He implores Jung to delve more deeply into these issues. He wants Jung to understand Zionism and its necessity and the fact that in Europe, true individuation of the Jews in the Jungian sense is really impossible. It is interesting to see how Neumann insists on the differences between Jews and non-Jews, a difference that, when pointed out by Jung, was regarded as anti-Semitic.

Jung soon replied to Neumann's letter on December 22, 1935.

> . . . What the European Jews do, I know already, but what the Jews do on archetypal soil, that interests me extraordinarily. . . The "*Kultur Juden*" are always on the road to being "not Jews." You are quite right, the way does not go from good to better but first downward, to the historical roots. I demand that most of my Jewish patients pay attention to the fact that they are obviously Jews. I would not do it if I did not see so often Jews who imagine themselves to be something else. For those to be Jewish is some kind of personal insult.
>
> . . . Your very positive conviction that the Palestinian soil is vital for a Jewish individuation is dear to me. How does the fact that the Jew lived generally much longer in other countries, rather than just in Palestine, relate to your conviction? Even Moses Maimonides preferred Cairo, though he could live in Jerusalem. Can it be that the Jew is so very used to being not a Jew, that he needs the Palestinian soil *in concreto* in order to be reminded of his being Jewish? I can, however, only enter with difficulty in my mind into a soul that did not grow on any soil.

Here we can see that Jung was indeed interested in Zionism and that he dearly regards the notion of Jewish individuation through a return to the land. Even his critical question regarding the Jewish preference for living in the Diaspora cannot be regarded as hostile. Jung's remark about his inability to identify with "a soul that did not grow on any soil" again demonstrates his personal difficulty in, perhaps even his resistance to, empathizing or identifying himself with the Jews and their history and culture, but that, too, cannot be regarded as anti-Semitism.

After *Kristallnacht* Neumann wrote a painful letter to Jung dated December 15, 1938.

> I do not know if you can imagine how difficult it is to maintain an inner relationship with a man who naturally feels, at most, a superficial connection to the events that injure all of us Jews. . . . It is understandable and natural for me to know that you live on quite a different level than ours. . . . On the other hand, it makes the approach difficult, though I am deeply convinced that I do not have to reproach you too much for being a distanced observer. I am sure you are involved in the events (as I experience daily) through your practice with your patients. Still I feel the need to write to you once again in order to sustain within me the feeling that even for a Jew like myself there still exists some piece of Europe.

I was considerably impressed by Neumann's almost desperate efforts to keep up his positive relationship with Jung. His hope to involve Jung seriously and deeply in Jewish issues failed, as did his expectation that Jung, following the aftermath of the terrible *Kristallnacht,* would speak out clearly against the Nazi persecution of the Jews. Even after *Kristallnacht,* which was a cruel physical assault on the Jews and their existence in Germany, Neumann continues to defend Jung. He is deeply convinced that he does not have to "reproach Jung too much for being a mere observer from afar." He makes a tremendous effort to hold on to Jung and sustain the feeling that even for a Jew like Neumann himself, "there still exists some piece of Europe." Jung represents this good piece of Europe that Neumann is so dependent on. Jung's speedy response came on December 19, 1938:

> You must not imagine that I retired to the snow-covered heights, above world events. I am even deeply involved and follow daily the newspapers on the Palestinian question and think often about my acquaintances there, who have to live in this chaos. . . . I have also predicted awful things for Germany, but when they really happen, it still will seem to me to be unbelievable. It can be said that here everyone is deeply shocked by what is going on in Germany. I have a lot to do with Jewish refugees and am permanently occupied with finding a place for all my Jewish acquaintances in England and in America. In this way I am in continuous connection with the events of our time. . . . I think you must be very careful concerning your opinion about your specific Jewish experiences. Truly there do exist specific Jewish traits in this development, but the specific Christian or Jewish traits have only a secondary significance. . . . Especially small is the difference between a typical

> Protestant and a Jewish psychology as far as the historical problem of time is concerned. Individual and race-related differences play only an insignificant role.
>
> It seems to me that the specific Jewish trait as well as the specific Christian trait could best be discovered in the way and manner in which materials from the unconscious are accepted by the subject. According to my experience it seems that the resistance of the Jew against them is more rigid, and therefore the attempt to resist much more vehement. I do not mean by this more than a mere subjective impression.

I was struck by Jung's insensitivity to Neumann's plea. In his opening words, he does not refer to *Kristallnacht* but rather speaks of the restlessness in Palestine. Later Jung writes that like everyone else in Switzerland he, too, is shocked by what is going on in Germany, but he offers no word of sympathy for the cruel fate of the German Jews, though he is very busy helping them. He goes on to say that the specific Christian or Jewish traits have only secondary significance. He writes that "race-related differences play only an insignificant part." Yet Jung insists on his subjective impression that the Jews are more resistant to materials from the unconscious than the Christians. Still, these views, which he reserves as subjective, could by no means be regarded as anti-Semitic.

On December 16, 1939, several months after the outbreak of World War II, Jung wrote to Neumann: "We here are naturally very much impressed by the direct danger of war in our own country, but in the meantime everything is still suspended. . . . In my lectures I deal with the Oriental position regarding the Yoga philosophy and the Western position regarding the Ignatian *Exercitia spiritualia.*"

As can be seen, it's business as usual for the Swiss, neutral Jung. Only after the beginning of World War II did Jung finally give up his position as the president of the International Psychotherapeutic Society, which practically ceased to exist at that time.

On January 13, 1949, Jung wrote to Jorg Firtz, an editor of *Die Weltwoche,* about Neumann and his book *Depth Psychology and a New Ethic:* "When I recommend his book, I do so mainly because he [Neumann] demonstrates what consequences can be reached when the ethical problem is exposed and explored without consideration and to the end. It should be taken into account that Neumann is a Jew and hence knows Christianity only from the outside, and in addition, we should know that it was demonstrated to the Jews in the most drastic manner 'that evil is always projected on the outside' as Neumann claims." Jung continues:

> But I am not the same Neumann, who was driven and pushed by a cruel destiny into a belligerent counterposition. If by doing so he brings difficulty to the world, causing some people to suffer, I am not astonished and I will not consider it disgraceful. . . . I also cannot be sorry should the so-called Christians suffer a little. They certainly deserve it. One always speaks about Christian morality, and I would once like to see the person who really performs it. Even toward Neumann they do not show the most quiet understanding, let alone "love for thy neighbor."

In this letter Jung is really supportive and empathic with Neumann the Jew. He claims that the Christians should suffer and that they deserve it. He attacks the Christians for lacking some understanding of Neumann and his ideas. Could it be that Jung also referred to himself, as a Christian who should suffer for his support of the Nazis and for his lack of empathy and understanding for the Jews, who themselves suffered so much from Christian compassionate love?

In a letter to Neumann dated August 28, 1949, Jung writes: "However, you have the tendency to judge the unconscious too pessimistically. It would be advisable to add to each negative comment a positive one; otherwise one may be impressed by a catastrophic tragedy without mercy from above. This would not be in keeping with the experience: 'God helps the courageous.'"

These remarks demonstrate the difference in mentality and approach between Jung and Neumann, the Jew who is still under the catastrophic impact of the Holocaust. Neumann, like the Jew Freud (who was also accused of being too pessimistic in his views of human nature and unconscious drives), sees the terrible dangers of an unrestrained, unbalanced, and erupting unconscious. In contrast, the naive and optimistic Swiss Jung really believes that "God helps the courageous."

In July 1950 Neumann wrote to Jung on his 75th birthday:

> In this little country [Israel], which is remote in many aspects and in many others productive and with good prospects for the future, I internally stand in solitude with a disintegrated Europe at my back and an Asia, dangerous in its awakening, in front of me. Just in such a situation, the connection with you meant to me vital support of decisive importance. . . . You were for me an internal guide, and this comforted me, especially because I, as a human being and a Jew, live, as you know, and experience things in many senses in a different and even opposite manner than you. Beyond the "incidents" and unpleasantnesses, I was always

left with a feeling of inner connection to you which is stronger than you imagine.

This letter demonstrates again why Jung's support meant so much to Neumann. The feeling of inner connection to Jung was more important than their different human experiences as Jew and Christian, or the incidents and unpleasantnesses that occurred between them.

On December 5, 1951, Neumann wrote to Jung about his not-yet-published book *Answer to Job:* "This is a book that conquered me to my depth. I think it is the most beautiful and deepest of all your writings. It can be said that it is not really a book. It is a dialogue and dispute with God, similar to that of Abraham, when he argued with God about the fate of Sodom. For me personally it is like an accusation sheet against God, who allowed six million of his people to be killed." Neumann is so enthusiastic about Jung's *Answer to Job* that he goes so far as to compare Jung to Abraham, the Jewish patriarch. Neumann identifies completely here with Jung in his charge against the Old Testament Jewish God Jehovah.

Jung's reply to Neumann's letter came soon, on January 5, 1952: "I thank you very much for your friendly letter and for the way that you understand me. This compensates for a thousand misunderstandings."

On February 28, 1952, Jung wrote to Neumann about his book *Amor and Psyche:* "I must humbly tell you how much your *Amor and Psyche* made me happy. It is excellent and written with a most powerful involvement." Here we can see that Jung, the generous, benevolent teacher and friend, supports Neumann and rewards him by admiring his strong involvement and his excellent work. How much Jung must have yearned for a similar attitude from Freud toward his work some forty years earlier. How different the father-son relationship of Freud and Jung from that of Jung and Neumann.

On October 11, 1958, Neumann wrote to Jung: "My relationship to you, as you know, does not depend on writing letters or conversations—better to say, is not dependent on them anymore—but each encounter with you always gives me a feeling of profound confirmation that cannot be found anywhere else." In another passage he says: "For me there exists a deep central attachment only with you yourself, and concerning all that is related to the mission of my work." Neumann feels no ambivalence toward Jung. He is now 53 years old, a writer and researcher who is much respected on his own merits. Yet he is very grateful for the "feeling of profound confirmation" he receives from Jung, which he cannot find anywhere else.

Neumann wrote his last letter to Jung on February 19, 1959, after reading Jung's manuscript for *Memories, Dreams, Reflections*. "For me it is the most beautiful of all your works, though I must admit that this has personal reasons. Of all that I have ever read, I cannot think of anything that is closer to my life perception and experience. . . . I have a life feeling that is very similar to that which speaks from your book."

In this letter we see not only that Neumann is grateful and admiring, but that he also feels deeply, beyond all the differences of religion, nationality, mentality, and age, that they share a very similar life experience. This letter, which was written two years before his death, best describes the depth and closeness that Neumann felt in his relationship with Jung.

Jung's last letter to Neumann is dated March 10, 1959: "Dear friend, For your deep and detailed letter from February 18, 1959, many thanks. . . . Without the reflecting consciousness of man, the world is of a gigantic meaninglessness. Man, according to our experience, is the only creature that can at all understand *meaning*." This was the last letter ever exchanged between them and the only one in which Jung addressed Neumann as *Lieber Freund* ("dear friend").

Erich Neumann died on November 5, 1960, after a short illness, in Tel Aviv. He was 56 years old.

Jung died on June 6, 1961, after a short illness, in his house in Küsnacht. He was 86 years old.

The relationship between Jung and Neumann was much closer and simpler than the very complicated, ambivalent relationship between Freud and Jung. Jung respected Neumann and supported him. He regarded him as a colleague, an equally creative personality, one who would continue and expand his work, and not as a dangerous adversary. He even defended Neumann to a certain extent against envious and competitive disciples in Switzerland.

The fact that Neumann was a Jew did not diminish in any way Jung's friendship toward him. Neumann's being Jewish did not increase his value in Jung's eyes, as was the case with Freud, who saw in Jung, the Christian, a real asset for the young science of psychoanalysis.

On the other hand, I cannot say that the fact that Neumann was a Jew and Jung a Christian did not play an important role in their relationship. It certainly had great meaning and significance, but anti-Semitism or philo-Semitism had nothing to do with it. Jung respected and appreciated the fact that Neumann was a proud Jew, a Jew who stood on his archetypal and collective roots. Jung believed in Neumann's Zionism as part of his true individuation and was enthusiastic about the return of the Jews to their native soil and roots.

Neumann guarded the positive relationship with Jung as something very delicate and precious. Jung symbolized for him the last and only positive spiritual bond between himself, the Jew, and treacherous Europe. He ignored, or perhaps even denied, the accusations that Jung was anti-Semitic.

Reading their correspondence carefully, I can detect no trace of anti-Semitism. Jung was objective toward the Jews and the Jewish problem. He disappointed Neumann because he did not get deeply involved in the Jewish question, as Neumann had expected, but almost all his expressions in the correspondence were free of anti-Jewish resentment or prejudice.

On the other hand, when reading about Jung's actions in 1934, and what he wrote, and knowing what was going on at that time in Germany and with the Jews, I am convinced that Jung was anti-Semitic in the full sense of the word. He was so at least until after World War II. His anti-Semitism was deeply rooted in his unconscious and erupted vehemently in the 1930s, just when anti-Semitism took its most brutal form in Germany. In Jungian terms, I would say that anti-Semitism was a component of Jung's shadow. It seems that he never came to grips with this aspect of his shadow. He never realized and confronted himself with his anti-Semitism and thus never suffered from the integration of this part of his shadow into his whole personality. Jung himself did not realize the full individuation and integration that he taught and sought all his life. Jung's anti-Semitism is an example of how, even in a great mind, when it has not been fully analyzed by an "other," there still lurk strong, unconscious, dark forces struggling without resolution.

CHAPTER 7

Aryeh Maidenbaum

Lingering Shadows

Aryeh Maidenbaum, Ph.D., is a Jungian analyst and director of the N. Y. Center for Jungian studies. Dr. Maidenbaum also serves as special consultant to The Jewish Museum of New York for its Educational Travel Programs. Among his publications are "Psychological Types, Job Change and Personal Growth" and "The Search for Spirit in Jungian Psychology." Co-editor of *Lingering Shadows: Jungians, Freudians and Anti-Semitism*, Dr. Maidenbaum, who taught Jungian psychology at NYU for many years, is the contributing Jungian author to *Current Theories of Psychoanalysis* (Robert Langs, ed.).

After discussing his personal difficulties in approaching this topic, and the path he took to Jung from his Orthodox Jewish background, Dr. Maidenbaum outlines his conclusions based on an examination of the record and interviews with people who had firsthand experience of the issues. He points to several areas that leave an inconclusive or conflicted impression, including the existence of a secret quota system for Jewish members of the Analytical Psychology Club of Zurich, which existed from the 1930s perhaps until as late as 1950. He concludes that, although Jung did not make policy for the club, he certainly must have known about the existence of the quota policy and clearly made no attempt to eliminate it. Thus, although Jung's own personal relationships with his Jewish students was unquestionably free of personal prejudice (indeed, at one point he went so far as to intervene on their behalf for admission to the club), on a public, collective level his refusal to address the topic is far from admirable.

This is a paper I did not want to write, on a topic I did not want to deal with, about a man whose psychology and ideas have played a most important part in my life. I come from a strong Orthodox Jewish background, and to this day Jewish history, culture, and tradition are a paramount aspect of the world I live in. Jung's psychology, in fact, helped me reconnect to my own Jewish roots and become a better Jew in the process. To have to deal with confronting this volatile and emotional issue of Jung's alleged anti-Semitism is not an easy task for me.

I discovered Jung through Rivkah Kluger, who was my first Jungian analyst, in Haifa, Israel. Dr. Kluger, whose own analysts included both Jung and Toni Wolff, was a very special woman, close to Jung and Jung's colleagues and friends in Zurich. In addition to being a Jungian analyst, Dr. Kluger was a scholar and student of Jewish and Near Eastern religion. In fact, two of her books, *Psyche and Bible* and *Satan in the Old Testament,* deal with building bridges to the world of the Bible through the application of Jung's ideas. Through Rivkah, a woman I loved dearly, I learned much about not only Jung's psychology but Jung the man. Certainly, to her, as someone who knew him well, there was no possible way he could be viewed as anti-Semitic.

My first indication that Jung's attitude toward Jews was in question came when, after completing my Ph.D. at the Hebrew University in Jerusalem, I applied for a postdoctoral grant. My request was initially approved, but afterward, when I indicated that I intended to use it for the purposes of study at the C. G. Jung Institute in Zurich, I was put on notice that this was not acceptable. Apparently, one of the committee members insisted that Jung had been not only anti-Semitic but a Nazi as well. I soon learned that this was a widely held view.

Through Rivkah's help, I was able to address the issue and refute some of the more blatantly false and ugly smears. It helped that Gershom Scholem had documented his own connection to Jung and had attended the Eranos Conferences, which Jung had been so much a part of. The committee ultimately approved my request, and I spent the next three years in Zurich, eventually completing my training as a Jungian analyst.

In Switzerland during these years, I was fortunate enough to meet, work, and study with a number of analysts who had been close to Jung, some of whom had even been in analysis with him. It was to these people, among others, that I turned, when the conceptualization of the "Lingering Shadows" conference became a reality, and the research I was engaged in took various turns and unexpected twists. It was for this reason as well that I enlisted the aid of a friend and colleague, Stephen Martin, to help plan the conference and conduct the research interviews in Zurich. We tried to keep an open mind in relation to the material at hand and approach this subjective problem on an objective level. We tried to be conscious of that aspect of the "transference" which might have inclined those who were in analysis with Jung to personalize their experiences and neglect to put the larger picture in perspective. In many ways, I have had to be careful and treat my own transferences (both positive and negative) in a similar manner, for I, too, feel personally connected to several of the people we interviewed, some of whom were quite involved with Jung during the turbulent earlier years and whose own actions are now coming into question. Dr. Martin helped me greatly in this process.

During the course of our research, interviews, and discussions, several conclusions have emerged for us:

1. Jung was neither a Nazi sympathizer nor a rabid, overt anti-Semite. Accusations along these lines are false and either unknowingly ignorant or maliciously slanderous.
2. Jung, as a consequence of accepting the presidency of the General Medical Society for Psychotherapy, was in fact able to reorganize that predominantly German group and, in theory, enable German Jewish psychotherapists to join a newly-formed international organization, with Jung as president. How many Jewish psychotherapists actually joined the newly formed international organization is not known.
3. Jung did, in fact, help many Jewish people, both personally and professionally, throughout his life, including the period in question.
4. Jung, however, was genuinely taken for a time with what he psychologically took to be a potentially positive resurgence in German nationalism during the early 1930s.
5. As part and parcel of this political activity, Jung had his own (perhaps opportunistic) agenda—to promote his ideas and himself. As many participants in the conference have agreed, the time has come to acknowledge this. From international activity to forming Jung institutes, Jung was understandably interested in seeing the work he was so involved in brought to a greater audience and attain widespread recognition.

6. Notwithstanding the shadow aspect of Jung's own personal positions, there appear to be "lingering shadows" among Freudians in their accusations against Jung. He is often portrayed as being guilty of much more heinous crimes than was the case. More often than not, even rudimentary knowledge of Jung's life and activities is lacking, leading us to understand that resistance to Jung's psychology and ideas plays more than a token role in this. In short, it is easier to discredit the man than deal with his psychology.
7. Finally, Jung himself said: "The greater the light, the greater the shadow." Jung, being indeed a "great light," had quite a large shadow, some of it revolving around his own attitude toward Jews, more on a larger, cultural, perhaps even *unconscious* level than personal, but there nevertheless. As a result of this, he got himself into trouble by picking an inappropriate moment in history to discuss the Jewish psyche—a time, moreover, in which he still knew very little about Jewish history, tradition, mysticism, or even as he put it, "cultural form." Undoubtedly, his complex and ambivalent attitude toward Jews was connected to his personal experience with Freud and his followers. Nevertheless, there appears to be no doubt that Jung did have his personal prejudices in this regard quite apart from Freud and the psychoanalytic movement.

There is nothing startling in reaching such conclusions. Even the most faithful and loyal of Jungians would accept this if they took the time to sift through the myriad primary and secondary sources available. There are, however, several areas that were particularly troubling, and we were hard pressed to explain them away.

First, what has troubled many Jungians all along has been the lack of a clear, distinct public statement by Jung dealing with his actions and more questionable pronouncements during the 1930s. And while he did disassociate himself from National Socialism and the politics of Germany, even in later years he did not unequivocally express regrets or show any understanding toward the sensitivities of Jews regarding his own, at best naive, earlier attitudes. In all likelihood, his personal admission to Rabbi Leo Baeck that he had "slipped up" must have been accompanied by a great deal of mutual soul searching for Baeck to have accepted Jung's apology.[1] But publicly, neither Jung, nor Baeck for that matter, ever said anything that would lead us to believe that Jung had come to terms with his own "Jewish shadow" issue of earlier years. In fact, even in his essay "After the Catastrophe," Jung discusses the Nazi distortions of "pseudo-scientific" race theories but neither mentions his own prewar writings, which lent themselves to similar misuse, nor directly refers to either the Holocaust or the catastrophe that had befallen the Jews of Europe.

Nevertheless, a most enlightening comment for one such article came from Siegmund Hurwitz. Dr. Hurwitz, eighty-six, is a deeply committed Jew who has written extensively on analytical psychology and Jewish topics. He told us that during the course of his own analysis with Jung (which took place over a period of ten years) he told Jung how troubled he was by some of Jung's earlier writings on the Jewish psyche, including the timing of his 1934 article titled "The State of Psychotherapy Today," in which he discusses the differences between "Jewish" and "German" psychology. Jung's reply to Dr. Hurwitz was: "Today I would not write this article in this way. I have written in my long life many books, and I have also written nonsense. Unfortunately, that was nonsense."

This was as close as we could get to an acknowledgment by Jung that there was anything wrong with what he had written and published in that period.

A second area that merited further investigation was the infamous manifesto written by Matthias Göring and inserted without Jung's knowledge and permission in the December 1933 edition of the *Zentralblatt.* It contained, in the words of Aniela Jaffé, "a declaration . . . by which the German branch of the society committed itself to Hitler's political and ideological principles."[2] Jung, as president of the international society, was the nominal editor of the journal. However, the journal itself was published in Leipzig, so that neither Jung nor C. A. Meier, his assistant at the time, could prevent what happened.

Unquestionably, this was done without Jung's knowledge. What troubled us was why Jung did not either write an editorial himself in a subsequent issue renouncing it and disassociating the international society from such a declaration, or even resign. We put the question to Dr. Meier, who made several points. First, Jung did no work at all on the journal. His understanding was that Meier would bear total responsibility, so that if anyone should have done something, it was Meier. And second, both Meier and Jung felt it was better to simply ignore the incident to avoid risking the breakup of the international society, which was able to protect Jewish psychotherapists.

In truth, acceptable answers for Jung's failure to make a public statement during or after the war do not exist. In general, the question—which we put not only to Meier but to a number of Jung's colleagues—as to why Jung did not apologize, renounce the 1933 *Zentralblatt* editorial, and/or resign the presidency elicited much defense but shed little new light. One possibility put forward was that Jung's anger at being attacked for an anti-Semitic bias he did not have pushed him in the direction of silence. Surely, if this was a factor, it served him poorly in the long run.

Notwithstanding Jung's private silence, an additional discovery during the course of our research proved even more difficult to come to terms with. Indeed, it was harder to ignore, owing to its overt content, rather than any omission. I am referring to the secret agreement limiting the number of Jews who could be accepted as members of the Analytical Psychology Club of Zurich. The club, with a membership of some fifty analysands of Jung and those active in Jung's circle, was a group that met regularly to hear lectures, discuss topics of Jungian interest, and socialize. Jung himself had no official capacity in the club but did attend meetings, and it is safe to assume that any policy decisions had to have his acceptance, if not blessings.

The document in question, dated December 1944, stated that, when possible, members of the Jewish faith should not exceed 10 percent and that "guests" (a separate category of membership that bestowed attendance but not voting privileges) should limit Jewish participation to 25 percent. It is important to note that this was an appendix to the by-laws, signed by members of the executive committee and apparently *not* circulated publicly to the club members. The president of the club at this time (and in fact for many years) was Toni Wolff, who, along with Linda Fierz David, is acknowledged to have been the prime mover behind this restriction. Naturally, the question that has to be answered is whether or not Jung knew about this restriction. There is no question but that he did.

After many hours of interviews and additional informal investigation, we realized there were no consistent or acceptable answers as to why this restriction was adopted. The date in question (December 7, 1944) was disturbing, but better understood in light of an acknowledgment that this policy had been unofficially in effect since the 1930s and only formalized in 1944. However, the reasons and justifications are far more difficult to pin down. Several of the responses of club members and even signatories were as follows.

There was a widespread fear of the club's becoming dominated by foreigners—a euphemism for German Jewish refugees who had made their way to Switzerland. Another rationale put forward was that Toni Wolff and Linda Fierz David (whose grandfather, incidentally, was rumored to have been Jewish) feared for Jung's life in the event that the Nazis invaded Switzerland. If Jungian institutions were kept free from a significant Jewish membership, they felt, both Jung and club members would be done a service.

Another reason put forward was that this had been an irrational time, in which a feeling of genuine hysteria prevailed. Most of those interviewed, including Jewish analysts, emphasized that unless one had lived in Switzerland during this period, one could not understand it. Several individuals remarked that there had been a feeling that an invasion by Germany was imminent. In short, Toni Wolff and Linda Fierz David, nicknamed "The Goddesses" in the club, were afraid Jung would be sent to a concentration camp if the Germans invaded and found too many Jewish Jungians in the club.

Finally, it has been suggested that this restriction was a form of "differentiation" and not "discrimination," an attitude that Jung himself held. Too many Jews would have changed the nature of the organization, and there was an obligation on the part of its officers to protect the Swiss character of the club.

To us, admittedly from the perspective and safety of over forty years' distance, none of these reasons is acceptable, although they all provide some psychological insight into the thought processes of the signatories. In this regard it is important to put some perspective on our findings—specifically, the additional research we feel is still needed before drawing definitive conclusions.

First and foremost is the question, not of whether Jung knew, but to what extent he was culpable. The fact that he knew is indisputable. Almost every person interviewed acknowledged that Jung was aware of the quota system then in effect. However, Jung's relationship to both the club and his individual Jewish analysands was a complex one. For example, Aniela Jaffé related the story that when her membership came into question, Jung made it clear that if she were not accepted as a member of the club, he would resign and have nothing to do with it. She was, naturally, accepted. Siegmund Hurwitz tells of the incident in 1950 when his membership came into question—a membership, ironically, that was sponsored and encouraged by Toni Wolff. When it was brought to Dr. Hurwitz's attention that he was being accepted despite the fact that Jewish membership was restricted, he informed Jung (who at first tried to defend the statute) that he was withdrawing his application, as he did not want to be a part of a club with such a policy. Jung called Hurwitz several weeks later and told him that the rule had been eliminated and he could now apply.

Amazingly, the elimination of the Jewish quota took place in 1950, five years after the end of the war. Thus, the nuances, as is always the case with Jung, are not so simple. Furthermore, the idea of a quota system was neither new nor limited to Switzerland, though given Jung's own history with the "Jewish issue," and coming *after* his meeting with Baeck, one would have expected him to be more conscious by this time (i.e., 1945–50).

When individuals active in the club were asked why this restriction had not been eliminated sooner, the response was that it had been forgotten about and not paid attention to—again, another area that clearly needs further research. For example, how many Jewish versus non-Jewish members were admitted during those years? Was there indeed a restrictive pattern in place as late as 1950? Unfortunately, when Stephen Martin and I tried to pursue this ourselves by examining the records of the club, we were told that the records were in shambles, making it impossible to piece anything together.

In conclusion, none of the people we interviewed was particularly proud of this piece of the club's history, and several were shocked, as they themselves had never seen this in writing before. Both Siegmund Hurwitz and Aniela Jaffé, for example, informed us that while they knew of the restrictions, this was the first time they had seen the document itself. And C. A. Meier, one of the signatories, acknowledged that such restrictions were in place since the 1930s but had no recollection of formally signing a document. His comment was that this should be taken in the context of its time, though when pressed he openly admitted that in retrospect it was an "ugly" thing.

Finally, however, what was heartening to us both was the honesty and trust shown by those we interviewed—individuals who are truly important figures in Jungian history. Their willingness to meet with us, openly discuss the topic, share their recollections, and confront this unpleasant shadow dimension of Jung was very touching. At times it was a painful experience, and we regretted having to witness their inner suffering. An excerpt from a letter sent to me by one of the individuals interviewed illustrates this point: "I myself felt tormented during the interview since I was in a difficult conflict between my loyalty to Jung and the necessity to tell the truth."

I know that many Jungians who are concerned with these issues carry similar feelings. Nevertheless, I feel confident that this is what Jung himself would have approved of—the search for truth, for conscious and unconscious realities.

Notes

1. Aniela Jaffé, "C. G. Jung and National Socialism," in *From the Life and Work of C. G. Jung*, p. 100.
2. Ibid., p. 81.

Chapter 8

Ann Belford Ulanov

Scapegoating: The Double Cross

Ann Belford Ulanov, Ph.D., Christiane Brooks Johnson Professor of Psychiatry and Religion at Union Theological Seminary, is a Jungian analyst in private practice and on the faculty of the C. G. Jung Institute of New York. She is the author of numerous books and articles, including *Wisdom of the Psyche*; *The Functioning Transcendent*; *Attacked by Poison Ivy: A Psychological Understanding*; and *The Female Ancestors of Christ*. Additionally, together with her late husband Barry Ulanov, she co-authored many books, such as *Primary Speech, A Psychology of Prayer*.

Somehow, in the Judeo-Christian tradition, scapegoating and redemption have become inseparable. This is what Ann Ulanov means by "The Double Cross," and she demonstrates the presence of this dynamic in Old Testament sacrifice and dietary proscriptions, the crucifixion of Jesus, anti-Semitism, and attitudes toward Jung, concluding that "we only scapegoat those who redeem us." She examines the scapegoating phenomenon in attitudes toward the Jews and in shadow projection in general, and questions how Jung, who professed a passionate attention to the existence of real evil, could have at first been blind to the evils of Nazi Germany.

Scapegoating and anti-Semitism are not subjects we can speak about objectively. We can only speak of them out of suffering—unconsciousness, abysmal pain and terror, rage and guilt, and a persistent longing to glimpse a way through their thickets of fear, sadism, violence, and despair.

Two crosses are always involved in scapegoating. The first cross represents suffering: we are nailed to cross-purposes, assaulted, brought to helplessness before the brute fact of evil. The opposites we would embrace pull us apart. The consciousness we strive for is opposed by unconsciousness. The help we offer turns out to hurt. The opposites do not just coincide: they clash; they collide. We are caught in a complex of opposites.

The second cross is the double-cross, the trick by one we trusted, the betrayal by someone or something that we counted on. In scapegoating we say to the other: "You carry the suffering and I will punish you for carrying it." Those we expect to help betray instead. Boatloads of Jews seeking refuge from the Holocaust were turned back from the shores of this country. Jung, the friend of many Jews, finally said to Rabbi Leo Baeck, "I slipped up."[1] Christians, who follow One who came to fulfill the law in love, often generate prejudice and persecution instead. The Jews, chosen by God, elected to be God's bride, seem left behind by God in the camps of Auschwitz and Dachau. Some Jews, for example, abandoned by neighbors and nations to abysmal suffering, appear to refuse to identify their suffering with the suffering of others—the miseries of blacks victimized by whites, of Ukrainians systematically starved by their government, of Cambodians massacred by the Khmer Rouge, of the millions buried alive in Soviet gulags.[2]

We must go further and ask whether we who are concerned to discuss anti-Semitism are prepared now to scapegoat Jung and Freud and other depth psychologists as a double-cross, to evade our own scapegoating. It relieves us to point to the prejudice of others, and especially such esteemed others as Jung and Freud, on whose work many of us have built our own work. Ultimately we double-cross ourselves by betraying our friends and befriending what betrays us.

Finally, the two crosses are one. The redemptive cross and the scapegoat cross are the same—someone or something to draw off the misery. We only scapegoat those who redeem us: Jesus, the Jew on the cross, double-crossed; the Jews, chosen by God, crucified as a people.

In Judaism (Lev. 16:1–28) two offerings must always be brought to the Lord—two doves, two turtles, two pigeons, two bulls, two rams, and finally two goats. The first goat is a sin offering. Its blood is sprinkled within the veil of the Holy of Holies before the Mercy Seat upon the Ark, where Yahweh will appear in a cloud. This goat's blood atones at the holy place for the uncleanness and transgressions of the children of Israel. Then the goat's blood is sprinkled outside the Holy of Holies on the altar, and the goat is taken outside the camp and burned—its own holocaust.

The second goat stays alive and is driven into the wilderness after the priest confesses in words delivered over it the iniquities of the children of Israel. This goat, loaded down with these sins, is sent away into a land which is not inhabited, into the desert outside the boundaries of community. These are the precincts of Azazel, the goat deity dwelling in the desert, to whom the sin offering is dispatched. Later, Azazel is called the leader of the fallen angels, the author of all sin (Enoch 6, 8, 10). Like Prometheus, he also instructs humans in essential human crafts. In later Jewish, Gnostic, and Mohammedan traditions, Azazel is called the leader of all demons. He is associated with the chthonic, demonic forces, both generative and destructive, sexual and combative, that prevail outside the boundaries of Israel.[3]

One set of sins is burned up outside the camp of Israel and the second set of sins driven away to the place beyond the bounds. We can see how the Jewish people have been identified with both goats, suffering holocaust and being driven outside the human community to the ends of the earth. More than any other people, they have been the archetypal scapegoat, carrying both kinds of crosses.

What then is scapegoating psychologically? This mechanism is well known to us. It forms a distinct chain of reactions that leads from personal repression to social oppression. Its defined sequence begins when we repress contents we dislike and dread. We disown them. We keep consciousness from such contents and we eject such contents from consciousness. Our ego recoils from connection to contents we feel are destructive to our ego position and from the disordered chaos from which such contents spring. We refuse consciousness to the annihilating forces we call evil. We either throw such contents out of consciousness into unconsciousness or we leave them blocked in unconsciousness, refusing them admittance to our awareness. Such refusal brings relief to our egos; we get rid—we think—of disturbing contents.

But such contents do not go away. They go unconscious. They remain in us as live bits of being, as volatile forces now out of reach of our ego and its restraining, civilizing effects. These contents regress and achieve still more powerful form, as a hungry dog we locked in a closet becomes a savage beast bent on killing to satisfy its hunger. A repressed content is like a tiny alligator we bring back from a Florida vacation that becomes increasingly inconvenient as it keeps on growing. We flush it down the toilet into our sewers. There it not only continues to grow but now, out of sight and out of reach, it joins all the other alligators flushed away by our neighbors. What we repress accumulates more life to itself, growing stronger, bigger, contaminating whatever else is in the unconscious. Pressure builds up that demands release into conscious life.

Such contents burst out finally in projections onto others—usually those different from us, alien, because of physical appearance or sex or background, or distant from us because we deem them inferior or superior to us. All that our egos judge unacceptable hurls itself in projection onto our alien or distant neighbor. We identify our neighbors with that bit of ourselves we put onto and into them. Thus we inaugurate a relationship of projective identification with our neighbors. We feel we must control them because they carry a feared bit of ourselves and fear them because we cannot control them. They carry the package of unconscious contents we dread in ourselves. Rather, we want to see ourselves as identified with the values and ideals we hold most precious. We contrast our good to our alien neighbors' bad. We draw a boundary around the good with which our egos identify, outlawing the bad with which we identify our neighbors.

We can understand that the initial function of such repression and projection is to differentiate good from bad, to become conscious of what we hold as good and to bind our group into a community, distinguished from other groups. Such initial differentiation and group consciousness might be all right, even furthering consciousness, if it did not go further, but it always does. For the repressed material, the howling dogs and snapping alligators, press to get out, press for contact. What begins as differentiation only too soon leads to a wide gap between our conscious ego identification with the good and our projective identification of our alien neighbor with the bad.

The line is drawn, from repression to regression and contamination of unconscious contents, to projection and projective identification onto our alien neighbor, to attitudes of prejudice from which grow acts of oppression, persecution, and finally, scapegoating. Like one or the other of the original scapegoats, the alien neighbor is seen as the carrier of our sins that we must get rid of in order to keep intact our commitment to the good. In the ironies of opposing consciousness and unconsciousness, we can indulge, even act out in frenzy, all the badness we disown in the name of defending the good. The disease attacks those who attack the disease. In the name of our ideal we attack, violate, persecute, and kill those on whom we have projected our badness. We are infiltrated by the very qualities we tried to control, depositing them in our neighbor.

What begins as initial differentiation of opposites ends by making a wide split between us and them, a split which soon becomes a yawning chasm filled with violence, misery, and suffering. That happens because we are unable to hold in consciousness the opposing values of good and bad. If we identify ourselves with the victims of such actions, we become the first goat, we become the victims who are burned up. In psychological terms, we fall into masochism. If we identify with the ones who accuse their neighbors, we see them as the second kind of scapegoat and ourselves fall into sadism, attempting to purge the community of their presence.

The temptations in scapegoating are double, and each brings its own cross. To get out of the coincidence of opposites—of the good and bad in each of us—we split them. To elude the cross of accepting and suffering the bad and good mixed in us, we double-cross our neighbor. Either way we avoid the real issue—what to do in the face of evil, where to put the alligators, how to hold the opposites within ourselves and our own community. In Jung's vocabulary, scapegoating introduces us to the shadow in ourselves, to the collective shadow in our society, and to the archetypal core that underlies the shadow.[4]

This connection between repression and scapegoating is true of all prejudices which are acted out in social oppression. What is specific to anti-Semitism? What do we repress and project and then identify with Jews? What is the specific archetypal core that informs and inflames the mechanism of scapegoating in anti-Semitism? The answer, in a word, is religion.

Although not at the center of the debate about anti-Semitism, often obscured by economic, political, and historical circumstances, and often put aside or denied by Jews in their self-appraisals, the religious issue rests in the background of anti-Semitism. It forms the distinct core of the package repressed by and projected onto the Jews.

Even to those who associate Judaism with ethnicity rather than faith, who see it as a culture rather than a religion, religion remains the inescapable fact, for this is a culture shaped by religion, whether it declares for or against the faith. The notorious resentment against Jews for their reputed intellectual superiority, for example, can be traced back to a religious origin. Judaism is the first of the three great monotheisms in human history, and the other two were clearly shaped by it. Islam itself traces its origins to Abraham. Jesus was a Jew.

Anti-Semitism is a religious scapegoating, not one of color, class, or sex. And religious scapegoating is the most violent of all because religion arranges the order of being. On the surface, anti-Semitism seems to follow the mechanisms of all prejudice—repression, regression, contamination, projection, projective-identification, prejudice, oppression, persecution, scapegoating.

At the core of anti-Semitism lies the specific archetype that ignites people against Jews. It is unmistakably religious. For the Jews are a people chosen by God, a people who have said yes to God's choosing, who have engaged in life-long dramas in yea-saying and nay-saying, turning to God, turning away. They complain that it is God who turns away and abandons them. And yet they know at the same time God is steadfast in demands upon them and in love of them.

It is almost commonplace to say that what has happened to Jews is what happens to God on earth. They have been hunted, hounded, excluded, trivialized, caricatured, mocked, betrayed, double-crossed. We persecute Jews because we persecute the addressing Ultimate, the calling to us to be Abraham or to be the bride, to be the feminine receiver and container who will make the transcendent manifest in this life.

Jung knew this addressing, this receiving womanliness. He described Yahweh as one whom we punch and kick back at for dislocating our hip, as with Jacob, or who plagues us as He did Job. Jung knew what a fearful thing it was to fall into the hands of the living God, to encounter the archetype of God in our own psyche. Such an experience is steel on stone, a defeat for the ego, and yet of such indescribable bliss, says Jung, that he will not, cannot breathe a word of it.[5]

The Jews symbolically represent those who want to say yes to God, a yes that will include questions, resistance, a simultaneous fighting and running away. In such speech with the divine, our bowels loosen, our stomachs heave, our voices fill up, our flesh trembles. We, like the Jews, dare now to be occupied with the Holy One who hovers over the Mercy Seat in the Holy of Holies, and we are frightened—and fascinated.

It is a miracle the Jews still survive, for they carry the projection of the primordial, not only our nay-saying, to the center, which is our sin, which we put on the scapegoat we drive into the desert, but also our yea-saying, that part of us that aches for the center, that wants to look, to see who will come through to us.

Jung crafted his whole psychology around this center. He discovered that we carry within our own psyches such a center, a self that is not

God but that within us which knows about God. It is a large knowing, a taste of that which transcends, not just the ego, but the whole psyche, the whole personal psyche, the whole group psyche.[6]

The deepest place of our dread of being is where the Jewish people stand, and they are persecuted for it. In them we persecute our own desire and fear of the center of being. In them we persecute our attraction to the center and our fear of it. What then happens when we scapegoat the Jews? We avoid compulsively, not only the mystery of our own shadows, both individual and collective, but the mystery of evil that we seek to eject from consciousness and project out of our communities.[7] That is the scapegoat we send into the desert. We also avoid the mystery of living in relation to the center and the burnt offering it seems to demand. That is the goat whose blood is offered at the altar.

We must look at one further thing that comes with all scapegoating, and particularly with anti-Semitism. Jews carry the necessity of drawing a boundary line when the finite comes in contact with the infinite. In repressing and projecting what we find bad, and thus insupportable, we are setting it off from the good. We are making boundary lines that help us to see evil and help protect us from its infectious nature. Such boundaries enhance consciousness and our sense of community.[8] To send the goat into the desert is to send it beyond the boundaries; to take the goat outside the camp to be burned is to define the boundaries of inside and out.

The anthropologist Mary Douglas tells us that this making of boundaries, which happens, for example, in the dietary law of Judaism, is an attempt to impose order on untidy experience.[9] It demarcates inside from outside, order from chaos, community from nameless wandering. Drawing boundaries marks off our belonging, living in relation to the center, from homelessness. God's blessing creates a space where being is always being-in-relation-to the center, and distinguished from non-being, which is to say from not-being-defined-in-relation-to, but choosing self-definition instead. We will make the boundaries. We will determine good and evil. We will know it all. We become know-it-alls. Pulling loose from such boundaries means taking to ourselves, our little selves, the big power to say what is good and what is evil—what was seen so unmistakably clearly in the death camps—the power to save or to kill.

Dietary laws in Judaism are like signs designed to inspire meditation upon what God has set apart as holy. Holiness is unity, integrity, completeness. Marion Milner, writing about painting, says the frame marks off a different kind of reality that is within the picture from what is outside. Our own psychoanalytical sessions do the same, marking off in time and space a special kind of reality that makes possible "that creative illusion that analysts call the transference."[10]

Drawing these boundaries, saying in effect that this is good and this is bad, this sacred, this profane, is possible only if connection to the transcendent is maintained. The goat's blood must be offered back to the Holy, whether at the altar or in the desert. When the scapegoating ritual pulls loose from the transcendent center, it falls into idolatry. Symbolic form becomes literal action, whether through inflation we identify with the chosen ones or through deflation become the literal victims of the double cross. When a ritual is literalized, it falls on real living people. Instead of asking what our relation is to the infinite, we take offense at those who claim a covenant: If we can destroy them, we can evade the whole question.

Jung mixed up the boundary lines, became caught up in them, and paid for it in his own experience of the double cross of scapegoating, both as accuser—drawing whole peoples into types, which inflamed persecution against them—and as accused—where he suffered, and his name goes on suffering, the label of anti-Semitism. Jung, so sensitive to the complexity of opposites, who never wanted to leave one of them out, was enmeshed in a complex of opposites. His strengths and gifts double-crossed him, in his weaknesses, in his blind spots. Jung shows us through his experience what it means to say scapegoating delivers us into fully acknowledging our shadow in ourselves and in the collective of which we are a part. We do not acknowledge our shadow from a safe perch in an observer's chair. It means to be pitched into the muck, coming up covered with it, stinking of it, smeared in our eyes so we cannot see clearly. That is the shadow. We slip onto it and into it, as Jung said. And we hurt others because of it. Jung also shows us, in his experience of the self and of the God-image in him, that a cross awaits any of us who struggle to relate to the Ultimate. Jung tried to keep the opposites together, and fell into them and into their splitting apart.

For example, Jung tells us that individuation can only occur in relation to tradition, to the collective, to the prevailing *Zeitgeist* from which we must differentiate ourselves and then relate to again, more consciously. We must become aware of the subjective premise from which we see objective truth, and know that our premise is subjective, so that finally, he wrote, we know that our vision of truth is only a "subjective confession."[11] But Jung himself was caught in the texture of his times with its bedeviling anti-Semitism. He was strongly influenced by his personal collectivity—generations of Christian pastors with all the ambiguity and deviousness of Christianity seeing Judaism as both its foundation and its rival. Christ the Jew, killed by Jews.

From another perspective, Jung remained embedded in centuries of Swiss traditions of neutrality, product of a country that observed the clashing opposite views of other peoples and chose to stand apart, to preserve neutrality for itself. Thus under his editorship of the journal of the International General Medical Society for Psychotherapy, Jung published both Nazi and Jewish doctors, expecting that scientific insight would be generated out of their opposing views.[12] Jung did not see in any of these collective and ostensibly objective worlds his own subjectivity, which colored not only his view of the Jews but also his hope of gathering insight from a sharp opposition neutrally observed.

Another example of where Jung was both crossed and double-crossed between opposites is in the realm of symbol. His great insight is into the openness of the symbol. It points to and evokes the living experience of the unknown, but never defines it exactly.[13] Yet Jung himself falls victim to attempts to define whole peoples in restrictive ways, which fed not differentiation, reconciliation, or insight, but separation and persecution. Jung reminds us again and again to open ourselves to the person before us, not to try to know what a dream means ahead of time, like a recipe, not to apply reasoning to spiritual paradoxes. He even declares his own typology is suggestive, never prescriptive. Yet here is Jung applying restrictive categories to whole races.[14] Jung's great, open consciousness, determined always to see the other, can also contribute to obliterating others by applying mass generalizations to them. Jung tells us repeatedly that the archetype is not a formula clapped onto persons, yet he himself falls victim to a fascination with the Wotan archetype and forgets the persons involved with the new invocation of it.[15]

Jung advocates the recovery to consciousness of the feminine mode of being, with his seminal insight into the contrasexual nature of the human, yet he himself suffered a benighted relation to his own anima during the Nazi years, as the "sick cow" dream and his illnesses of the heart show. Yet growth continued in him, and true openness, as his near-death vision makes clear. He saw himself being fed kosher food by a maternal anima figure, whom he joined in a "mystical marriage," seeing himself cast as "Rabbi ben Jochai, whose wedding in the afterlife was being celebrated."[16] Jay Sherry suggests that the sick-cow side of Jung's anima—the nurturing feminine with "life-promoting milk"—fell ill from Jung's fascination with the Wotan archetype, suddenly alive again in Nazi Germany, and from Jung's bitterness about Freud after the breakup of their relationship.[17]

Jung, noted for bringing insight into the feeling and sensate levels of the unconscious, was tripped up by the limitations of his own feeling and sensate functions.[18] He expressed his dubious views about archetypal factors in Jewish psychology at a time of racial fanaticism in Germany, where even to be a Jew was enough to put one's life in danger. To put forward for scientific discussion the topic of racial differences in such a climate, even to think in such terms, was a grave error. Jung missed on the feeling and sensate levels—in terms of his typology his own inferior functions—the reality of the evil being visited upon the Jews. He wrote and spoke about racial characteristics, both during and after the war, in a way that was bound to further inflame the persecution of a whole people. Caught in his own emotions about the Wotan archetype, and his own resentments against Freudian analysis, he did not see the harm he himself was causing.

Jung is singular among depth psychologists in his intense interest in evil, in taking up good and evil as moral categories, in probing the mystery of conscience.[19] Yet Jung did not at first recognize one of the greatest examples of evil in history when it confronted him in its immeasurable brutality. Jung's incessant protests and objections against the Christian understanding of the force of evil, as described in the doctrine of *privatio boni,* can be understood as that excessive protestation we all fall into when we are fascinated by something and cannot really see what it is that so absorbs us.[20] Jung insists that the doctrine misses the fact that evil really exists, that it is really there savaging our lives. To anyone who grasps the doctrine, Jung's reading grossly misses the point. But the point here is that Jung missed the brute facts of Nazi evil.

Perhaps the two missings—of evil in itself and of the Nazi evil—are linked. In the *privatio boni,* evil is indeed understood to exist, but in a very different way from good. Good is simply being in relation to God, related being, created being, being within the circle of dependent connections to the Creator. Evil denies that connection, seeks to destroy it, to defect from it. Evil exists as denial, betrayal, deficiency, a ruthless attempt to put "nothing" in the place of something.[21] Evil exists outside relation to a transcendent center, usurping the center for its own version and vision of reality. Isn't this exactly what the Nazis attempted?

Aniela Jaffé understands Jung's error about the Jews and about Nazism as the product of a one-sided consciousness. She says his "romantic consciousness" got caught in fascination with the objective psyche displayed in National Socialism, particularly through the Wotan archetype. The "classic" type of consciousness which, Jaffé says, Jung acquired toward National Socialism was not fooled for a moment.[22]

At first, Jung missed the evil so clear to so many others in the rise of the Nazis because of his faith in his own theory of consciousness. He missed it because of his conviction that healing power is released when consciousness can expand to include all the opposites, when a small ego can behold the *complexio oppositorum* of the self. Jung described the self as the God-image within us manifest in the psyche. He described the self—his image of God—as the *coincidentia oppositorum* and as the *complexio oppositorum.* Jung faced cross and double cross when he equated his image of God with God. What he relied upon betrayed him, and he betrayed what he relied upon. Like any person who really risks encounter with the living God, Jung was stripped of his God-image. When we identify our God-image with what it points to, as in some ways some of the time we must, because our image acts as a bridge between us and that unknown center to which it leads, it will break beneath our feet, for what it leads to is radically different from our pictures of it.[23] Jung's faith in consciousness was betrayed. It did not work. It double-crossed him. Consciousness of the opposites and writing about them in categories of Aryan and Jew, of the Germanic and the Jewish, harmed instead of helping, brought attack instead of a healing clarity.

What is to be done? Jung slipped up because of areas in his large personality of incomplete individuation. They resulted, these areas of absence and deprivation, from the collective *Zeitgeist,* from his own tendencies to type instead of to see symbolically, from his own underdeveloped feeling and sensate functions, from his own anima problems, from the resulting blindness to the stark reality of Nazi evil, from his over-determined reliance on consciousness of opposites. Do we, then, dismiss everything Jung has to say? Hardly. That would be for us to fall into the double cross—either accusing or defending Jung or thinking we can stay out of the whole mess with a neutrality only too much like his at its worst. Seeing Jung caught, we should turn to our own enmeshment in scapegoating, for anti-Semitism is still here, still active among us. What is so powerful about this particular brand of scapegoating that it still persists, after all the horrors of the Holocaust?

The specific scapegoating of anti-Semitism introduces us not only to our own evil in collective and individual form in the myth of expelling evil, but also to our own God-image, our own relation or lack of relation to the transcendent. Whether we are Jewish or not, whether we practice or repudiate religion, the spiritual question is constellated: What is our relation to the center?

One of the reasons anti-Semitism endures is that we all need to take up two issues: how to deal with the shadow and how to relate to the self. Jung's insights and Jung's cross and double cross will help us enormously here.

The shadow issue poses itself in a series of additional questions. How do we mark off boundaries to consolidate ego-consciousness without discriminating against those who have different boundaries? How do we differentiate without repudiating?[24] Or, to put the same issue in social terms, how do we each set off order from disorder without disowning our neighbors? How do we think in terms of a whole society while at the same time risking commitment to our particular part of society? How do we get rooted firmly in our soil and remain hospitable to those who root differently or in different earth?

Jung's failures and insights point the way. Our consciousness must develop differently. A double intercession matches the double cross. We intercede for shadow and for ego both. Consciousness intercedes for the left-out bits of shadow in our personality and in our society, while at the same time respecting our need for boundaries. Consciousness also intercedes on behalf of our ego-point-of-view in relation to the opposite points of view that live inside us and around us. The *complexio oppositorum* which Jung sees as essential comes home to us. It becomes our everyday reality. This is living toward the self. We try to intercede on behalf of what we believe in and on behalf of what others believe in, too. For this we urgently need the help of the Hebrew Bible and the feminine mode of being.

To do this work with the shadow means neither expelling evil nor burning it up. It means not identifying with either scapegoat, for both are offerings to the transcendent—the altar deity or the desert deity. It means moving on to the Prophets and the Psalms in the Hebrew Bible, where God says, I do not want burnt offerings, I want a broken and contrite heart; I do not want burnt offerings, I want a faithful and loving spirit. But to make this shift means changing the way we become conscious. The old way was to differentiate opposites—good from bad, us from them, inside boundaries from outside boundaries—by splitting them apart. But in that way the split widens to a point where we cannot bring the opposites together again, and millions of people perish in the gap left between them. Differentiation then turns into discrimination. Consciousness means repression. The opposites do not belong together as parts of a complex whole, coinciding all at once, but instead proceed serially, sequentially, to a killing exclusivity.

What the texts of the Hebrew Bible are after in the shift from burnt offering to heart offering is inclusion of a feeling, sensate, bodily kind of awareness, where, although different each from the other, we are still all members of the one body. This perception is fostered by the feminine mode of being that goes into the midst of living experience and differentiates aspects of it by a both/and instead of an either/or method of apprehension.[25] The split does not widen to expel opposites nor move to exclude any one of them. The opposites are held in tension to discern and integrate all of them.

The feminine mode of consciousness allows a holding in being of what one is separating in thought. It is a holding in feeling of what we discern differences in, a holding of boundaries to make space for the commitments of the particular persons and groups that together compose the whole. The feminine mode recognizes evil both without sentimentality and without enthusiasm for grand ways of fixing it. Evil is a fact to be reckoned with and, if necessary, to be fought or suffered. The feminine approach helps the ego in its space-making function, enlarging awareness so the coinciding opposites can be experienced as complexly related to each other and to the whole of which they are parts.[26] Those coinciding opposites make up different parts of our society, different groups rooted in different commitments, just as much as they make up different segments of each person's personality.

In gaining consciousness of our own scapegoating tendencies, and interceding for another way, we are pushed to become conscious of how we experience the center of existence, of how we experience what it is all for and thus what really matters.

This consciousness of our own images of the center, of what Jung calls our God-images, makes us struggle with mystery as it touches us. If we are in any way to lift from the Jews what history has scapegoated them for—self-conscious relation to the center—then we must take up that task, their task, ourselves, in our own groups, in our own lives.

This is not to say everyone must become a defined Jew—any more than Muslim or Christian or Buddhist or atheist. It is to say that we must direct our consciousness to the center and decide to struggle with it and about it, to know its great positive qualities, its abiding difficulties, ourselves. That will keep our neighbors safe from the unconscious spiritual burden that we only too easily project onto them.

If we take up this task we will know the cross and double cross, but differently now, as a necessary ritual in relation to the transcendent. We will enter that radical experience that Jung exemplifies, of disidentifying our God-images from God, for relating to the infinite means being stripped of our finite images of it. That which we rely upon will pin us to the cross and will double-cross us. We will be forced to identify what our images of God are, forced to disidentify them from the transcendent itself. This means simultaneously committing ourselves in time and space to belief in whatever our version of the center is and opening to whatever our symbols evoke and point to but never capture or define, let alone prescribe for others. It means drawing boundaries that are both binding and open-ended. In religious terms, it means witnessing rather than proselytizing. In psychological terms, we are brought to true consciousness of opposites, rather than coercion. This is a paradoxical knowing and unknowing simultaneously. It is a seeing into the dark ground of the God who presides over both goats, both crosses, within boundary and beyond, the world of deity and of desert.

Notes

1. Aniela Jaffé, "C. G. Jung and National Socialism" in *From the Life and Work of Jung,* pp. 97–98.

2. See Richard L. Rubenstein, *After Auschwitz: Radical Theology and Contemporary Judaism* (Indianapolis: Bobbs-Merrill, 1966); see also Richard L. Rubenstein and John K. Roth, *Approaches to Auschwitz: The Holocaust and Its Legacy* (Atlanta: John Knox, 1987); John G. Gager, *The Origins of Anti-Semitism* (New York: Oxford University Press, 1983); Rosemary Ruether, *Faith and Fratricide: The Theological Roots of Anti-Semitism* (New York: Seabury, 1974); R. M. Lowenstein, *Christians and Jews: A Psychoanalytic Study* (New York: International Universities Press, 1952).

3. *The Oxford Dictionary of the Christian Church* (London: Oxford University Press, 1974); see also Sylvia Brinton Perera, *The Scapegoat Complex: Toward a Mythology of Shadow and Guilt* (Toronto: Inner City Books, 1986), pp. 18–19, 89.

4. See Erich Neuman, *Depth Psychology and a New Ethic,* Eugene Rolfe, trans. (New York: Putnam's, 1969; Boston: Shambhala Publications, 1990), *passim* for discussion of the many facets of repression and their effects on society. See also C. G. Jung, "Shadow," in *Aion, CW* 9, II, ¶ 13–19.

5. See C. G. Jung, *Letters,* vol. 2, p. 156. See also C. G. Jung, *Mysterium Coniunctionis* 14, ¶ 778.

6. See C. G. Jung, *Psychological Types, CW* 6, ¶ 789–790. See also C. G. Jung, *The Archetypes and the Collective Unconscious, CW* 9, I, ¶ 5, 442, 572, 626.

7. See C. G. Jung, *Two Essays in Analytical Psychology, CW* 7, ¶ 27, 35, 41–42, 70–78, 152–154, 185. See also C. G. Jung, *Psychology and Religion: West and East, CW* 2, ¶ 140; see also ¶ 509–513, 738–789.

8. See Neumann, *Depth Psychology and a New Ethic,* pp. 64–66.

9. Mary Douglas, *Purity and Danger* (New York: Frederick A. Praeger, 1966), pp. 1, 4–5, 29, 50, 53–54, 57, 63–64.

10. Marion Milner, "The Role of Illusion in Symbol Formation," *New Directions in Psychoanalysis,* M. Klein, P. Hermann, and R. E. Money-Kyrle, eds. (New York: Basic Books, 1957), p. 86; also cited in Douglas, *op. cit.*, p. 63.

11. See C. G. Jung, *Civilization in Transition, CW* 10, ¶ 1025, 1034. See also C. G. Jung, *Modern Man in Search of a Soul,* W. S. Dell and C. F. Baynes, trans. (New York: Harcourt, Brace & Co., 1933), p. 220.

12. See Jung, *Civilization in Transition,* ¶ 1026–1032.

13. See Jung, *Letters,* vol. 1, pp. 32, 59; See also Jung, *Psychological Types,* ¶ 814–829; see also Ann Belford Ulanov, *The Feminine in Jungian Psychology and Christian Theology* (Evanston: Northwestern University Press, 1971), chap. 5

14. See Jung, *Civilization in Transition,* ¶ 400–487.

15. See ibid., ¶ 371–399 and especially 385, 391.

16. C. G. Jung, *Memories, Dreams, Reflections*, p. 294.

17. See Jay Sherry, "Jung, the Jews, and Hitler," *Spring,* 1986, pp. 170–174, for full presentation of this idea.

18. Jung, *Psychological Types,* ¶ 595–609.

19. See Jung, *Civilization in Transition,* ¶ 825–886.

20. See Jung, *Letters,* vol. 2, pp 52–54, 58–61, 71–73, 268, 281, 484, 519. See Jung, *Psychology and Religion: West and East,* ¶ 274, 541 *f,* 470, 685.

21. For further discussion of this denying role of evil, see Ann Belford Ulanov, "The Devil's Trick," in *The Wisdom of the Psyche* (Cambridge: Cowley, 1988).

22. Jaffé, "C. G. Jung and National Socialism," p. 96. Jung describes the two kinds of consciousness, linking them with extraversion and introversion, in his *Psychological Types,* ¶ 543, 544, 548, 549, 550.

The romantic type tends to be extraverted, swift in his reactions, expressing himself and needing to make his presence felt, "because his whole nature goes outwards to the object. He gives himself easily to the world in a form that is pleasing and acceptable. . . ." Enthusiasm "flows out of his mouth." He appears interesting, empathetic. He publishes early and wants to make a name for himself.

"The classic type is slow to produce, usually bringing forth the ripest fruit of his mind relatively late in life." He needs "to stand unblemished in the public eye" and does not set other minds on fire. He always keeps his personality in the background and tends to be introverted, hiding "his personal reactions and suppressing his immediate reactions." He lets "his work speak for him and does not take up the cudgels on its behalf." He seals his lips over enthusiasm and appears commonplace.

As usual with any typology, neither of these descriptions fits Jung precisely. But Jaffé's referral to them as helping to explain Jung's trials with the Nazis is most interesting.

23. See Ann Belford Ulanov, *Picturing God* (Cambridge: Cowley, 1986), pp. 164–171, 179–184.

24. See Ann Belford Ulanov, "When Is Repudiation Differentiation?" unpublished paper, 1987.

25. See Ann Belford Ulanov, *The Feminine in Jungian Psychology and in Christian Theology,* Part III; see also "Between Anxiety and Faith: The Role of the Feminine in Paul Tillich's Theological Thought," in Jacquelyn A. Kegley, ed., *Paul Tillich on Creativity* (Lanham, MD: University Press of America, 1989).

26. See Ann Belford Ulanov, "The Ego as Spacemaker," unpublished paper, 1981.

Part III

The Jungian Collective: Reactions, Responses and Comments—The Paris Workshop

Chapter 9

Jerome Bernstein

Collective Shadow Integration of the Jungian Community: Atonement

Jerome S. Bernstein is a Jungian analyst and clinical psychologist with a private practice in Santa Fe, New Mexico. He was founding president of the C. G. Jung Analysts Association of Greater Washington, D.C. and past-president of the C. G. Jung Institute of Santa Fe. He is the author of *Power and Politics: The Psychology of Soviet-American Partnership*, and numerous articles on the application of analytical psychology to groups and nations as well as to clinical issues. His book, *Living in the Borderland: Discriminating the Pathological from the Sacred*, is due for publication in 2003.

Allegations that Carl Jung was anti-Semitic have been swirling around since his break with Freud in 1913. Controversy over this issue has picked up steam since then—including allegations that Jung was pro-Nazi—and is as charged as it ever was, if not more so. What I have set out to do here is to discuss the salient history of the Jungian collective itself (professional clinical practitioners and professional and lay Jungian organizations) in dealing with the issue of Jung's alleged anti-Semitism. The record of Jung's writings and sayings that have been construed as pro-Nazi and/or anti-Semitic has been documented in *Lingering Shadows: Jungians, Freudians, and Anti-Semitism*[1] and in publications since 1990 including new material contained in this volume. Based on the documentation available to me, I see so little evidence to support the charge that Jung was pro-Nazi. I will not pursue it further.

My focus here is history and the historical record. None of us can invent that history—although some, cited below, attempt to out of their own motives. We can only state the truth that we know and try to understand its meaning with regard to the man. I believe that it is in Jung's best interest to let the record speak for itself. Jung taught us that we all have shadows, no matter how conscious we are, and that great men have great shadows. It is only in trying to further an image of Jung as something trans-human that we need hide his shadow. And attempts to hide Jung's shadow stimulate and further the most negative projections onto the man himself. Certainly, such attempts do not protect him. In the absence of an accurate historical record, the worst is more likely to be projected. From my perspective, Jung the man, as do other great men, becomes more real the more three-dimensional his image. With the shadow hidden away, these figures come across only as two-dimensional. And the more two-dimensional they appear, the more likely the "missing" dimension will be projected, and the worse the projection will be.

"Projection" involves the unconscious attribution to others of psychological and emotional traits and qualities that are incompatible with our own self-image or the image of someone or some group that we either idealize or despise. As Jungian analyst Edward C. Whitmont puts it: "The fundamental law of preservation of energy applies to psychological functioning as well as to physics. What is expelled, repressed from individual [and collective] consciousness, reappears in projection upon another person, group or figure."[2]

Jung's theories, more than most, have stood the weather of time. Revelations regarding any anti-Semitic aspects of Jung's shadow, no matter what they are, are not likely to destroy his work. Since his death, his theories are increasingly embraced by and permeate almost all schools of psychology. And if Jung's work cannot survive his shadow, then perhaps there is something in this that we, his followers, must face and integrate.

Because I fervently believe that both history and Jung are best served by presenting the most accurate record possible, this chapter contains material either never published or not published in sources readily available to those in pursuit of relevant information on the topic. Some of the material may be perceived as controversial. I am presenting it not to rekindle conflict, but to show how difficult it is to work through shadow problems of this sort. The record presented below refutes some of the calumnious accusations by some of Jung's most dedicated detractors. It also acknowledges some of their charges. We need to document the former—rather than argue them on the basis of faith without the support of the historical record—and we must face the implications of the latter. In some cases, we must also look at our own complicity in facilitating distortions and slanders toward Jung. In other cases, it is to the credit of the Jungian community that many of the most damning allegations against Jung that are supported by evidence have come from within the Jungian collective itself.

I must begin this discussion with an account of my personal history regarding Jung and anti-Semitism. My own history is a part of our collective history as Jungians, and how we have arrived at this point in time still wrestling with this question. The emotional/feeling drama is a central part of that history. There are some who think that history should be reported only in cold and dispassionate terms. However, it seldom is merely cold and dispassionate in the making—in the reporting, yes, but not in the making. I choose this less orthodox approach because it feels more whole and more honest.

Although rumors and allegations of anti-Semitism have surrounded Jung for most of the 20th century, to my knowledge the issue has been openly discussed by the Jungian collective in conferences only since an informal meeting in Jerusalem at the 1983 Congress of the International Association for Analytical Psychology (IAAP). As will be discussed below, subsequent IAAP conferences addressed the issue, specifically regarding the "Jewish quota" of the Analytical Psychology Club of Zurich. This last provides a good clinical case study in shadow resolution on the collective level. To me, the shocking thing in life's reality is not that we fall into the shadow. On the contrary, it is noteworthy that shadow issues can be resolved, particularly on the collective level.

The Genesis of the Paris Workshop on Jung and Anti-Semitism

The XIth International Congress of the International Association for Analytical Psychology (IAAP)[3] was held between August 28 and September 2, 1989, in Paris. On two of those days, a workshop titled "Jung and Anti-Semitism" was held as part of the Congress program. I proposed the workshop and acted as chair of the proceedings. Although there were three workshops that ran concurrently, the workshop on Jung and Anti-Semitism was far and away the most heavily attended. Each of the two days of the Jung and Anti-Semitism workshops had to be moved to larger rooms to accommodate standing room attendance. There were over 150 attendees at the first day of the workshop and nearly 250 at the second—nearly a third of those in attendance at the Congress based on the IAAP estimate of 750 attendees. I mention the heavy attendance to give some notion of the importance attached to this topic by the international Jungian analytic community. The presentations given in this workshop were published in *Lingering Shadows.*

I had proposed the workshop on Jung and Anti-Semitism to pursue and clarify the extent to which the accusations that Jung was anti-Semitic and pro-Nazi were true. Consciously, I did not seriously consider that those accusations could be true—certainly nowhere near as true as Jung's many detractors asserted. As it turned out, I have come to realize that there was much about my proposal for that two-day workshop at the XIth Congress that was naive and unconsciously driven.

No doubt, part of my unconscious reason for wanting such a workshop was to defend Jung. I had entered Jungian analysis in 1969 with my life in shambles, hanging on by my fingernails, and experiencing more psychological pain than I had thought possible. Carl Jung, through the medium of my analyst, was responsible for saving my life and soul, and I owed a debt of gratitude to both Jung and his work. As I saw it, how could a man who played such a direct role in reconnecting me to my soul—including, specifically, my Jewish soul from which I had become alienated—be anti-Semitic? Later, when Jung became my teacher through his writings as well as through my analysis, I came to understand that self-righteous judgment is one of the greatest threats to human survival, and that shadow integration and consciousness-raising are the hardest challenges we face as humans.

Two years or so into my analysis, I overheard a conversation where Jung was referred to as anti-Semitic. That was the first time I had ever heard such an allegation. I was stunned by it since I respected both parties to the conversation and could not dismiss it. Later that week, in my regular analytic session, I raised the question with my analyst. He assured me that although such rumors had been around for a while that there was no substance to them. I respected his opinion highly, and knew he had met Jung and many of Jung's associates. Further, he himself was Jewish, and would be aware of such a prejudice. That was that, I thought. The issue dropped from my consciousness. I still had a life to put together.

Twelve years or so later, in 1983, after having completed my Jungian analytic training, I attended my first international Jungian Congress. As it happened, it was the first Congress to be held in Jerusalem. I spent many days before, during, and after the Congress wandering/exploring the streets of Jerusalem. I experienced my Jewishness in ways I had never imagined. I remember one sunny afternoon just walking down the street feeling specifically Jewish and not a minority. As an eight- or ten-year-old, a group of older kids actually stoned me because I was a Jew—one of too numerous experiences of overt anti-Semitic behavior towards me. For the first time in my life, I felt pride at being a Jew.

Early on at this Congress in Jerusalem, I passed a message board in the lobby of the meeting area. On it was a simple note stating something like: "Anyone interested in discussing the emotional impact of attending a Congress in Jerusalem meet at 8 p.m." I don't believe that the writer of the note was identified.[4] I attended that meeting—participation in which has had a continuing profound impact on my life.

As I recall, there were about 70 to 80 people in that small room. Roughly a quarter or so were Germans, nearly half were Jewish with only a smattering of Israeli Jews, and a quarter "other." There were two or three (perhaps more) people who had no connection to the Congress or to Jung. They had seen the same note on the message board and decided to attend. There we were, facing each other with no agenda, all of us aware that it was our emotions—negative as well as positive—that brought us face-to-face with one another. I don't recall how the discussion began or who said what. What I do remember is a number of the Germans who spoke, most of them in their 30s and 40s, and how surprised I was at what they revealed. To a person they had expressed great fear and trepidation at coming to Israel. Most acknowledged painful dreams or anxiety attacks. One acknowledged a panic attack on the way from the airport and a need to flee the country; one or two acknowledged throwing up from anxiety since being in Israel. None had been born before World War II began in 1939. They were either small children during the War or had been born after May 1945 when the War in Europe ended. There was much talk on all sides about collective guilt. Clearly the German attendees were experiencing it profoundly.

Emotionally, I was a believer in collective guilt. But I had not given much thought to the notion of collective guilt. And now I was facing it in the anguished faces of those Germans present. The burden of their fate was powerfully present in that room. I found myself feeling sympathy for their caughtness, their dilemma. The hideousness of the Nazi evil was still claiming even more victims, these young Germans among others, nearly forty years after the end of the war.

What followed, not discretely recalled by my mind but very much engraved on my emotions and soul, was a long and rambling discussion about the Holocaust, questions about how one heals, and the pain, and excitement, of attending a conference in Jerusalem with all that this implied symbolically. Repeatedly, the discussion returned to the feelings of collective guilt on the part of the Germans. Jung's name came up a few times. And each time it did, it was in the context of Jung's "anti-Semitism." (As I recall, there was only one reference to his "pro-Nazi" leanings.) The word "alleged" was not used in this context and the accusation was put forth as a matter of course. No one, not a single individual in a room containing many analysts, raised a question about this assertion, nor even about an assertion of Jung's "pro-Nazi" leanings.

There was pain, fear, sadness, dread, anger, rage, and dismay in the room. I, particularly, was gripped by the horrible caughtness of the young Germans present—by how, of course, they would feel responsible for that which they could not be responsible. I acknowledged my observations and feelings in the group and expressed my sympathy for how they, along with many of the rest of us, also had been victimized by the evil of Nazism. (I was eight years old, in the United States, when the war ended in Europe; yet I felt personally victimized by Nazism.)

That comment, that expression of sympathy for the young Germans present—which I hold to today—outraged a number of Jews in the room. "How could you possibly compare any non-Jewish German to the Jewish victims of the Holocaust?" "How could you be sympathetic to Germans in the heart of the Jewish state that was founded on the ashes of the Holocaust?" There were some other statements I don't recall; I only feel their cuts eighteen years later. I was accused by someone of being anti-Semitic. Then came the harpoon, thrown by one of the non-Jungian people in the group who purported to be a rabbi from Connecticut: "You are a traitor to your people and your heritage and you soil the memory of those who died in the Holocaust." That one stuck. He hit where it hurt, since the side of me that believed in collective guilt would agree with him. At the same time, my feelings and soul told me that these anguished Germans were also victims of the Nazis and, in some cases, of their very own parents and family members who were active Nazis (and whatever it was/is in the German collective psyche that acted out the Holocaust). They were victims of a different sort to be sure, but victims nonetheless. I also experienced quite painfully the ruthless daggers of Jewish prejudice. By the end of the evening, there had been some kind of coming together. I can't put words to it, but some kind of healing took place. The impossible—Germans coming to Jerusalem and Jews facing Germans in Jerusalem with all that this implied and carried with it—had been approached, and spoken, and touched. Virtually everyone in the room felt it. It was quite palpable.

The next morning was to be a plenary session at the Congress. Several people who had attended the meeting the evening before had a discussion at breakfast and it was decided that indeed something psychologically important had taken place the night before, and that a short report should be given at the Congress on the events of the previous evening. Although I had not attended the breakfast meeting, it was also decided by those who had met, that I should be the one to give the report. What ensued that morning before the plenary meeting was an embittered conflict between some members of the Israeli Society who held that such a report should *not* be given, that it had nothing to do with the Congress proceedings and hence was inappropriate. Other members of the Israeli delegation were just as adamant that a report should be given. The tug of war went back and forth and got ugly. One prominent member of the Israeli Society resigned over the internal conflict within the society around the issue. Shadow elements that were present the night before clearly had arisen again. Unlike the healing feeling that prevailed the previous evening, no such feeling was forthcoming from this confrontation. Finally, the question was put to those present for a vote from the floor at the plenary session to be held later that morning: Should a ten-minute report on the events of the previous evening be given to the Congress? The vote by the Congress delegates was in favor of a report, although not by a large margin, perhaps 3 to 2 in favor. So, one of the Germans in attendance at the meeting the night before and I gave a less-than-10-minute report. In a way that I can neither understand nor articulate, our presentation seemed to move the delegates. The report was received enthusiastically.

Contemporary Context and Relevance

With regard to Jung and his alleged anti-Semitism, there is more than the historical record and interest that is at stake here. In the past ten years or so there has been an increasing crescendo of those who would throw out the body of Jung's work and theory on the basis of his alleged anti-Semitism and so-called Nazi leanings, lack of proof notwithstanding. To discredit the man is to discredit his work, so the thinking seems to be. There are others whose agenda seems intent on invalidating Jung's psychology and who appropriate the issue of Jung's alleged anti-Semitism in service to their goal. Nevertheless, alternatively, there is legitimate question as to whether Jung was anti-Semitic and, if so, the degree to which he was. The lives and history of all great men and women are of interest to many. In this context, Jung's life and history is part of the public domain, and must be examined whether we, as Jungians, like it or not.

A good example of how this issue refuses to disappear is the tempest that has swirled around the contemporary works of Richard Noll (*The Aryan Christ* and *The Jung Cult*,) Frank McLynn (*Carl Gustav Jung*) and Walter Kendrick (reviewer for *The New York Times Book Review*), among others. In this storm there are the too-often-repeated charges that Jungians are only "mythologists" and "apologists" for Jung, that they are not interested in recording an honest history of their own movement, and worse, that they cover up and suppress it.[5]

The Jewish Quota in the Psychology Club of Zurich

First revealed at the "Lingering Shadows" conference in New York, it was shortly thereafter brought to the attention of those attending the Paris workshop that the Psychology Club of Zurich[6] had employed a secret quota beginning in the 1930s that remained in effect until 1950. The quota limited Jewish membership in the Club (which consisted of analysts and non-analysts who met bi-monthly to hear lectures by Jung and others) to not more than 10 percent, and "guest attendance" by Jews to no more than 25 percent. It was also asserted that Jung, in all probability, knew of the quota.[7] Alluding specifically to Jung's alleged anti-Semitism and pro-Nazi leanings, and to the secret Jewish quota in the Analytical Psychology Club of Zurich, Richard Noll states that "as of this late date (1996) no one in Zurich...has ever attempted to make a formal apology for these attitudes or actions."[8]

As revealed in *Lingering Shadows*, the history of allegations that Jung was anti-Semitic goes back to the break between Freud and Jung, to Freud's suggestion that "he [Jung] seemed ready to enter into a friendly relationship with me and for my sake to give up certain racial prejudices which he had previously permitted himself."[9] Since that time, the issue has been broached, pro and con, in numerous Jungian and non-Jungian professional articles, journals, histories, newspaper articles and editorials, book reviews, presentations at conferences, and the like. It remains a hotly debated topic in the psychoanalytic field, i.e., the world of Freudian and Jungian psychology. (See Bibliography.)

The topic was addressed at the 1986 IAAP Congress in Berlin, during a discussion titled "Destructiveness in the Tension Between Myth and History" (among three German analysts, Arvid Erlenmeyer, Anne Springer, and Klaus Winelmann). The Berlin workshop covered a number of topics relevant to the history of the psychoanalytic movement in general and the Jungian movement specifically, including the Nazi era and some of the allegations against Jung. However, the workshop was not specifically focused on the allegations of Jung's anti-Semitism and pro-Nazism.

Beginning in 1989 the larger Jungian community took upon itself to openly discuss the subject more directly. The issue was first embraced and pursued formally in a series of events beginning with the Lingering Shadows Conference which was held and sponsored by the C. G. Jung Foundation of New York in the spring of 1989, followed by the two-day "Workshop on Jung and Anti-Semitism," which took place at the XIth Congress of the International Association for Analytical Psychology (IAAP) in Paris on August 31 and September 1, 1989. The Preface to *Lingering Shadows* states that the Paris workshop grew out of that conference in the Spring of 1989. However, the impetus for my proposal to deal with this topic at the Paris conference grew out of my experience in Israel. I had made my workshop proposal to the Congress Planning Committee months prior to the Lingering Shadows Conference and indeed had no knowledge of the conference until after my proposal had been approved. It is symbolically fitting, given all that Jerusalem symbolizes, that Aryeh Maidenbaum in the Preface to *Lingering Shadows* states that, for him, "The seed for this book was planted in Jerusalem, germinated in Zurich, and blossomed in New York," some fifteen years later. For me, the seed for the Paris workshop also was planted in Jerusalem, but at the 1983 meeting described above. Thus, several similarly-focused Jungian conferences bring us to the present moment: first, the informal meeting at the Jerusalem Congress in 1983, followed by Berlin in 1986, the Lingering Shadows conference in New York, the two-day workshop at the Paris Congress, and, finally, the Chicago Congress in the fall of 1992.

It is important to note that the Paris workshop could only have taken place with the approval of the Congress Program Committee, an administrative arm of the IAAP, to whom I submitted my proposal for the workshop. Although the IAAP Program Committee approved the workshop as part of the Congress program, it had no role in structuring its focus or determining the presenters. I personally chose the presenters. A major criterion I used for selecting presenters was my assessment of their capacity for objectivity and willingness to be open and honest. I felt it important that this workshop address objective history—to the degree it could be ascertained—on the subject of Jung's alleged anti-Semitism. The record needed to be clarified for the sake of an accurate history of the Jungian collective and the history of analytical psychology, no matter how Jung came off in the picture. For the most part, I think that this vision did become reality at the Paris workshop, albeit with complications.

It is also important to note that the fact of the secret "Jewish quota" within the Analytical Psychology Club of Zurich from the 1930s to 1950 was first revealed publicly by Aryeh Maidenbaum at the New York Lingering Shadows Conference in the spring of 1989.[10] When this piece of history was exposed again at the 1989 Paris Workshop, the reaction was electric: shock and anger. Ultimately, it mobilized the Jungian collective to take decisive action in addressing this piece of history at the 1992 IAAP meeting in Chicago and subsequently catalyzed a broader focus on the shadow of the larger Jungian collective, as evidenced in this volume. However, I wish to emphasize that I neither knew of nor attended the 1989 Lingering Shadows Conference in New York and had no knowledge of the "Jewish quota" issue until shortly before the Paris workshop later that year. In retrospect, I regret not having specifically invited members of the Psychology Club of Zurich to appear on the panel at the Paris Workshop. It was a serious omission for which I here apologize to the Club. I had received the information about the Jewish quota only weeks before the advent of the Paris Workshop.

Atonement: Shadow Integration

As a finale to the 1989 workshop on Jung and Anti-Semitism in Paris, the very last comment made in the workshop proceedings was by San Francisco Jungian analyst John Beebe, who stated his conviction that seeking some act of atonement from the Analytical Psychology Club of Zurich regarding the Jewish membership quota is essential for moving forward and for healing. Dr. Beebe's position clearly implies that not only the integrity of the man, Jung, but our own integrity as a community of Jungian analysts, hinges on our capacity to express atonement for a serious injury to others and to reject anti-Semitism and, indeed, all prejudice. His suggestion was met with approbation by those in attendance.[11]

In accordance with Dr. Beebe's suggestion, as chairperson of the Paris workshop, I entered upon a three year correspondence with the president of the Analytical Psychology Club of Zurich as a follow-up to the Paris workshop. I conveyed to the president of the Club the sentiment expressed by Dr. Beebe at the end of the Workshop and invited—later pressed for—some formal acknowledgment of the Jewish quota by the Club and some expression of atonement. The effort was frustrating and unfruitful.

Because the Paris workshop had been attended by a third of the Congress participants, and because Dr. Beebe's suggestion was met with such enthusiasm, I felt that I owed it to my colleagues and to the process of shadow revelation and integration begun in Paris, to give a follow-up report at the XIIth Congress in Chicago in 1992. I did so, and that report was sent out as part of the Minutes of the Plenary Session of the Chicago Congress in a separate mailing to each of the international societies. However, and significantly, it is not contained in any published report on the proceedings of the Congress. The report was placed under the heading, "miscellaneous," item 9.C., with no heading or title indicating content. Anyone researching this issue would virtually have to know specifically what one was seeking and where it was in order to obtain the information.

My report to the XIIth Congress, which is published here in Appendix B, pages 259–271, was direct, factual, and critical.[12] The delegates were moved and angry at what appeared to be a stonewalling by the president of the Analytical Psychology Club of my efforts to engage the club in some kind of acknowledgment and act of atonement for the secret Jewish quota. After an animated discussion the delegate assembly formulated a statement protesting the lack of forthrightness in the responses I received from the club president. A formal resolution was passed regarding non-discrimination within the IAAP and its member groups:

> RESOLUTION:
> We request that the constituent societies of the IAAP establish and follow a policy of nondiscrimination regarding race, religion, ethnic origin, gender, or sexual orientation to apply to membership in professional societies, training programs, and events for the public at large sponsored by them.

After giving my report in Chicago, I took no further formal action. I assumed that members of the Analytical Psychology Club of Zurich who were present at the Chicago IAAP Congress in 1992 probably had had no knowledge of my three-year correspondence with the president of the Club, and would, after hearing my report, raise the issue within the Club. This assumption proved to be true. Subsequently, in August of 1993, I received a letter and a committee report, dated July 12, 1993, signed by the current Executive Committee members of the Club and by the members of a study group established by the Club to examine the issues raised in my correspondence with the Club president between

1989–1992. The operative sentences of that letter state: "There is no question that today we regret the events in the Club of that time. In other respects we sincerely hope—and unfortunately it is only a hope—that all discrimination against anybody, especially anti-Semitism, is a matter of the past."

> For Transgressions Against God, the Day of Atonement Atones;
> But for Transgressions of One Human Being Against Another,
> The Day of Atonement Does Not Atone until
> They Have Made Peace with One Another...
>
> —*The Mishna*[13]

On January 10, 1994, I responded to the Analytical Psychology Club of Zurich as follows:

> Jerome S. Bernstein, M.A.P.C., NCPsyA.
> January 10, 1994
>
> Dear Members of the Executive Committee, The Study Group, and Club Members:
>
> I wish to thank you for your personal correspondence to me dated 12 July 1993 regarding the historical issues of the Jewish quota in the Club during the 1930s through 1950. 1 particularly found details of the Report of the Study Group of interest since it contained some information of which I was not aware.
>
> My apologies for not responding sooner. I have waited until now to respond to your July communication to me because I wanted to let it sit and digest—I wanted to be clear about how I felt—before responding.
>
> I appreciate the sentiment expressed in the last paragraph of the Memorandum dated July 12, 1993 and signed by the Executive Committee of the Club. It feels sincere and genuinely concerned with healing wounds resulting from that period in the Club's history. As a result, I consider the charge of following up on some act of atonement on the part of the Club as having been met and that I have no further formal role in this matter.
>
> It is satisfying to know that colleagues in the Club faced an unpleasant shadow issue with integrity. I was personally touched by the symbolism of having received what appears to be an original copy of the Memorandum of the Executive Committee signed in ink by all members. I take that symbolic statement as a recogni-

tion of the nature of my initial contacts with the Club and therein feel some personal healing with you.

I send you best wishes for the New Year and look forward to meeting some of you at the next International in Zurich.

Sincerely,
Jerome S. Bernstein, M.A.P.C., NCPsyA.
Chairman, Workshop on Jung and Anti-Semitism
XIth Congress of the IAAP
cc: John Beebe
Thomas B. Kirsch, M.D., President, IAAP

More Lingering Shadows: Shadows Closer to Home

Unfortunately, there are still lingering shadows concerning the politics surrounding the issue of Jung's alleged anti-Semitism—specifically, the role of the Jungian collective in clarifying and bringing information to light and/or in suppressing relevant information. Providing light where there has been none may be of some help.

In the fall of 1993, I received an inquiry from the Association of Graduate Analytical Psychologists of Zurich (AGAP) regarding further developments that had transpired since the XIIth Congress in Chicago in August 1992. (AGAP is a professional association of Jungian analysts who are graduates of the C. G. Jung Institute of Zurich. It is separate from the Analytical Psychology Club of Zurich, whose membership consists of lay individuals as well as graduate analysts.) In a response dated December 6, 1993, to an inquiry from AGAP, I observed:

> The experience in pursuing this matter was an extraordinary one for me. What I found so astounding (in retrospect I shouldn't have) was the inability of not only the club's president, but a number of other colleagues, in particular the then-president of the IAAP, to have a feeling relationship to the issue nor to be able to perceive that the actions taken by the Club during the period in question had relevance today, had caused injury, then and now, to colleagues, non-Jewish as well as Jewish. There seemed to be no recognition or concern that there were "lingering shadows" over this issue which raised fundamental ethical questions not only about the Club, but about Dr. Jung and about the ethical integrity of the larger Jungian community as well as our profession. There seemed to be no awareness or concern for how this issue would sit in the history of the analytical psychology move-

> ment and how it could be used to further the irrational assault on Jung and Jungians which had continued with intensity since the 1930s. Were these statements made of any group, they would be reprehensible. That they pertained to analytical psychologists whose professional training and commitment involves raising to consciousness of unconscious material I found astounding, dismaying and fascinating.
>
> I take the Club's July 1993 response to be a sincere acknowledgment of, and act of atonement for, the actions for the Club during the period in question as well as more recent actions taken in the Club's name. In all, the experience was enlightening for me personally and as a member of the larger community of Jungian analysts. There is no question in my mind that the response of delegate members at both the XIth [1989] and XIIth [1992] Congresses played no small role in raising consciousness within our community and an ultimate resolution of this specific issue. I also respect the forthrightness of the larger membership of the Analytical Psychology Club of Zurich when they had at their disposal facts surrounding the issue.
>
> Once again we learn that consciousness, and with it, ethical responsibility, is never easy—even for those of us who have a diploma acknowledging special abilities to wrestle with those issues. I am happy to report that, with struggle, this effort has been successful....

At the same time, it is important to be aware of how shadow issues of this kind activate our most difficult complexes on both sides of the issue. Often we operate under the illusion that our reactions are limited to the issue at hand. However, in my experience, highly emotionally laden shadow issues—particularly on the collective level—usually activate our core complexes. I often find myself in an intense wrestling match with those ancillary complexes that threaten to take over the issue at hand. For a Jew, anti-Semitic shadow issues will almost always activate some of one's most primary complexes. They can challenge the very essence of his/her identity and soul. In any case, on a collective level, this problem did not detract club members from a responsible, conscious resolution of this issue of the Jewish quota. The fact that the process itself—that is, the process by which the Club came to issue its statement of atonement—was difficult, resisted at some levels, painful, resented, and complexed, was to be expected. The group ego, no less than the individual ego, does not like being called to task. The fact of the resistance in some quarters did not detract from the genuineness of the ultimate outcome. If anything, it heightened the integrity of the process.

Moral Consciousness

Moral consciousness is indispensable to an ethical attitude and the prevention of falling headlong into a destructive power complex. That individuals and groups have shadows certainly is not news. However, when either rises to the challenge of their own destructive shadow contents and owns and acts to integrate those contents, that is news. What began as an ignoble and wounding chapter in the history of the Club concluded with an admirable and, in some ways, exemplary process of consciousness-raising, shadow integration, and healing within our own collective. The process engaged in by the Analytical Psychology Club of Zurich ultimately reflected the finest spirit of Jung's teachings. For personal reasons, I did not attend the 1995 XIIIth Congress in Zurich. I regret that decision. I would have preferred to have given a more extensive report on the follow-up with the Psychology Club and the statement of atonement which did issue from the Club.

Dr. Beebe gave the final report on the effort since the Paris workshop to obtain an "act of atonement" from the Analytical Psychology Club of Zurich regarding its imposed Jewish quota. His report included a reading of the operative statements in the club's "statement of atonement." I would have liked to have seen a more comprehensive report given, one that reflected the psychological and spiritual struggles surrounding this piece of our history, delineating the process itself—it worked!—and one which would have acknowledged the character strength of our own larger collective when called upon to face our own shadow. It was, difficulties notwithstanding, one of the Jungian community's finer moments. It is with this desire that I write this now to complete the record.

This latter point is no small matter. In the absence of a full and open record of this process, we are open to the kinds of charges and scurrilous attacks that some would lay at our feet. Indeed, we contribute to them! For example, in *The Jung Cult*, Richard Noll cites the secret Jewish quota in the Analytical Psychology Club of Zurich as a reprehensible example of Jung's anti-Semitism. He says, "To my knowledge, even as of this late date (1996) no one in Zurich—certainly no one in the Jung family—has ever attempted to make a formal apology for these attitudes or actions."[14] Paradoxically in this case, most of the documentation and information that was suppressed would have put the lie to some of

Dr. Noll's accusations, and would have shown our collective, including the Analytical Psychology Club of Zurich, in a more favorable light. To some degree, some of the material would have shown Dr. Jung in a less negative light given that in 1950 it was he who insisted that the Jewish quota policy be eliminated.

What is Anti-Semitism?

"Anti-Semitism" is a term bandied about by many people, Jewish and non-Jewish. Both in my observations over the years and in the literature I have read, the term is virtually never defined. Everyone assumes they know what they mean when they use the term and that those with whom they are talking know its meaning and psychological implications. But do we? Anti-Semitism has been used to refer to everything from the Nazi horrors to an experience my wife had at a high school baseball booster meeting where someone, as it turns out innocently, used the term to "Jew down" a sports store selling equipment to the high school. When the mother of another team member approached the person after the meeting and pointed out that the expression "Jewing down" someone is quite offensive to Jews, the person was taken aback, stating that he had just grown up with the term and it had never occurred to him that it would be offensive to another. In fact, he had no idea that the phrase had anything to do with Jews at all—it had never occurred to him. An apology followed. The anti-Semitism in the case of the Nazis is obvious; much less certain on a personal level is the baseball meeting example. Cultural prejudice, as opposed to personal prejudice, is carried on the collective level and absorbed by the individual through the cultural *ethos*. The "learning" of the prejudice, usually, is almost totally without personal reflection and is essentially impersonal for the carrier of the prejudice. When the prejudice is reflected upon, the carrier either rejects it as incompatible with his/her personal values or retains it as consistent with theirs. At this point, it becomes more than a cultural prejudice and is now a prejudice of the individual. Of course, the cultural prejudice remains in the collective culture. In my own case, for years I used the word "gypped," when referring to a situation where I felt that I had been taken advantage of. I had "picked up" the expression in the vernacular of the culture I lived in. In my early 20s, someone pointed out that the word was a pejorative derivative from the word "Gypsy," an association I had never made. I immediately ceased consciously using the word, "gypped," although a month ago it slipped out of my mouth, much to my surprise!

So, what is anti-Semitism—what are we talking about? In the first place, not all anti-Jewish prejudice constitutes anti-Semitism. Anti-Semitism, in my mind, represents a particularly virulent form of anti-Jewish prejudice. It carries an emotional implication, consciously or unconsciously, ultimately pointing toward genocide.

As Richard Levy points out in his book, *Anti-Semitism in the Modern World: An Anthology of Texts*, "Many ordinary Europeans of the middle and upper classes harbored all sorts of negative attitudes about Jewry in general without this mind-set seriously affecting their personal relations with individual Jews, even up to and including marriage."[15] Levy states:

> The difference between Jew hatred and anti-Semitism, then and now, is not one [just] of degree. Anti-Jewish feeling was too ubiquitous before and after 1879, too much a part of the common outlook of Westerners (including a good many Jews), to be considered the acid test for anti-Semitism. Although a certain "critical mass" of hatred has been reached, the anti-Semites betray no consistency in this matter. Some were rabid and obsessional, others appeared to be no more than ordinarily prejudiced, and a few maintained cordial relationship with Jews while exploiting the anti-Jewish feelings of others.
>
> Judged by prejudicial feelings alone, nearly everyone would have to be labeled an anti-Semite.[16]

The Chambers English Dictionary defines "prejudice" as any "judgment or opinion formed beforehand or *without due examination*: a prejudgment."[17] As we know, there are as many forms of prejudice as there are groups: "Spics" (Hispanics or Mexicans); "Wops" (Italians); "Dagos" (Spanish, Portuguese, or Italians); "Kikes" (Jews); "Chinks" (Chinese); "Nips" (Japanese); "Niggers" (Blacks); "Honkies" (Whites), etc. More often than not these terms, as in the case of the term "Jew down" used at the high school baseball meeting, are culturally derived and embedded and are passed on through the culture "without due examination." And, indeed, one can frequently hear any of these terms used by individuals of the target group itself when referencing themselves and/or others of their ethnic/religious group. The degree of reprehension attached to any of these prejudicial terms for individuals within a given target group varies from none at all to extreme. In this context, anti-Jewish prejudice may not constitute anti-Semitism.

Anti-Jewish prejudice has been, more often than not, culturally transmitted over the centuries. For reasons I will not explore here, some cultures such as the Germanic have a higher prevalence of anti-Jewish prejudice than others. In the case of the latter, it is not surprising that the nature and degree of German anti-Jewish prejudice gave rise to, but was not subsumed by, new forms and the need for a new word—"anti-Semitism." In other words, both forms exist at the same time in that and other cultures.

Jungian analyst Richard Stein points out that everyone "has a shadow, which includes racial prejudice to one degree or another."[18] In this context, "defensive moves to contain the Good in subjectivity while projecting the Bad in objectivity, are dynamic defenses used in early childhood to establish boundary between self and other, which are similar to the dynamics of racial prejudice."[19] Since differentiation is the primary tool for forging individual and group identity, the dynamics that give rise to racial and other forms of prejudice are bound up with the formation of individual and group identity. In other words, like it or not, all of us carry the tendency toward prejudice of one form or another as the price of our individual development. Our choice is not whether we will or won't carry prejudices; rather the choice that we can have is the degree of consciousness we struggle to attain and the responsibility we take toward the prejudices we carry within us.

Carl Jung points out that regarding individual differences, individual consciousness develops out of an original state of unconsciousness. In other words, without differentiation, we would all exist in a state of some form of participation mystique in a manner not unlike the child's identification with the parents. He says, "Differentiation is the essence, the *sine qua non* of consciousness."[20] Differentiation, and thus identity, inevitably involves the dynamic we call "prejudice." In this sense, "prejudice" is a natural by-product of the differentiation of the archetype of the Self, i.e. it has archetypal roots. By "archetype" I mean universal psychic forms that structure and influence, if not direct, human development and behavior. Thus, in this instance regarding the archetype of the Self, that archetype assures that the "Self" in all of us develops in the same manner—not to become the same person, but with the same psychodynamic process. Moreover, on the collective level, pseudo-speciation—a psychodynamic process wherein a given human group has a sense of sociocultural separateness as if it were a distinct biological species—has been essential for producing the cultural differentiation and conflict essential for the evolution of civilization as we know it.[21] In short, self-development means differentiation; and differentiation means an emphasis on difference. The word "prejudice," however, is used almost exclusively in the context of groups or individuals who are members of groups targeted as "different."

Thus, psychodynamically and archetypally speaking, there is no avoidance of prejudice in individual or group development. There is only the choice and the degree to which we apply "due examination" as the definition of prejudice implies. The more we apply "due examination," the less prejudiced we are likely to behave; the less we do apply "due examination," the more prejudiced we are likely to behave, and the more susceptible we become ultimately, individually and collectively, to, for example, anti-Semitism.

Note that I have stated that with due examination we would be less likely to behave in a prejudicial manner. I deliberately did not say that we would not be prejudiced. We seem to have better luck at controlling our behavior in this regard than in determining what prejudicial feelings we may carry.

On an emotional level, we tend to react to most prejudice on a personal level and see it as personally motivated. From an archetypal standpoint, prejudice (as distinct from anti-Semitism) has a large, impersonal dimension. This point becomes important in the context of how we perceive and react to prejudice. Treating an impersonal dynamic as if it were personally motivated could, in fact, bring about the very reaction we wish to avoid.

In this context, Levy tends to see anti-Semitism more in political terms. He says that, "Anti-Semitism is not merely emotional; it is activist....what was new and menacingly different about anti-Semitism [was] its politicization and embodiment in permanent political parties, voluntary associations, and publishing ventures—in short, its institutionalization."[22] He goes on to offer a definition of "anti-Semitism" as

> ". . . a willingness and a *commitment*[23] to act against Jews over long duration for either of two aims:
>
> 1. To render Jews harmless by some means or other, thus negating the [supposedly] enormous power they had illegitimately gained or
>
> 2. To accomplish other political goals not directly bearing on the well-being of Jews.[24]

In my opinion, Levy's definition is too narrowly political and unpsychological for our purposes here. I would offer the following definition for "anti-Semitism" as distinguished from anti-Jewish prejudice:

Anti-Semitism is an attitude wherein the ego identifies with anti-Jewish prejudice and compels anti-Jewish behavior on a consistent basis and does not permit itself a differing viewpoint or behavior, even upon focused examination.

This definition seems to address the political and the nonpolitical and psychological characteristics of anti-Semitism.

One of the reasons I have so carefully delineated the difference between anti-Semitism and anti-Jewish prejudice is because it does not serve the needs of Jews (nor any other minority group) to lump anti-Semitism and prejudice together. For one thing, prejudice regarding Jews and other minority groups is much more easily dealt with than its much more deeply entrenched and virulent forms such as anti-Semitism. The contemporary knee-jerk reaction of "playing the race card" wherein a defense of a minority person—regardless of whether the individual is guilty of a crime or not—is based on a counter-charge of prejudice, facts notwithstanding, has seriously confounded the problem on all fronts. We have seen this dynamic played out in the case of O. J. Simpson, for example, and it is still being played out in the case of Jonathan Pollard, an American Jew convicted of spying against the United States on behalf of Israel.

The word "anti-Semite" (and its derivative, "anti-Semitism") first appeared in Germany in 1879, coined by Wilhelm Marr in his essay, "The Victory of Judaism over Germandom."[25] The impetus for a new term for a particular kind of anti-Jewish prejudice reflected a wide recognition that historic patterns and motives for anti-Jewish prejudice had so changed that a new word was needed. Although there were extreme forms of anti-Jewish prejudice prior to 1879 (acts and behaviors that would be called "anti-Semitism" today such as in the Crusades, the persecution and expulsion of Jews from England, France, and Spain, the Inquisition, and so forth) most of these earlier forms were acted out primarily in the name of religion and/or the church. The new term "anti-Semitism" was coined, it appears, to refer to extreme and particular forms of anti-Jewish prejudice at large in the society at that time. In essence, it was a new sociological term that came to symbolize a new dimension of anti-Jewish prejudice reflected in the larger collective. But what was that new dimension of anti-Jewish prejudice that required a new term?

What the term connotes goes beyond prejudice, in the colloquial sense of the word and as I have attempted to differentiate above. One clue that may help us identify the new dimension that required a new term for anti-Jewish prejudice can be found in the title of Marr's 1879 essay, i.e. "The *Victory* of Judaism over Germandom." (Italics added.) In other words, apparently there was a conviction in Germany at that time that Judaism, and all of the black magic projected onto it, was sufficiently powerful to take over and destroy "Germandom," i.e. German values and ethos. Judaism, in other words, was perceived to have sufficient power to enslave the German people and culture. This attitude, subsumed in the coining of the word "anti-Semitism," carried the German collective cultural projection of the devil. I believe that a new term was needed to address a projected underlying/unconscious irrational feeling of racial, religious, and cultural threat to the dominant group(s) that was beginning to become liminal. It was easier to hold on to an irrational conviction that the devil is "out there,"—projected onto Jews—than to face the implications of dealing with one's own internal devil, individually and collectively. This projection of the devil imago in the form of anti-Semitism was so powerful that it coined a new word that stuck within the German culture as well as internationally, and subsequently was adopted by the target group itself. Less than sixty years later, it became the basis for the "final solution," by the Nazis to the "Jewish Question."

In the modern era since the end of World War II, where exaggeration and extremism in almost all forms of communication seem to have picked up ever-increasing momentum, the term "anti-Semitism" has come to be used for any and all forms of anti-Jewish prejudice. Similarly, any international conflict is often referred to as "genocide"—for example, those in Israel/Palestine, Chechnya, and Iraq—which is a gross distortion of the meaning of the word. Anti-Semitism, in my opinion, correctly used, would apply only to extreme, consciously committed forms of anti-Jewish prejudice, ultimately pointing toward the extreme of genocide. I have intentionally distinguished between anti-Jewish prejudice and anti-Semitism because both the nature and psychological intention of each is quite different. Few people carrying the anti-Jewish prejudice prevalent in their culture would consciously subscribe to the kind of anti-Semitism leading to the Holocaust. This distinction is quite important also when addressing the question of Jung's alleged anti-Semitism.

Was Carl Jung Anti-Semitic?

With regard to the published record regarding Carl Jung, I believe that the evidence indicates that Jung, like many of his culture, carried cultural anti-Jewish prejudice. Based on the record I have seen to date, I see little factual evidence supporting a charge of personal anti-Semitism. Nevertheless, my concern with Carl Jung regarding the allegations of his personal anti-Semitism is much less with what he did say than with what he did not say. As Elie Wiesel has often reminded us, "the opposite of love is not hate but indifference."[26] He points out that with indifference, there is no reciprocity. Micha Neumann's presentation in *Lingering Shadows* regarding Jung's indifference to the heart-wrenching pleadings of his father, Erich Neumann, Jung's protégé, for Jung to express himself publicly on the plight of European Jewry, especially after the advent of *Kristallnacht* on November 10, 1938, is particularly telling.[27] For Erich Neumann and his son Micha, Jung was one of the loudest silent onlookers of this pillage and murder. Jung's cold analyses and pontifications without any expression of human compassion leave me, still, chilled to my core. The Talmud says, "Silence easily becomes acquiescence."[28]

"I slipped up"[29] is defensive, shallow, and shockingly unfeeling as Jung's only recorded (and second-hand, at that) personal commentary regarding the Holocaust; this, from a man who, since before WWI, commented repeatedly on man's morality or lack thereof, and on threats to world peace and human survival from unintegrated shadow dynamics and uncontained archetypal dynamics. His public silence on the subject of the Holocaust leaves me aghast.[30]

To quote Adolf Guggenbühl-Craig (former president of both the Jung Institute in Zurich and the IAAP) on this matter:

> Everyone in Europe, with perhaps the exception of the Italians, was anti-Semitic in the last century, and in the centuries before that, as well as in this century. Anti-Semitism was and is part of the collective mythology, originating from the Christian religion. The Jews were considered to be the killers of Jesus Christ. . . .
>
> Jung was on the one hand a psychological genius and on the other hand a very average middle-class man, a bourgeois, with all the mythological beliefs, images, and ideas that his class possessed. Anti-Semitism was, and partially still is, the darker side of this belief system. . . . The anti-Semitism of Jung was . . . part and parcel of the collective he belonged to.[31]

Although Dr. Guggenbühl-Craig does not differentiate between anti-Jewish prejudice and anti-Semitism, he is saying that Jung was like most other Swiss—and, for that matter, like most other Europeans of the era—with regard to anti-Jewish prejudice. In other words, he understands Jung's anti-Jewish prejudice as coming from the Swiss/Germanic/European cultural collective.

The operative phrase in the dictionary definition of prejudice that I quoted earlier is "without due examination." In this context,

I believe it to be a crucial and defining phrase in distinguishing between anti-Jewish prejudice and anti-Semitism. We must be careful here also to not confuse "due" or "undue examination" with "conscious" or "unconscious." One can be quite aware of one's prejudice without having duly examined it. A pertinent vignette: On the way to the XIth International IAAP Congress in Paris in 1989, where I would be chairing the two-day workshop on Jung and Anti-Semitism, my family and I spent an afternoon with Jung's son Franz, in his home (formerly his father's home). It was an exceptionally pleasant and amiable afternoon and Franz Jung could not have been a more warm, friendly or gracious host. During that time, we discussed many topics about his father, himself, and the Jung family. After a few hours, Franz began to make some tea and refreshments for us. While he was doing so I informed him about the Paris workshop and asked him what he thought about the charges of anti-Semitism against his father. He dismissed them with a wave of his hand and said that there was no substance to the charges. He then followed with a short discussion about "those people," referring to Jews, obviously not having the slightest notion that his tone and the phrase "those people" had any pejorative connotation. There is no question that he knew that I was a Jew and it was apparent to both my wife and me that he neither intended any insult nor had any awareness of the prejudice that came with his comments. Neither of us was offended by his comments, since it was clear to both of us that his Jewish prejudice was both impersonal and not "duly examined." To me it was a prime example of the cultural prejudice that seeps into individual members of any collective.

There is, of course, the unpublished record—letters and other material retained by the Jung family and others. No doubt, much of this could shed additional light on the question of Jung's alleged anti-Semitism. In the absence of the rest of the documents that could further clarify this picture, there seems to be a rush to judgment. There are those both within the Jungian community and without who are ready to condemn Jung for the worst; and there are those who would defend Jung until the end. In time, what of Jung's material that is being withheld by the Jung family and why, will likely come to light. We know what we know and we don't know what we don't know. Judgment is a poor substitute for historical fact. Jung's writings emphasize over and over to hold the tension of the opposites in the absence of clear resolution between them; this is the only ethical and psychological stance of integrity, unique circumstances notwithstanding. As Matthew Bernstein has writen, in an unpublished 1997 paper titled "Carl Jung and Anti-Semitism: A Historical Approach":

> It is tempting to either slap Carl Jung with the anti-Semitic label or completely exonerate him of ever having done wrong. I choose to do neither. We must remain faithful to history in our examination of this intricate matter. Carl Jung was neither completely guilty of anti-Semitism, nor wholly against it. He lived in troubled times and . . . never could shake loose the demons of Hitler and the Holocaust.[32]

I look upon the reality of the Jewish quota within the Analytical Psychology Club of Zurich as reflecting the nature of the times as well as those individuals and groups involved—repugnant nonetheless, but understandable in context. The primary issue today is not to pass judgment but rather to redeem what can be redeemed. Redemption frequently does not come cheap. In this case it came with some struggle. But in my view the outcome was both healing, for the most part, and ethical.

To my mind, the challenge for the Jungian collective from this point on is to commit to the process/struggle of continuing to bring more information and clarity on the painful subject of Jung's alleged anti-Semitism. Whatever information might come to bear, it seems to me that ultimately it will be less damaging than colluding with Jung's shadow or our own. And, whatever information might come to light about Carl Jung in this arena, surely there is something redeeming—even for Jung himself—in the fact that those who employ his psychology and carry his name take the lead in bringing to light whatever truth demands telling. As Stephen Martin observed in the Introduction to *Lingering Shadows*, "It seemed imperative that we, the Jungians, should inaugurate the dialogue and initiate the rapprochement, because to look into the darkness, personal or collective, was, in Jung's mind, the cornerstone of a psychologically authentic and ethical life."[33] This applies no less to Carl Jung as it does to us. We need to continue what we have begun.

Each day of your life is the Day of Atonement; every word spoken from the heart is the name of the Lord.[34]

Notes

1. Aryeh Maidenbaum and Stephen A Martin, eds., *Lingering Shadows: Jungians, Freudians, and Anti-Semitism* (Boston: Shambhala, 1991).

2. Edward C. Whitmont, *Return of the Goddess* (New York: Crossroad, 1982), p. 63.

3. Jungian psychology is also known as "analytical psychology."

4. I will take this moment to thank her/him for catalyzing the events that took place and for the process that the meeting thrust me into.

5. See Richard Noll, "The Rose, the Cross and the Analyst," op. ed. column, *New York Times*, October 15, 1994, *The Jung Cult: The Origins of a Charismatic Movement* (Princeton, Princeton University Press, 1994; London: Fontana, 1996), and *The Aryan Christ: The Secret Life of Carl Jung* (New York: Random House, 1997); and Frank McLynn, *Carl Gustav Jung* (New York: St. Martin's Press, 1997). Also see Anthony Stevens, M.D., "Critical Notice," in *The Journal of Analytical Psychology* 42, no. 4 (1997): 671–690.

6. See chapter 3 in Sonu Shamdasani, *Cult Fictions* (London: Routledge, 1998) for a more detailed history of the origin and history of the Club.

7. See Aryeh Maidenbaum, "Lingering Shadows: A Personal Perspective," in Maidenbaum and Martin, eds., *Lingering Shadows*, pp. 291–300.

8. Noll, *The Jung Cult*, p. xii.

9. See Appendix A in Maidenbaum and Martin, eds., *Lingering Shadows*, p. 362.

10. See Maidenbaum, "Lingering Shadows: A Personal Perspective," op. cit.

11. Ibid., p. 328.

12. The full report is contained in the Minutes of the Delegates Meeting of August 26, 1992, which was sent to the Presidents member societies of the IAAP by the President of the IAAP on January 20, 1993. A summary report is contained under "Miscellaneous," item 9, and the full report is contained at the end as "Exhibit No. 4."

13. Quoted in Chaim Stern, *Gates of Repentance: The New Union Prayerbook for the Days of Awe* (New York: Central Conference of American Rabbis, 1978), p. 324.

14. Noll, *The Jung Cult*, p. xii.

15. Richard S. Levy, *Anti-Semitism in the Modern World: An Anthology of Texts* (Lexington, MA: D. C. Heath and Company, 1991), p. 4.

16. Ibid., p. 3.

17. Sidney I. Landau, *Chambers English Dictionary* (Cambridge, England: 1988), p. 1152. Italics mine.

18. Richard Stein, "Jung's 'Mana Personality' and the Nazi Era," in Maidenbaum and Martin, eds., *Lingering Shadows*, p. 90

19. Polly Young-Eisendrath, "The Absence of Black Americans as Jungian Analysts," *Quadrant* 20, no. 2 (1987): 42. Quoted in Stein, op. cit., p. 90.

20. C. G. Jung, *Two Essays in Analytical Psychology*, 2nd edition. *CW* 7, ¶ 329.

21. See chapter 8, "Paranoia between Groups and Nations" in Jerome S. Bernstein, *Power and Politics: The Psychology of Soviet-American Partnerships* (Boston: Shambhala, 1989).

22. Levy, *Anti-Semitism in the Modern World*, p. 4.

23. "Commitment" implies awareness *and* "due examination." Italics mine.

24. Levy, op. cit., p. 5.

25. Ibid., p. 2.

26. Elie Wiesel, *And the Sea is Never Full: Memoirs, 1969*(New York: Alfred Knopf, 1999), p. 372.

27. See Micha Neumann, "On the Relationship between Erich Neumann and C. G. Jung," on pp. 73–86. *Kristallnacht,* also known as the "night of the broken glass," refers to an orgy of massive public assaults on Jews and Jewish establishments in Germany and sympathizing countries such as Austria, officially sanctioned by the Nazi German government. "Some 195 synagogues were burned, more than 800 shops destroyed and 7,500 looted. The streets of Germany were littered by the shattered shop windows. . . . Twenty thousand Jews were arrested and taken to concentration camps. Official German figures listed thirty-six killed, but newsmen and diplomatic observers counted many more deaths. (Arthur D. Morse, *While 6 Million Died: A Chronicle of American Apathy* [New York: Ace Publishing, 1968], p. 182). The *New York Times* reported on November 11, 1938, "Huge but mostly silent crowds looked on and the police confined themselves to regulating traffic and making wholesale arrest of Jews 'for their own protection.'" For Erich Neumann and his son Micha, Jung was one of the loudest, silent onlookers of this pillage and murder.

28. Wiesel, *And the Sea Is Never Full*, p. 7.

29. See Appendix A in this book, pp. 219–257.

30. See, among other writings, "After the Catastrophe," in *CW* 10; *CW* 18, *The Symbolic Life*, especially chapters xi, "Civilization in Transition," pp. 551–641 and XII, *Psychology and Religion*, pp. 645–744. Also see William McGuire and R. F. C. Hull, eds., *C. G. Jung Speaking: Interviews and Encounters* (Princeton: Princeton University Press, 1977).

31. Adolf Guggenbühl-Craig, "Reflections on Jung and Anti-Semitism," in this book, pp. 141–146.

32. Matthew David Bernstein, "Carl Jung and Anti-Semitism: A Historical Approach," unpublished paper (New York: Columbia University, December 1, 1997), p. 27.

33. Maidenbaum and Martin, eds., *Lingering Shadows*, p. 2.

34. S. Ansky, *The Dybbuk*, as quoted in Stern, *Gates of Repentance*, p. 236.

CHAPTER 10

Adolf Guggenbühl-Craig

Reflections on Jung and Collective Anti-Semitism

Adolf Guggenbühl-Craig is a psychiatrist and Jungian analyst in Zurich, Switzerland, and the author of several books, including *Power in the Helping Professions* and *Eros on Crutches: Reflections on Psychology and Amorality.* In his contribution to the workshop, he suggests that we should not be alarmed by Jung's anti-Semitism, as it was a byproduct of his bourgeois Protestant background and in no way detracted from his psychological genius. He urges us to confront our need for an idealized, shadowless father figure in Jung, and to accept that he was, ultimately, simply an ordinary person of his time.

Guggenbühl-Craig makes the uniquely Jungian argument that generalizations about nations and races are valid in that they are ultimately mythological in nature, and therefore true expressions of collective fantasy.

The center of our discussion seems to be the impact of Jung's anti-Semitism on the credibility of his ideas, and the injuries that we have suffered as a result of Jung's darker side. I may be the wrong person to talk about this topic, as I feel neither injured nor disappointed by Jung.

In 1943, when I was 20 years old, I started to read Jung. My father warned me, "Why are you interested in that man? Don't you know that he is an anti-Semite, he flirts with Nazism, he flatters rich ladies, and who knows what else?" At that time, I had the same political ideas as my father. For both of us anti-Semitism was *the* crime. We knew that the Germans had begun to exterminate the Jews. I was at that time so shocked by this fact that I started to learn Yiddish, a feeble attempt to honor the threatened Jewish people. And I continued, in spite of my father, to read Jung.

My father's opinions of Jung were not particularly original. He had never read Jung himself. His psychological hero was Freud. The ideas he had about Jung were collective, shared by a large number of Swiss, who saw in Hitler's Germany a deadly danger for Switzerland and the whole liberal democratic world. When later, as a psychiatrist, I joined the Jungians, my father was very disappointed. He could never fully understand how I could betray my family and myself by joining what to him was a half-fascistic crowd. That's why, to use James Hillman's images, I was never a white, innocent Jungian; I was "yellow" from the beginning. But all the same, the topic interests me. How do the dark sides of Jung affect us, as Christians and as Jews, or whatever our identity may be? I will try to give a precise answer to this question now and go into details later.

The dark sides of Jung should not affect us at all. We should ignore them; they should not worry us at all. For us, the second-generation Jungians, the dark sides of Jung are a pseudo-issue, a non-event. If it affects us all the same, then there is something wrong with us. We have to examine ourselves to find out what is wrong.

But first of all, let us turn to Jung. As far as I can see, Jung was certainly anti-Semitic, but in a less ideological, conscious, yet deeper way than Andrew Samuels believes. Everyone in Europe, with perhaps the exception of the Italians, was anti-Semitic in the last century, and in the centuries before that, as well as in this century. Anti-Semitism was and is part of the collective mythology, originating from the Christian religion. The Jews were considered to be the killers of Jesus Christ. James Kirsch has written very convincingly about the religious roots of Jung's anti-Semitism. (See the article by James Kirsch in *Lingering Shadows.*)

Jung was, on the one hand, a psychological genius, and on the other hand, a very average middle-class man, a bourgeois, with all the mythological beliefs, images, and ideas that this class possessed. Anti-Semitism was, and partially still is, the darker side of this belief system. There are many bright sides, too: ideas of freedom, justice, decency, honesty, social justice, democracy, and so on. The anti-Semitism of Jung was a sheer banality, part and parcel of the collective to which he belonged.

As an ordinary man, Jung displayed positive and negative sides. He was, for instance, an appeaser: don't make the beast angry, don't anger

Hitler, and so forth. Again, this was a typical collective attitude. Europe was, until 1939, largely dominated by appeasers. Remember Chamberlain's "Peace for our time" after Munich? "Be nice to the beast, save your skin," amounted to an argument in favor of survival at all costs.

Appeasement is not always a mistake; it is one way to deal with the dark forces around and within us. Heroes have done as much damage, and as much good, as appeasers—and in the collective psyche, sometimes the appeaser is stronger, while at other times the hero is.

Jung was intellectual, again in a very collective way. Intellectuals are much inclined to admire power. The French speak of a *trahison des clercs,* a phrase that translates literally as "treason of the clergy" or "of the intellectuals." We should not forget that hundreds of European intellectuals, writers, and sophisticated professors paid homage to Stalin while he was walking knee-deep in the blood of Russian peasants. They admired even his macabre purges. While Mao was killing millions of Chinese farmers, many intellectuals went on praising him as the creator of a new and better world. This admiration of power among intellectuals is probably a compensation for their fascination with the spirit. Obviously, not all intellectuals are blinded by power; there are always a few original individuals who can resist it. But the bulk of them, insofar as they are part of the intellectual collective, tend to be attracted by power.

And so Jung, as a collective intellectual, was fascinated by Hitler and Mussolini. This is not very original. But even the greatest genius can only be original in a small part of his psyche; the bigger part belongs to the collective psyche. And Jung, at least after World War II, did not follow the collective crazes for the mass murderers Stalin and Mao.

I repeat: Jung had many sides. On one side he was a unique psychological genius, on the other side he was an average member of the upper middle class, an anti-Semite, an appeaser, and sometimes an intellectual who admired power.

However, if we are chagrined by the contradictions in Jung, we are not true Jungian psychologists; we are then missing some points of Jungian psychology, because Jung taught us the following: human beings are many-sided, composed of many archetypes, psychoids, complexes, all of them having their own consciousness. The different sides might have little to do with each other, not only in schizophrenics, but in all of us.

In dealing with my wife, my children, and my friends, I have to take all sides into account. With Jung this is not the case. Jung was not my friend. His contradictory sides might have been a problem for his analysands, but his aura was so overpowering that often the critical faculties of his analysands melted away and they slipped into an eternal happy glorification of the master. We Jungians today have to listen to his genius; the rest should be of no interest to us.

There was a movement in American literary criticism that coined a phrase, "The author is 'out,'" meaning that personal information about a writer is of no interest, and only his or her work counts. This certainly applies to Jung.

But we still have to ask: why this disappointment in Jung? Why is this disappointment so widespread among Jungians? I believe that this disappointment stems from a deep need for a perfect leader, a perfect saint, someone who guides us, who becomes a guru. And so, if a genius appears, we make him into a saint, a prophet, and a leader. But even though we are psychologists and know about archetypes, we are still not conscious of this longing for the messiah or for the second coming of Christ. We are then, of course, disappointed when our hero, apart from being a genius, turns out to be a very average human being.

Nevertheless, I must confess that I was very disturbed a few years ago when the changes in the statutes of the Jungian club in Zurich during the war, limiting the number of Jewish numbers, were revealed. What the club did—whoever the club was at that time—is very difficult to understand. It was similar to kicking a dying man in the face. But then again, who wants to throw the first stone?

Granting Jung his shadow of collective beliefs frees us from our messianic projection onto him. Yet there is another important issue, which has been raised by Andrew Samuels: is there something inherent in the ideas of Jung that could lead to anti-Semitism or to Nazism? That is, in my opinion, the only issue that we have to worry about, and this only within limits. By way of comparison, Christianity contains inherent ideas that, when misunderstood and abused, led to the burning of thousands of men and women as witches and to pogroms, and yet some of us are still Christians.

Andrew Samuels has mentioned Jung's fascination with nations. He thinks that this fascination should be suspect. Here I have to defend Jung. In this instance I see evidence of his psychological genius.

Nations are a very impressive psychological phenomenon. It makes no difference if Germany only existed officially since 1871, or if already in olden times one spoke of the *römischen Reich deutscher Nation* (the Roman empire of the German nation), or if the Italians became a nation only in the 19th century, or if the British nation is really four nations. The fact is that in the past centuries, millions of people died in Europe and elsewhere for their nation, often voluntarily. Nations are an extremely powerful phenomenon and, like all important psychological phenomena, they cannot be explained; they can only be approached by mythological images.

We all talk about the characteristics of different nations. For instance, we say that the Italians have lots of feelings, the French are rational, the Swiss are sober, the English are gentlemen and ladies; but it is pure mythology. I hope that Jung realized this when he talked about Germans and Jews in this way. This talk about the characters of nations and peoples is all fantasy—extremely powerful fantasy. Maybe Jung was at times inclined to take these fantasies too literally; from the point of view of Jungian psychology, these fantasies can be treated as pure mythological images.

The problem of the different characteristics of groups and nations, of women and men, is not whether they are inborn or acquired, but that they are a powerful collective phenomenon of mysterious origin, only able to be described by mythology. Jung tried to do just that, to understand this powerful phenomenon by the collective fantasies and the mythologies lying behind them.

The collective fantasies, or at least the fantasies of some nations, became ill during this century, as we saw in Nazi Germany. Our job as psychotherapists, analysts, and psychiatrists is to treat psychotics and neurotics, with the help of the insight analytical psychology gives us. Our job is not only to talk to ladies and gentlemen about their fancy dreams—or only to train trainees to become, in turn, training analysts for trainees. When we have patients with delusions, hallucinations, horrible perversions, it's no use pointing to reality. First we have to join with the psychopathology of the patient and accept it. We even have to do this half unconsciously, and only when we make this connection and become fascinated can we go further with the patient and eventually help him or her.

Jung, the genius, did exactly that. He let himself be drawn into the collective madness of Nazism, of which anti-Semitism was only a part. He was fascinated by the phenomenon, and out of this fascination he was able to formulate and describe precisely what this phenomenon was and is. His little book *Wotan* is still, even today, the best, most frightening mythological description of Nazism. All other explanations, based on economy, inflation, sociology, and the like, look poor compared with the tremendous mythological images by which Jung tried to approach

National Socialism. Jung was in many ways a very average man, but once he was caught by a psychological phenomenon, his genius always got the better of him.

But now you may ask: What can we do when we are attacked because of the dark sides of Jung? To that question I can only answer: If you are afraid of being attacked, you should not become analysts or psychotherapists, but honest accountants at Lafayette or Marks and Spencer.

We can forget about the little average collective man Jung, the appeaser, anti-Semite, and admirer of power. We have mainly to be inspired by Jung's passion for psychology. I say passion, not detached observation, but burning, even self-damaging passion for the human psyche in all its appearances.

CHAPTER 11

Marga Speicher

Jung, Anti-Semitism, and the Nazi Regime

Marga Speicher, Ph.D., is a Jungian analyst in private practice in San Antonio, Texas. Past faculty member of the C. G. Jung Institute and of the C. G. Jung Foundation in New York, she was also chairperson of the Institute's Board of Trustees. In this paper Dr. Speicher describes her personal connection to the subject of anti-Semitism and the Nazi regime. She details her own personal path to consciousness on this issue and urges the Jungian community to deal straightforwardly with this component of Jung's shadow.

Why did I agree to serve as a panelist in the workshop that seeks to explore Jung's relation to Germany in the early 1930s and his stance toward Nazism and anti-Semitism? A personal matter led me to agree readily: one of the major struggles in my life has centered on facing the issue of Germany in World War II, of Nazism, and of the anti-Semitism that exploded so virulently and that led to holocaust and genocide. Fate stuck me right in the middle of this thorny issue and I participated in the workshop to bring my own personal dimension to bear on this topic. I will speak about what coming to terms with Nazism and anti-Semitism, with the collective shadow, has involved for me as a person and what it involves for me as a Jungian analyst.

I was born in Germany in 1934 and grew up in a Catholic family in a small industrial town. In my family I was told of the Nazis as a godless regime opposed to religious practice. My father was censured for being a practicing Catholic. I directly experienced the existence of the police state. As a Catholic, I prayed during the Good Friday liturgy "for the conversion of the unbelieving Jews," as all Catholics did until the reforms of Vatican II. I knew of Jews only in an abstract sense; the term was not connected to any individual person.

Immediately after the war in 1945, we were confronted with the horrible occurrences of the Holocaust. The textbooks issued by the Occupation forces contained stories of concentration camps and death camps that profoundly marked my eleven-year-old psyche. However, while the horrors of the Holocaust were thrust into the eleven-year-old's being, the subsequent years of schooling were notable for the lack of study of Nazism, anti-Semitism, and the Holocaust. From what I understand now, this silence on recent history was typical of German education in the late 1940s and early 1950s. There was focus on current events—the establishment and workings of the postwar democracy and the movement toward European unity.

I came to the United States in 1956 and spent the next fifteen years in South Texas acquiring a professional education and working as a psychotherapist. I moved to New York City in 1972. It was then and there that life forced me to confront squarely my German background, anti-Semitism, the Holocaust: collective shadow and collective guilt. These were issues that I had managed to avoid, contents that I had split off and had let sink into the unconscious, where they were wreaking havoc with my life.

A concern for dealing at a deeper level with blockages in my life led me at that point into another analytic exploration. New York City, with its large Jewish population, where the annual Holocaust Remembrance Week not only is observed in synagogues but enters public consciousness, provided the outer stimulus for the confrontation that I had avoided for so long.

Jung's essay "After the Catastrophe" (1945) was profoundly meaningful to me. Jung speaks at length about collective guilt: of German collective guilt and of European collective guilt. And he calls for an acknowledgment of psychic participation in the fall into shadow, lest a person "compound his *[sic]* collective guilt by the sin of unconsciousness." He speaks of the need for "a proper *rite de sortie,* a solemn admission of guilt" so that we can "escape the contaminating touch of evil."[1]

In my inner confrontation, it became essential for me (1) on a personal level, to recall as much as I could of the years I spent in Germany during and after the war; (2) on a wider level, to know as much as I could of Nazism, anti-Semitism, Holocaust, and genocide;

(3) most importantly, to come to a personal stance in relation to collective issues.

My personal confrontation with Nazism, anti-Semitism, Holocaust, and genocide occurred about thirty years after the war's end, when I was around forty years old. It was a late confrontation and I have asked myself, "Where was I, psychically, in the interim?" The details of that answer are not relevant to this discussion, but the fact of the delay needs to be noted. A few years after this confrontation, I met and married a Jewish man. With and within that important relationship, life did thrust me closer to the experience of the Jewish minority in Western civilization.

When I look at our topic, the relation of the Jungian community to Jung's position toward Nazism and anti-Semitism, I see an odd similarity between the course that awareness of collective shadow issues took in my life and the course that our communal awareness of Jung's shadow issues has taken so far and where it is today. Both share a long period of silence; an awakening to the issue at the IAAP Congresses in Jerusalem and Berlin, where outer environment contributed to the raising of the questions; the conference in New York, aptly called "Lingering Shadows"; and, finally, the workshop on Jung and anti-Semitism at the Paris IAAP Congress.

What was Jung's position in regard to anti-Semitism and the Nazi regime? I have reviewed much of the available material and listened carefully to the material presented at the New York conference. It is my belief at present that Jung shared in the anti-Semitism that was rampant throughout Europe and that his position toward Nazism in its early years, on one hand, was naively apolitical and, on the other hand, was fed by overly optimistic views of the archetypal energies that he saw activated.[2]

We can look at Jung's anti-Semitism in terms of his family history, of the culture of his time, and especially of the intellectual environment at the turn of the century. We can also see how the conflicts with Freud and the remnants of disappointment, hurt, and anger after their parting contributed to his ethnocentric emphasis on the differentiation between Jewish and Germanic psychology, which pervades his statements of the 1920s and early 1930s. We can, furthermore, see how Jung, in the 1930s, seized the opportunity to focus on his contributions to psychotherapy that were acceptable in the Germany of the 1930s when Freudian views had fallen into political disfavor irrespective of their merit. I do not believe that Jung was anti-Semitic on a person-to-person basis nor that he held conscious anti-Semitic views. Jung's orientation was firmly German-Swiss and Protestant-Christian. In the underground waters of that orientation there flowed ethnocentrism and anti-Semitism that remained unconscious, in shadow, but that influenced his views and actions. The ethnocentrism and anti-Semitism in Jung formed a background attitude similar to the racism and ethnocentrism of many today who are consciously neither racist nor ethnocentric.

When we look at Jung's relation to Germany in the early 1930s, we see that Jung was taken by the archetypal dynamic of Wotan, which he saw as underlying the nationalistic stirrings in Germany. He valued its awakening and held hopes that it would yield long-term positive contributions.[3] It is easy for any of us at any time not to see clearly the earthly reality whenever we focus on archetypal energies.

In the 1930s, Jung fell into shadow, into the anti-Semitism lurking in the psychic underground waters, and into the fascination with the potential of an archetypal awakening in Germany. He also fell into the shadow of being apolitical. He said repeatedly that he was a physician and not a political man.[4] He overlooked or ignored the fact that he lived in a body politic, like it or not, and that every action or nonaction makes a political statement, overtly or covertly. This is especially evident in the life of a prominent person; and Jung was a prominent person.

I wish Jung had spoken out strongly against anti-Semitism. I know that there was censorship and fear in Switzerland, especially in the 1940s, as the Swiss tried to stay uninvolved in the European conflicts. Nonetheless, I wish Jung had spoken out against anti-Semitism. I wish Pius XII had spoken out. I wish leaders in the United States had spoken out and had acted firmly and directly to aid persecuted groups in Germany and under German occupation. I am grateful for each person, prominent or unknown, who did speak out as well as for each person in the underground and Resistance who was able to stand against the tide.

Jung did not speak out clearly and publicly against anti-Semitism because he fell into shadow. That is the human condition.

Jung defended himself vigorously against charges of anti-Semitism and acquiescence. In 1946, he published a long list of excerpts[5] out of his earlier writing to show how he had foreseen and warned against the eruptions in Europe. He had seen and named the archetypal dynamics in their positive and in their negative aspects, but he had not attended actively and publicly to the horrible human manifestations. It has been said: "Too much psychology, not enough political action." Jung's reply to that point would be, again, that he is a physician, not a political man. But that is an easy reply: we are all involved in the political world, be it by action or omission. Omission is also a political act.

Jung wrestled with the events of Nazism and of the Holocaust. In "After the Catastrophe" in 1945, he wrote: "While I was working on this article I noticed how churned up one still is in one's own psyche. . . . I must confess that no article has ever given me so much trouble, from a moral as well as a human point of view. I had not realized how much I myself was affected. . . . This inner identity or *participation mystique* with events in Germany has caused me to experience afresh how painfully wide is the scope of the psychological concept of *collective guilt*."[6] He speaks of participation in collective shadow that is to be faced by the German and by the European, and he calls for recognition, consciousness, a *rite de sortie*.[7] One can read the essay as his way of acknowledging collective shadow and collective guilt that touched him also.

I do not know whether Jung ever wrestled with the anti-Semitism in his shadow. I have not seen an indication of such a struggle in anything I have read or heard. I have seen denial in his writings.

What I miss in Jung is a clear acknowledgment that he had fallen into the shadow of anti-Semitism, of fascination with archetypal energies, of the apolitical stance. I wish he could have come to a clear, open acknowledgment of the fall into shadow. (We do not know what his private acknowledgment might have been.)

What is my relation as a Jungian analyst to Jung's shadow issues? The very same as for all shadow issues: to see them, know them, and name them; to acknowledge them as human and let them be what they are: shadow—without condoning or whitewashing or denying. That is the stance we take toward shadow: know it, name it, be with it, and then ask: how do I live with it? what does it require?

Jung died in 1961. World War II ended in 1945. The most questionable period in Jung's life falls into the early and mid-1930s. The time is here in which we as a Jungian community[8] can see and name Jung's shadow issues of anti-Semitism, fascination with archetypal energies, the apolitical stance; the time also in which we can seek to understand the dynamics as far as we can; and the time in which we can grow through this process. Why have we as a community stayed away from this process for so long? Where have we been, psychically, in the interim? Shadow issues claim to be recognized. When we block them out, a price has to be paid.

I want to urge us as a Jungian community to give the necessary recognition and acknowledgment to Jung's shadow, his anti-Semitism, his fascination with archetypal energies, and his apolitical stance as well as to the shadow of the Jungian community in those very same matters. We have to ask ourselves continually: (1) Where do the underground waters of ethnocentrism, anti-Semitism, racism flow at the present time? (2) When and where does our recognition of archetypal energies turn into fascination and cause us to lose sight of earthly reality? (3) Where do we claim an apolitical stance in a rather routine manner without due consideration of the political impact of such a position?[9]

Such an exploration of Jung's fall into shadow can lead us, on the one hand, to a better understanding of shadow, personal and archetypal, individual and collective, and, on the other hand, to a better understanding of the ever-present pitfalls inherent in personal and communal life as well as to the pitfalls inherent in the theoretical and philosophical positions we hold.

I will close with Jung's words from "After the Catastrophe": "We must all open our eyes to the shadow who looms behind contemporary man [*sic*]. . . . It is indeed no small matter to know of one's own guilt and one's own evil, and there is certainly nothing to be gained by losing sight of one's own shadow. . . . Anything that remains in the unconscious is incorrigible; psychological corrections can be made only in consciousness."[10]

Notes

1. C. G. Jung, "After the Catastrophe," *CW* 10, ¶ 400–443. The quotations are from ¶ 404 and 410.

2. It is beyond the scope of this brief paper to present the basic data on which my conclusions are based. The data are contained in Jung's writings as published in the *Collected Works* and in his letters. A critical review and evaluation of Jung's views, words, and actions can be found elsewhere in this book. See especially Appendix A, "Significant Words and Events."

3. C. G. Jung, "Wotan," *CW* 10, ¶ 371–399.

4. In responding to criticism over his involvement with the General Medical Society for Psychotherapy in Germany and with the International General Medical Society for Psychotherapy in the 1930s, Jung refers to himself as uninterested in politics but only interested in assisting the German psychotherapists. For instance, he wrote to Abraham Aaron Roback on 29 September 1936: "As a matter of fact, I am quite unpolitical."

5. C. G. Jung, "Epilogue to 'Essays on Contemporary Events,'" *CW* 10, ¶ 458–487.

6. Jung, "After the Catastrophe," *CW* 10, ¶ 402.

7. Ibid., ¶ 404, 411.

8. While individuals in our midst have struggled with these issues, as a community we have been silent about them. It is important that we see Jung the man separate from Jung the original creative thinker and psychologist; that we see and name the flaws of the man while we reap the benefits of his psychological creativity, which are the basis of our professional orientation.

9. I am speaking of the position that each of us as an individual holds in relation to these issues. As a community, we have not called much attention to the manifestations of these issues in our individual lives. That is a lacuna. In regard to political matters, I consider it important that each person's consciousness and conscience direct her or his political stance. I am not thinking of these issues in terms of taking action or expressing views as a group nor as so-called psychological experts.

10. Jung, "After the Catastrophe," *CW* 10, ¶ 440.

Part IV

Personal Reflections

CHAPTER 12

Werner H. Engel

Thoughts and Memories of C. G. Jung

Werner H. Engel, M.D., a psychiatrist and Jungian analyst, is a Life Fellow of the American Psychiatric Association. He was born in Berlin in 1901, worked as a farmer, and came to the United States as a refugee from the Nazis in 1940. During the war, he volunteered for the U.S. Army Rehabilitation Service; from 1957 to 1977 he served as a psychiatric examiner to the German General Consulate for restitutions for victims of the Nazis. He was president of the New York Association for Analytical Psychology (1965–1972) and was founder and medical director of the C. G. Jung Training Center Clinic (1975–1983).

As a participant in the "Lingering Shadows" conference, Dr. Engel was invited to submit his paper to this book, although he did not present it at the conference. He presents here his perspective on Jung and the Nazi era through personal reminiscences of Jung and memories of conversations with several of his Jewish followers. This is the story of a Jew, a survivor of Nazi Germany, a psychiatrically trained physician, and a Jungian analyst who has found in Jungian psychology a meaningful context in which to place the events of his personal life. Not disregarding the shadow element in Jung, Dr. Engel faces it in full recognition of the special category of Jung's personality.

The 1989 conference "Lingering Shadows: Jungians, Freudians, and Anti-Semitism" brought memories to my mind that I regard as milestones in my relationship to Jung's person and Jung's work.

I am aware that such memories are necessarily incomplete and subjective.

In Berlin, in 1929, when I was 28 years old, a meaningful coincidence had brought me to my first analyst, James Kirsch, M.D. In 1933, before leaving for Palestine to flee the Nazis, Kirsch called my attention to the presence of C. G. Jung in Berlin, where I saw Jung for the first time.

I remember Jung's next time in Berlin in 1934. He was giving a seminar in the Architects' Building which was located on a very wide street, I believe, Hardenbergstrasse. Through that street a military parade was scheduled for the reception of Mussolini by Hitler.

Jung had started speaking when the parade came nearer and nearer, brass, drums, and all else increasing. He was standing on the stage, with the usual big Nazi flag on his left side and, on a chair to his right, a uniformed Nazi officer who had been assigned to monitor the lecture according to the ruling for assemblies. Soon, with the noise growing louder and louder, Jung had to stop. Only we who were seated in the front could hear what he said in his normal, well-grounded voice: "Lassen wir die Weltgeschichte ruhig an uns vorbeimarschieren!" (Let world history quietly pass us by). His stress was on the *vorbei* ("by").

Now, the word *vorbei* in German has both a literal and a connotative meaning. Literally, as I translated above, Jung merely stated that world history was passing by. But *vorbei* can also connote the hope that something will be over. This is precisely the meaning we heard Jung express, in a rather tongue-in-cheek manner: his hope that this Nazi period of world history would soon be over.[1] Those of us sitting in the front, in fact, were so sure that Jung had implied this second meaning that we were staring in fearful tension at the SS-officer. He was as close to Jung as we were. Had he noticed what Jung had so forcefully expressed with his "*vorbei*"? We had expected some consternation or even some action, as he was there to guard against exactly what had just happened. Yet there was not a move—so he was apparently under the fascination of what happened outside those windows.

I was most powerfully impressed by Jung's sentence. Something in me knew that I had heard the real Jung, and that knowing has crystallized more and more over time.

Jung strongly believed in that *vorbei*. At the time, he shared that belief with an unknown number of others: that Germany would wake up to see what was going on. A strong idea of transition, a strong belief in transformation toward what he wished Germany to be, must have been on his mind in those dark and beclouded days. That man whom I just had seen and heard was certainly not a Nazi.

Marie-Louise von Franz, known as a sharp-thinking critic, has stated that in all the years that she knew Jung personally, from 1933 to his death, she "never perceived the slightest conscious or unconscious trace of any such attitude . . . referring to the oft-repeated slander that Jung was a National Socialist and/or anti-Semitic."[2] She speaks of a "therapeutic optimism" that must be considered before Jung's mistakes are to be discussed. Jung had "admitted his illusions about people when it came to Nazism and he could never have imagined that such abysmal evil could come to the surface and break out."[3]

In the same year, 1934, Jung acted directly against the most basic Nazi rulings and principles, the destruction of anything Jewish, when he officially reinvited Jewish psychotherapists, whom the Germans had *gleichgeschaltet* (i.e., deprived of their professional standing and more), back into his international organization by using his position as president to make a basic change of the constitution of this organization. He announced this change at the time of the Congress in Bad Nauheim, in the midst of Nazi ruling. The publication of this pro-Jewish constitutional change could not be released in Nazi Germany and was therefore added as a special unbound page of the *Zentralblatt für Psychotherapie* for subscribers outside Germany. This page was used by Ernest Harms for his paper "Carl Gustav Jung—Defender of Freud and the Jews," in which he revised widespread misconceptions about Jung.

Harms, the chief editor of the scientific journal *The Nervous Child,* had been my coordinator when I was in charge of a psychiatric child guidance clinic in New York City. I remember that he reported difficulties in finding the special page containing Jung's reinvitation to the Jewish therapists in New York City libraries, but had found it in an out-of-town library. He left the question open whether anyone in New York City might have been interested in preventing Jung's pro-Jewish activities from being known in wider circles.

That article by Harms is a well-researched history of Jung's activities around the year 1934 and could well be a compensation for the various misinterpretations of that period. Jung has frequently described the difficulties he had taken on himself in this chaotic period. They do not need repetition. I was in Berlin, my birthplace, during the Hitler years from 1933 to 1940, because various emigration attempts had failed for political reasons. Only later, in New York, in Zurich, and other places, did I hear or read about Jung's activities for the support and assistance given to Jews and his organized efforts to help assure the victory of the Western Powers. I am not sure whether Jung has received proper credit for these various activities.

I have rather experienced the opposite. What I mean is what I prefer to call the "formula" with the wording: "How can you . . ." Innumerable times and at a great variety of places where I met with Jews, I met with the "How can you. . ." formula. That means: How can you who are a good Jew associate with that Nazi or anti-Semite Jung!

The basis for this formula is the archetypal concept: treason, with in-built duplicity: treason against my collective, my tribe on the one hand; treason against my inner knowing, my conviction, on the other. This was where the silent memory from the noisy moment of the *vorbei* found its proper place, and its answer: Who of the questioners really wants to know who that man Jung really is, or was? Very few; the rest just simply knew better, they had read it all.

I remember when Dr. M. Esther Harding, an outstanding representative of Jung in New York, once arrived with pounds of anti-Jungian letters and articles, her years-long collection. Today such a collection would be much heavier. There is a great amount of energy invested there, even—or especially—when it appears repetitive. It is certainly worth examining. To be satisfied with describing a person from his dark side only, his or her shadow, does not show the total person. But the method is of great interest and frequently applied. It does not leave room for the light—for values. It is the method of anti-Semitism: you isolate and enlarge the shadow qualities, even invent or project them, and you diminish, neglect, or deny what is valuable and acceptable. That is the nature of the prejudicial element in anti-Semitism. It expressed itself clearly in that special formula "How can you...!"

The difference was that this time it was not pointing at a Jew, but at the non-Jewish Jung.

In a more organized form, the principle of concentrating on the shadow without leaving much space for the positive values of a person and his work can even appear under the title "Lingering Shadows" here relating to "Jungians, Freudians, and Anti-Semitism." Unless a listener is well aware of what Freud as well as Jung actually means for our time, facing the volume of those lingering shadows could lead to a distortion of the image of these personalities.

On the other hand, there is no doubt about the necessity of clarifying and truthfully researching those elements that could have an influence on freeing the emotions that may have blocked the acceptance of the total personalities of either of these two highly creative men.

The emotional element of acceptability is also the basis for loyalty toward a person, which may contain the acceptance of unified opposites of dark shadow and bright light. This factor—acceptance—may well be preceded by a painfully felt dilemma which faces the individual with a special task of healing, starting with the internal one.

In my early analytical years 1929 to 1933 and later I had established my collection of Jungian books and related literature that were ready to be packed when the American consulate proceeded with the acceptance of affidavits for visa to the United States, where my wife's family had resettled. The time was 1938 when I found out that whatever I wanted to take out of Germany would undergo inspection in my district of Berlin. I also heard that the inspectors were not all alike in letting the restricted Jungian books pass, but mine was especially strict and to try to bribe him could be deadly.

A friend, Heinz Westmann, who had fled to England before his goods could be packed, had asked me to be present at the packing of his lift-van. That inspector, I found out, was open to financially supported persuasion, and so my bookcase with Jungian books went first to England. One thing was clear: the Nazis had learned between 1933 and 1938 that Jung was not one of them, but the opposite, a declared anti-Nazi. The inspectors knew that Jung's books were blacklisted. The Nazis knew in 1938 what some people do not seem to know fifty years later.

Besides the paper by Harms, many efforts have been made to study the life of Jung around 1934. There are individual statements like "Jung, the Jews, and Hitler" by Jay Sherry in *Spring* 1986 and repeated chapters on Jung and National Socialism in the books of Aniela Jaffé and many others.

I was highly impressed by James Kirsch's paper "Reconsidering Jung's So-Called Anti-Semitism."[4] Kirsch, an outstanding Jewish Jungian analyst from Berlin, deeply rooted in his Judaism, had known Jung since 1928 and, with some interruptions, had worked with Jung in Zurich about once a year for decades, until Jung's death. His paper brings, with great openness and clarity, the facts that have contributed to Jung's reputation as an anti-Semite, including the "quite devastating" fragment of a letter to W. M. Kranenfeldt.

Kirsch concludes that Jung's unacceptable and insufficiently informed statements derived from residues of his tragic and painful relationship to Freud, and that facing the immensely powerful god-image of Yahweh in his later book *Answer to Job* had resulted in conquering in depth any residues of potential anti-Semitic traces. "Through this brutal act of fate he finally overcame the anti-Semitic feelings which originally had been activated in him through his experience of Freud."[5] In his way Kirsch has worked out that the Jewish question was for Jung not a matter of politics, but essentially a deeply intrapsychic experience with its consequences.

In this connection it could be said that the attempts of Emma Jung and Sabina Spielrein to accomplish a reconciliation of these two men, Jung and Freud, in an early period would have been most senseless if they, two women who knew Jung intimately had noticed anti-Semitism in Jung's motivations.

In my conversations with Siegmund Hurwitz, a Jewish Jungian in Zurich deeply involved in Kabbalah studies, he told me what happened in 1939 when Hitler was preparing to march into Austria. Freud was in Vienna. Jung and the Riklin family, of whom the son was a friend of Hurwitz, prepared a basis for an escape for Freud to Switzerland or any safe place, and the son of Riklin traveled to Vienna to Freud's house to deliver the monetary support in person. At the door he received the answer that Freud would not accept help from his enemies.[6]

It would certainly be a daring speculation to imagine what could have resulted from that invitation if Freud had not reacted with that basically not surprising rejection. Jung may have had an extraordinary potentiality of a totally new contact in mind, maybe even a reversal of the father-son transference on a higher spiritual level.

But all that stayed was prolonged pain.

Hurwitz also confirmed to me that Jung, occasionally with Hurwitz's assistance, had undergone intensive studies to deepen his knowledge of Judaism, including Isaac Luria's kabbalistic writings.

In this connection it is of interest that on November 16, 1937, Jung wrote to Professor M. H. Göring, editor of the *Zentralblatt für Psychotherapie* in Berlin. Jung had heard that Göring planned a book review of the author Rosenberg, who had made the statement that the Jews have contempt for mysticism. Jung responded that this was an extremely regrettable error for anyone who knew Jewish history, especially Chasidism. He said that no mention should be made of such writing: "I cannot cover such derailments *(Entgleisungen)* with my name."[7]

When the time for him had come, Jung must have felt a powerful urge to rebuild or restore the personal side of his relationship with a most highly qualified and most deeply rooted representative of Judaism. That opportunity arose when Rabbi Leo Baeck came to Zurich. Rabbi Baeck had stayed, caring for his congregation in Berlin, until the Nazis deported him and them to the concentration camp Theresienstadt, where he stayed until the last ones were freed.

Great credit is due to Aniela Jaffé for having given, in her well-known essay "Jung and National Socialism," a most impressive description of the highly important meeting of Jung and Rabbi Baeck. She let Gershom Scholem from Jerusalem tell the story. Aniela Jaffé writes:

Those who had an opportunity to converse with Jung personally were in a better position than an outsider to see the shadow side of this great researcher and to accept it. As evidence of this, I will quote from a letter which Gershom Scholem wrote to me in 1963 and has kindly permitted me to publish. It reports a conversation he had about Jung with Leo Baeck. With this report of a subjective experience I will end my attempt to give an account and interpretation of the facts.

Jerusalem

Dear Mrs. Jaffé: 7 May 1963

As you are so interested in the story of Baeck and Jung, I will write it down for your benefit and have no objection to being cited by you in this matter.

In the summer of 1947 Leo Baeck was in Jerusalem. I had then just received for the first time an invitation to the Eranos meeting in Ascona, evidently at Jung's suggestion, and I asked Baeck whether I should accept it, as I had heard and read many protests about Jung's behavior in the Nazi period. Baeck said: "You must go, absolutely!" and in the course of our conversation told me the following story. He too had been put off by Jung's reputation resulting from those well-known articles in the years 1933–1934, precisely because he knew Jung very well from the Darmstadt meetings of the School of Wisdom and would never have credited him with any Nazi and anti-Semitic sentiments. When, after his release from Theresienstadt, he returned to Switzerland for the first time (I think it was 1946), he therefore did not call on Jung in Zurich. But it came to Jung's ears that he was in the city and Jung sent a message begging him to visit him, which he, Baeck, declined because of those happenings. Whereupon Jung came to his hotel and they had an extremely lively talk lasting two hours, during which Baeck reproached him with all the things he had heard. Jung defended himself by an appeal to the special conditions in Germany but at the same time confessed to him: "Well, I slipped up"—probably referring to the Nazis and his expectation that something great might after all emerge. This remark, "I slipped up," which Baeck repeated to me several times, remains vividly in my memory. Baeck said that in this talk they cleared up everything that had come between them and that they parted from one another reconciled again. Because of this explanation of Baeck's I accepted the invitation to Eranos when it came a second time.

Yours sincerely,
G. Scholem[8]

Siegmund Hurwitz had later told me that not only Scholem but also Rabbi Baeck had joined Jung at an Eranos meeting at Ascona. In addition, James Kirsch reported that Baeck stayed in Jung's home for two weeks in 1947.[9]

When leaders so deeply rooted in Judaism as Rabbi Leo Baeck and Gershom Scholem were able to accomplish the final healing of their relationship with Carl Jung, those who cannot might consider going more deeply and seriously into themselves, assisted by the inner opening for meeting the total personality of this man Jung.

The powerful energy that had driven Jung not to let Leo Baeck go without the opportunity to meet him face to face must have been harbored in Jung since those years around 1934. *Ausgerutscht,* which appears translated as "slipped up," means much more than the simple "slipped up" to a Swiss mountain climber, as Jung was. It means to lose one's footing, and in the quest to conquer those great Swiss mountains, to lose one's footing is an occurrence of truly serious and potentially deadly nature. It was of a matter on such a level that Jung referred to when he said, "Ich bin ausgerutscht." For him, the "slippings" of 1933–1934 were now seen as the tragic and deadly serious missteps that they had been. And it was to this context and to this meaning that Leo Baeck must have resonated in their important meeting of reconciliation.

Jung did not believe in whitewashing. Aniela Jaffé has, in a different connection, preserved Jung's opinion by the following: "Keiner darf sich vom andern 'die Würde seiner Schuld' nehmen lassen." ("No one shall allow another to deprive him of the dignity of his guilt.")[10]

The question of loyalty to Jung played a significant role in my relationship to Jewish Jungian analysts in my early years. It was clear that each one had found his or her own loyalty to Jung in an individual way.

Specifically I remember such loyalty discussions with James Kirsch in New York and Los Angeles, Max Zeller in Berlin, Gerhard Adler in London, Ernst Bernhard in Rome, and with Erich Neumann on his balcony looking out to the Mediterranean in Tel Aviv. The meeting with Erich Neumann at which we discussed loyalty to Jung stands sharply in my memory because of the wide and beautiful expanse of the Mediterranean visible from that balcony. In more recent years Julia Neumann remarked to me how sad she was that that very view was obscured by new buildings that had gone up.

The memory of that wide view corresponds symbolically to my memory of the inner attitude that leads to the acceptance of Jung as a total personality. These five Jewish analysts whom I have mentioned had all originally come from Berlin.

Some extended analytical work with Rivkah Schaerf (later to become Rivkah Kluger) in Zurich had led, on the basis of a dream, to the first of my many trips to Israel.

I have mentioned six Jewish names of analysts, early followers of Jung. If I wanted to extend that list beyond those six I would have to mention a very long list of analysts, all devoted Jewish followers of Jung. The length of that list could well remind one of the fact that for a while the group of Freud was described by others and himself as representative of a "Jewish science." Considering the length of that list, one can well say that here Jung is not too far behind Freud, as far as Jewish followers are concerned.

The meeting between Jung and Baeck was personal, eye-to-eye between these two great men.

I want to conclude with an account of my last meeting with Jung in 1954, an encounter that struck me then and has remained with me ever since as being representative of that outstanding man.

I had had many sessions with Emma Jung at that time. A frequent topic had been the many forms of pain. She even wanted to be informed about the various patents of American reclining chairs, apparently stimulated by her desire to sit and rest more comfortably, maybe related to an early discomfort that may have foreshadowed her tragic end only one year later.

I remember that my topic on this particular occasion was my seven Hitler years in Berlin and, later, my mother's suicide in Berlin. My mother took her life after receiving the order to report to Alexanderplatz, which meant concentration camp, unaware that my visa and ticket for her to the United States were in the mail, to arrive the next day.

Then Emma Jung stood up, walked around her long table, and stretched out her hand. I, standing, took her guiding hand, and she led me all the way to Jung's room. She opened the door, said my name, and when Dr. Jung, from his seat, gestured to me to be seated, she had left.

Jung's strong voice was nearly inaudible. I heard, in the beginning, a few words relating to his German origin. The rest was silence, with powerful waves of silent communication between us. No way to say whose pain, whose darkness, was around—and no need. Three and a half decades later there is no loss of intensity.

I had felt at the start surrounded by a sea of pain and very slowly entered the inconceivable deepening of the numinosum in that nonexisting time.

The comradeship in silence with this radiant man whose universal creativity had given my life guidance and meaning was on a level far out of the reach of the categories of those "lingering shadows."

For me, what was felt as grace was the recognition that a time shared in human comradeship, in deepest silence, was more convincing of the true category of that extraordinary man than any reading or even speaking could be or have been.

This communion of silence was a powerful bridge from the totality of one man's life to that of another and even, potentially, into life beyond. That silence, that uniting communication took its own time, and when I had the feeling that it was time to go, I arose in silence, no words, no formalities. I just got up and left, filled with the numinosity of that utterly powerful togetherness.

A last look at the well-known inscription over the front door—*Vocatus atque non vocatus, Deus aderit* ("Called or not called, the God will be present")—and I was out in great silence on the walkway to the street, into the little world of Seestrasse.

Notes

1. From Hella Adler in London I learned how Gerhard Adler, who had been present, had described Jung saying those same words: "with a twinkle in his eyes."

2. Marie-Louise von Franz, *C. G. Jung: His Myth in Our Time* (New York: G. P. Putnam & Sons, 1975), pp. 63–64.

3. Ibid.

4. In Daniel M. Young and Estelle Weinreid, *et al.*, *The Arms of the Windmill: Essays in Analytical Psychology* (1981).

5. Ibid.,p. 2.5.

6. For details, see Robert S. McCully, "Letters," *Quadrant* 20, no. 2 (1987): 73–74. Conversation with Riklin, Jr.

7. C. G. Jung, *Briefe,* vol. 1, 1906–1945 (Freiburg: Walter Verlag, 1972), p. 302.

8. Aniela Jaffé, "Jung and National Socialism," in *Jung's Last Years and Other Essays,* pp. 96–99.

9. James Kirsch, "Interview with David Serbin," *Psychological Perspectives,* Fall 1985, p. 172.

10. Aniela Jaffé, *Aus Leben und Werkstatt von C. G. Jung* (Zurich: Rascher Verlag, 1968), p. 120.

CHAPTER 13

J. Marvin Spiegelman

A Personal Reflection on Jung and Anti-Semitism

J. Marvin Spiegelman, Ph.D. is a Diplomate of the American Board of Psychology and of the C. G. Jung Institute in Zurich. Past faculty member of UCLA, Dr. Spiegelman has been a Visiting Professor at USC, the Hebrew University of Jerusalem, and Pacifica Graduate Institute. He is the author of nine books, co-author of five books in the fields of psychotherapy and of psychology and religion, as well as three books of fiction. He is a member of the International Association of Analytical Psychology and the Society of Jungian Analysts of Southern California and consulting editor of the Journal of Analytical Psychology and of the Journal of Psychology and Judaism. Dr. Spiegelman has been in private practice in Los Angeles for over forty years.

The issue of Jung's anti-Semitism was simultaneous with my living introduction to his psychology. In the fall of 1948, when I began graduate school in Psychology at UCLA, one class I enrolled in was called "Critical Problems in Psychology," given by the esteemed Professor Gengerelli. I chanced to sit next to an "older man" (he was about 44, I was 22!) and wondered why such a person would be enrolled in this class but said nothing at that point. The professor began to speak about art, surprisingly, and said, to my astonishment, that one day there would be a mathematics of that activity. I blurted out, unintentionally, "nonsense," but the professor did not chastise me. Instead, my neighbor, who had been looking at my handwritten notes, said, "Very interesting handwriting! Musical and creative." I gazed at him in wonder. What was a graphologist doing in the behavioristically-oriented psychology department at this university? After class, I asked him about this and he said that he had practiced graphology, along with Jungian analysis, in Germany before the war. In all naiveté, I asked, "But you are Jewish aren't you? Wasn't Jung a Nazi?" This question, based on mere gossip and no knowledge, was asked in all sincerity. Dr. Max Zeller, as I learned his name, replied that this was not true and that he, himself, was not only Jewish but had spent some time in a concentration camp. Now intrigued as well as astonished, I asked whether I might speak to him about Jungian psychology some time, and he graciously agreed.

Some days later—after Dr. Zeller realized that he did not, after all, need to take academic psychology courses in order to become qualified for the forthcoming licensing requirements and, therefore, ended his brief entry into our University—he invited me to his house, and I accepted gladly. When I arrived at his pleasant, but hardly wealthy home, in a Jewish part of town, I was taken with its European cultural atmosphere of books, paintings, piano, music. I met his charming wife and his elder son served me tea, while his daughter and younger son were attended to in the kitchen. Dr. Zeller then began to tell me about Jungian psychology by recounting a dream, which was much like a fairy tale. I was entranced by this, as well as by the man and his warmly loving home, resolving to undergo analysis with him when I could afford it. I had no intention, then, of becoming an analyst, but was happy in the prospect of being a professor and researcher.

Two years later, when I was a teaching assistant and earning a princely sum of $112 per month, I went to Dr. Zeller with the request for analysis and he graciously accepted me at a reduced fee. Thus began, in 1950, my lifelong association with Jungian psychology.

Jewish issues emerged fairly early in my analysis, although (perhaps because) I was not very observant. I had undergone Bar Mitzvah, of course, and had enjoyed high holy-day observances in the temple with my grandfather, as well as celebrating feast days with the entire family, but, like my father, was just respectful of the tradition and inclined to be secular. My dreams brought up my grandfather quite a lot and I then began to see this deeply religious man frequently in that last year of his life. He died at 97. A crucial dream and an accompanying active imagination cemented matters in this regard. After only three months of analysis, I brought this dream and my first active imagination, titled "Purple in the Blue" to my analytic session. In the waiting room, I found several volumes, just arrived, of the Zohar. I was only vaguely familiar with the title of this classic of Jewish mysticism but when I opened a volume at random, I was astonished to find a fantasy which jibed, amazingly, with what I had written and drawn. Shaken, I went upstairs to my analytic hour and was overcome with this instance of synchronicity. So profound was the impact of this event upon me that I waited until I was 40 to study the Zohar and Jewish mysticism, despite the fact that my myth was deeply ecumenical and my "Jewish" dreams quite important. Indeed, I subsequently realized that I needed to learn all that I could about Christianity, Buddhism, Hinduism, etc. until I was ready to go more deeply into Jewish mysticism. I was also amazed to discover that it was also part of the Jewish tradition that one not study Kabbalah until one was 40! So, it was clear that Jungian psychology was not only instrumental in bringing me more deeply into the religious heritage into which I was born, it was crucial.

That same first analysis also produced questions about the shadow that demonstrated my own anti-Semitism as well as anti-Christian sentiments, all of which required deeper reflection and emotion, and themselves led further into philo-Semitism and philo-Christianity, with experiences, from within, which enabled me to truly appreciate these varying paths to God. I also learned that Dr. Zeller had himself been shocked with how Nazi he had become when he was in England, as a consequence of the German spirit at the time. All of this deepened my understanding of the shadow, personal and collective, but it was hard to convey this to others who had not undergone such things in relation to the unconscious. The fact that the founders of the Los Angeles Jungian group, as well as the majority of members, were Jewish at that time, carried weight as well. When Rivkah Schaerf, one of several visitors from Zurich to lecture in Los Angeles, presented biblical seminars, as well as a summary of Jung's as-yet-unpublished-in-English *Answer to Job,* I felt that I was truly at home in every way.

Reading Jung's papers of the 1930s touching on Jewish questions, such as "Wotan," were somewhat troubling, but I was, by then, no longer negatively sensitive to the idea of there being a "'Jewish psychology," although I understood that the *use* of this term was indeed perilously close to associating it with the prejudices of Nazism. But the theme of Jung's anti-Semitism remained peripheral.

All the same, when I began my formal training at the C. G. Jung Institute in Zurich some years later, I felt called upon to ask my analyst, Professor Dr. C. A. Meier, if he were anti-Semitic. His answer endeared him to me at once. He responded, "Not more than average!" I understand that he answered this question when posed by others with the reply, "Not more than the average Jew!" Meier's cogent admission made me feel safe: not only was he fully aware of his shadow, he could admit it, even in a delicate situation. This consciousness enabled me to go deeper into my own shadow, as well as the collective shadow of Western civilization, confident that there would be acceptance as well as understanding. It was, therefore, utterly wonderful to read *Answer to Job.* Here, at last, was a truly "Judeo-Christian" work that got at the core of our Western historical soul, its vicissitudes, problems, and future. I also realized that it would take just this kind of consciousness, rare in both Christians and Jews, to address issues of cultural prejudice.

During my training days in Zurich, many of the students were Jewish. These included my fellow Americans Jim Hillman and Robert Stein, the Egyptian Molly Tuby and the Swiss Gustav Dreifuss. All became and remain good friends of mine. Dr. Dreifuss, as is known, emigrated to Israel after we graduated and has had a rich career there. All of these Jews, along with the many that I have known in Los Angeles and elsewhere, have had an understanding about Jung's anti-Semitism similar to my own. It is hard for us all, I think, to tolerate the relatively shallow level of criticism engaged in.

All of the foregoing is prologue to what I understand in relation to Jung's anti-Semitism, as well as my own and that of others. And this is what occurred to me one night some years ago, when Andrew Samuel spoke in Los Angeles on this issue and read selected and disturbing quotes from Jung. I was seated next to an Orthodox Rabbi and an Israeli woman pupil at the time, and felt compelled to respond to the lecture by stating that I did not recognize the Jung that I knew from the material presented. The years since have seen workshops, papers, and so forth, on this theme, but I found that the excellent answers by Aniela Jaffé and Thomas Kirsch, for example, have been insufficient. I shall here attempt my own answer, feeling that my own will be hardly more effective. I shall leave to the end why I think this is so.

First of all, was Jung anti-Semitic? Of course he was! But so were (and are) most people in Western civilization! All of us, Jew and Gentile, before the Holocaust, were born into the deep myth of our culture that held the Jews responsible for the death of God! This produced a wide variety of other treatments and beliefs (no citizenship, no ownership of land, limited entrance into skills, crafts, and professions, etc.) which kept the Jews apart until the Emancipation of the 18th and 19th centuries. Jung, as an educated man, was rather less anti-Semitic than most people. He was interested in and supported Freud, for example, when the rest of the psychiatric world was extremely hostile and practically blatantly anti-Semitic about him. Yet how could Jung not be otherwise, until he had his own experiences of shadow and depth in this area? His insights about ethnic psychology and so forth were profound but his knowledge about the political ramifications of what he had to say, I think, was abysmally ignorant. To even talk about "Jewish psychology" and "nomadism" during the Hitler time of the 1930s was a grave disservice, not because Jung wanted this but because he did not realize the extent of damage and, like the Swiss generally (as we only know now) had more than a little of the Germanic anti-Semitism in their psyche.

All the same, Jung had numerous Jewish pupils, even early on, Gerhard Adler, Erich Neumann, Thomas Kirsch, Rivkah Schaerf Kluger, Siegmund Hurwitz, and others from my own 2nd generation of analysts. From these, and from his own experiences of the unconscious and of life, he was able to learn about Jewish mysticism and the Jewish psyche more generally. He was thus able to see that this ethnic portrayal of the psyche (Kabbalah) had many similarities to his own experience. When, in his seventies, he had the visions he reports in his *Memories, Dreams, Reflections*, of the mystical unions in Judaism (with the Shekhina), Christianity (Marriage of the Lamb), and Pagan Greek (*Hierosgamos*), he clearly found a unity in his soul of Western consciousness. I think it would have been impossible for an anti-Semite to have had his experience of the union with the Shekhina, the feminine presence of God. Furthermore, Jung's book, *Answer to Job* is, I think, one of the chief spiritual texts of the 20th century, truly combining Judaism and Christianity in the soul, in a seamless connection, honoring both and seeing where modern consciousness requires revision and development of our traditions. So, to see the aging Jung as still anti-Semitic is to be blind to his development.

My own experience of Jung when I studied in Zurich, in several lectures, one seminar and a final session where I went to receive his blessing for my analytic work, were those of a tremendously religious and charismatic man who was so sensitive to the movements of the soul that he knew what I was asking before I asked it. This capacity, born of his own life-long struggle and relationship to the Self, was experienced by others as well. So, I am satisfied that the charges made against him, although based on outrageous things he sometimes said, are often out of context and/or were made during earlier periods of his life. The Jung I knew could not have been guilty of such charges.

I need to say a further word about what I experienced personally with Jung, beyond the powerful impact of his personality and his profound work (especially *Answer to Job*). I must tell that at age 18, just before

I went overseas during World War II, my ancient and deeply religious grandfather called me to him to give me his blessing. This was not only a blessing, connected with God, which asked for my safety, but was also a direct bestowing, like that for Jacob, of our family energy and commitment to serve God. This had a powerful impact on me and was in my mind as I was completing my studies in Zurich 15 years later. As I was completing my studies, I went to Jung with an unexpressed request for him to also bless my work and service, not as part of a biological or ethnic family, of course, but in the context of being a part of a community of individuals on a common spiritual path. Without speaking of details, I need to say that this took place. I felt so blessed and so connected. Ever since, I have always felt both Jung and my grandfather standing behind me in my work, rather like those images that Asian gurus have of their teachers in back of them as they do their work. Thus, in contrast to the oedipal rebellion in the Greek psyche, as Freud adumbrated, I see myself continuing two ancient traditions and serving what is behind both of these "fathers" (including my own loving father). The divine feminine, both Sophia and Shekhina, has joined this pair, over the years, as both men would have wished for me and as they found for themselves.

What remains in our present connection, however, is the deeper question of why Jung continues to be subject to these vicious attacks. My view is that Jung's experience of the Self, combining good and evil in their ultimate wholeness, is impossible to understand for those with "straight-line" kinds of consciousness, such as academics committed to an exclusively rational approach to the psyche, fundamentalists who can not permit any deviation from a "right" way to think or be, and others who are threatened by this paradoxical receptivity to the divine and to life. Among these "types" are those who also need to destroy Jung because of what he discovered and what he taught. I can understand this, but certainly deplore it. Among Jungians, at least, I would hope for greater and larger understanding of what it means to experience the "dark side of God" as did Jung and, I presume, any of us experience if we go to any sort of depth in the psyche. Jung's empiricism in these matters is quite simple. All one has to do, really, is employ his attitude toward dreams, be careful in the dialogue with the unconscious, including a continuing use of active imagination, and one will turn up what he found in the psyche also, without regard to any particular names for these qualities, dynamics, or activities. It is just useful to use words like shadow, anima and animus. We now know that these concepts can have unexpected and unintended political effects. Yet anyone who has done this work on his or her own shadow, anima, or animus, and has arrived at a relationship to the Self, will know that humans are all brothers and sisters with the divine, and even with our animal cousins. We should all at least know about the continuing human predilection for projection, and how this works out in our endogenous/exogenous kinship libido, making for attraction and repulsion to the Other, no matter how or where it turns up. Ultimately, we all pursue our own individuation, which relates us to the Self within and the Self as manifested in our group, nation, tribe, or religion and that of humankind. For this knowledge, and for providing a way to connect with my own tradition and my individuality at the same time, I am deeply grateful to C. G. Jung.

Addendum

Recent experiences of a more subtle anti-Semitism, even among enlightened, creative, educated, modern people, such as Joseph Campbell and T. S. Eliot, along with the even more subtle use of the epithet of anti-Semitism hurled at Jung by contemporary scholars or therapists have made me reflect further on this theme.

Take, for instance, Joseph Campbell, that pioneer mythologist and peerless lecturer in the field of comparative religion, whom we all have read and admired in television interviews. I recall having heard him lecture, in my native city of Los Angeles, many years ago, as well as much earlier at the Eranos conference in Switzerland in1957. He was less well-known when he spoke at that meeting where Jung also lectured and, I am afraid I have to say, I was less impressed with him than the others. Yet he did develop and his later work was indeed magnificent. When I heard him speak a few years before his death, however, I was surprised to hear a not-too subtle negativity toward the Jewish God. As he even spoke the not-to-be-spoken name of Yahveh, his mouth made a sign of distaste as if he had ingested a very sour herring. Sure enough, it may well have been his negative attitude toward the monotheisms, but the Jewish God came in for particular enmity. The same subtle negativity was found in the sensitive and profound T. S. Eliot and others. Now these are not just some pre-psychological academic fascists, but people who knew about the Holocaust, were acquainted with psychology, etc. But were they analyzed? Did they have occasion to discover and work on their own shadows? I doubt it, and this is surely a source of much of our distress over projection, as I mentioned earlier. The same can be said about reviewers such as Richard Noll and Jeffrey Masson, who clearly do not have a clue about what Jung experienced and wrote about in terms of the archetypal unconscious. The same, alas, can be said of not a few others, even some Jungian analysts. So the shadow of unknowing hangs heavily in this area.

Yet there is something more. Both the educated elite and the boorish peasant often still share the continuing anti-Semitism of our two-thousand-year-old Christian civilization. And the latter has succeeded even in having its prejudice (witness the "Protocols of the Elders of Zion" forgery) embraced full-heartedly by many in Islam and even in parts of Asia. True, the Jewish shadow is painfully visible and, like that experienced by black people, particularly in America, the shadow qualities projected by white non-Jews are often compelled to be enacted by the projectees. Anti-Semitism is just part of the Western Christian shadow, connected with a "hook" in the receiver of projection, as we say in the analytic community, but based itself on an archetype.

To me, this says that anti-Semitism may change in individuals, as a result of consciousness brought about by analysis and education, but will remain in Western culture until a new myth embraces us all. And that is particularly where Jung, in his quite remarkable book, *Answer to Job,* has brought us. He, practically alone in my opinion, has truly presented the often-used term, "Judeo-Christian" consciousness as a seamless web, probing deeply, honestly, and empathetically into the archetypal shadows of both faiths, and has shown us where the needed development of our God-image now brings us. The millennium which we have just begun will no doubt continue this expansion of our consciousness, at least individually if not collectively, and it is this deeper, ongoing dilemma of the soul from which these outcroppings of hatred and unknowingness reverberate. It is indeed a paradox that one who is continuing to be called anti-Semite was he who has shed the maximum light on the depth of these issues in the Western soul and it is he, alas, who is so little understood and so much maligned. Paradoxically, this is much like the suffering experienced historically by the chief archetypal actors in the psyche in this event, the Jewish image of God, the Jewish Jesus and the Jewish Mary.

CHAPTER 14

Sanford L. Drob

Jung, Kabbalah, and Judaism

Sanford L. Drob, Ph.D. is Director of Psychological Assessment and the Senior Forensic Psychologist at Bellevue Hospital in New York. In addition to his numerous publications in clinical, forensic, and philosophical psychology, Dr. Drob's books, *Symbols of the Kabbalah: Philosophical and Psychological Perspectives*, and *Kabbalistic Metaphors: Jewish Mystical Themes in Ancient and Modern Thought*, were published by Jason Aronson in 2000. Dr. Drob is currently completing books on Jung and Jewish mysticism, and Kabbalah and Postmodern thought. This article originally published in the *Journal of the American Psychological Association* as "Jung and the Kabbalah."

In a letter to the Rev. Erastus Evans, written on 17 February 1954, Carl Jung described the excitement of his first encounter with the Kabbalistic symbols of *Shevirat ha-Kelim* (the Breaking of the Vessels) and *Tikkun ha-Olam* (the Restoration of the World):

> In a tract of the Lurianic Kabbalah, the remarkable idea is developed that man is destined to become God's helper in the attempt to restore the vessels which were broken when God thought to create a world. Only a few weeks ago I came across this impressive doctrine which gives meaning to man's status exalted by the incarnation. I am glad that I can quote at least one voice in favor of my rather involuntary manifesto (Jung, 1973, vol. 2, p. 157).

Several years later, in a letter to a Ms. Edith Schroeder, who had inquired regarding "the significance of Freud's Jewish descent for the origin, content and acceptance of psychoanalysis," Jung replied:

> One would have to take a deep plunge into the history of the Jewish mind. This would carry us beyond Jewish Orthodoxy into the subterranean workings of Hasidism. . . and then into the intricacies of the Kabbalah, which still remains unexplored psychologically (Jung, 1973, vol. 2, pp. 358–359).

Jung then informed Schroeder that he himself could not perform such a task because he had no knowledge of Hebrew and was not acquainted with all the relevant sources.

In point of fact, Jung, in the last decades of his life, had taken a deep interest in the psychological aspects of a number of Kabbalistic symbols and ideas; ideas to which he had been exposed primarily through his reading of 16th- and 17th-century alchemical texts, and especially through the writings of the Christian Kabbalist and alchemist Christian Knorr Von Rosenroth (1636–1689). As a result, Jung's last great work, *Mysterium Coniunctionis* (1955–1956/1963), completed in his 80th year, in 1954, though ostensibly a treatise on alchemy, is filled with discussions of such Kabbalistic symbols as *Adam Kadmon* (Primordial Man), the *Sefirot,* and the union of the "Holy One" and his bride. These symbols became important pivots around which Jung constructed his final interpretations of such notions as the archetypes and the collective unconscious and his theory of the ultimate psychological purpose of humankind.

Yet as great as Jung's acknowledged affinity is to the Kabbalah, his unacknowledged relationship was even greater. For every reference to the Kabbalah in Jung's writings, there are several to Gnosticism and perhaps dozens to alchemy: yet the interpretations Jung places on Gnosticism (itself a close cousin to the Kabbalah), and the very texts Jung refers to on alchemy, were profoundly Kabbalistic, so much so that one could call the Jung of the *Mysterium Coniunctionis* and other later works a Kabbalist (albeit a Christian one) in contemporary guise.

Jung has frequently been called a Gnostic. It is interesting that Jung's main accuser in this regard was the Jewish philosopher Martin Buber, who is well-known for, among other things, his work on Hasidism. Buber held that Jung was Gnostic because he reduced God to the inner divine spark in humans and identified religious experience with a turning inward into the self, as opposed to a participation in relations with others as the vehicle for relating to a transcendent God (Buber, 1952; see also Dourley, 1994). Conversely, the Christian "death of God" theologian, Thomas J. J. Altizer, hailed Jung's "Gnosticism" as part of his proof of the death of a transcendent God, which, through Christ, had become completely immanent in humankind (Altizer, 1959, see also Segal, 1992).

For reasons that I detail in this article, it is my view that Jung is far more Kabbalistic than he is Gnostic, and he is "alchemical" largely to the extent that the alchemists borrowed from and relied on Kabbalistic ideas. I also argue that in the 1930s, when Jung was formulating a psychology based on his reading of alchemy, he had a strong motive to suppress the "Jewish" origins of many alchemical ideas.

In this article, I show that Jung ultimately read Gnosticism in such a manner as to transform a radical anticosmic, anti-individualistic doctrine into a world-affirming basis for an individual psychology. Furthermore, I show that he interpreted alchemy so as to extract its Kabbalistic spiritual and psychological core. Had Jung been sufficiently familiar with the Kabbalists (and Hasidim), his task could have been far easier, for their writings would have provided Jung a psychologically richer and more sympathetic symbolism than either the "other-worldly" theories of the Gnostics or the radically material practice of the alchemists. Indeed, in some instances the Gnostics, the alchemists, and the Kabbalists share the same symbols and images (e.g., the "sparks," "Primordial Man"), but in each case the Kabbalistic approach to these symbols is the closest to Jung's own. In short, by providing a "this-worldly" interpretation of Gnosticism, and a spiritual-psychological interpretation of alchemy, Jung arrived at a view that was in many ways Kabbalistic in spirit. Indeed, Jung, in his interpretation of alchemy, succeeded remarkably in extracting the Kabbalistic "gold" that lay buried in the alchemists' texts and methods. His work can then be profitably understood as falling in the tradition of those thinkers such as Pico della Mirandola; Johannes Reuchlin (1983); and Knorr von Rosenroth, who created a distinctively Christian Kabbalah (Scholem, 1974, pp. 196–201).

Jung can be interpreted as a contemporary Kabbalist yet one who provides the basis for a radical *psychological* interpretation of the Kabbalists' symbols and ideas. Such an interpretation was not altogether foreign to the Kabbalists themselves, who, on the principle of the microcosm mirroring the macrocosm, held that their own descriptions of cosmic events were also, and equally profoundly, descriptions of the dynamics within men's souls (Idel, 1988, 1995). Indeed, such an interpretation of the Kabbalah provided the major impetus for the doctrines of the Hasidim. Still, Jung took this psychologization process further than either the Kabbalists or the Hasidim, living in a prepsychoanalytic age, could ever have hoped to do themselves.

The Kabbalah

The Kabbalah, the most developed expression of Jewish mysticism, is a vast subject that today commands its own field of study. Rooted in early Jewish mysticism, and regarded by many as a Jewish form of Gnosticism (Scholem, 1941/1961. 1960), the Kabbalah achieved its own unique expression in the anonymous *Sefèr ha-Bahir,* generally regarded as the earliest extant text in this mystical genre (Scholem, 1962/1987). It is in this work that the theory of the 10 *Sefirot,* the value archetypes (Will, Wisdom, Understanding, Kindness, Judgment, Beauty, Glory, Splendor, Foundation, and Kingship) that the Kabbalists all held to be the essence of creation, begins to take form. The *locus classicus,* however, for the *Sefirot* and other Kabbalistic symbols, is the *Zohar* (Sperling and Simon, 1931–1934; Tishby and Lachower, 1989), traditionally attributed to the rabbinic sage Simeon ben Yochai (with whom, as we shall see, Jung identified himself) but thought by contemporary scholars to have originated in Spain some time in the 13th century. The *Zohar,* which is written as a loose and far-reaching commentary on the Torah (the Five Books of Moses), is the source of much of the "wedding symbolism" (unifications of the various *Sefirot)* that preoccupied the alchemists studied by Jung. Its homilies on the nature of the unknowable infinite, the masculine amid the feminine, and the relationship between good and evil can provide much of interest to analytic and archetypal psychologists. Jung himself quoted a number of Zoharic passages and appears to have been acquainted with both a German and an English translation of portions of this book.

It is, however, the radical reformulation of the Kabbalah, initiated by Isaac Luria (1534–1572) and recorded by his disciples—notably, Chayyim Vital (1542–1620)—that is of the greatest interest from a Jungian perspective. Luria's ideas were little known outside orthodox Jewish circles, however, until Gershom Scholem brought them to the attention of the intellectual world in the 1930s and 1940s (Scholem, 1941/1961). The Lurianic Kabbalah is of interest in part because of its systematic and dynamic treatment of many of the symbols and conceptions of the earlier Kabbalah (see Elior, 1993; Jacobs, 1987; Schochet, 1981; Scholem, 1973, 1974).

Jung's Familiarity with the Kabbalah

Jung does not appear to have had any in-depth knowledge of the original texts of the Kabbalah. Although *Mysterium Coniunctionis* includes citations of Sperling and Simon's English translation of the *Zohar* (first published in 1931–1934), as well as of a German translation of the *Zohar* by Ernst Mueller (Jung, 1955–1956/1963, pp. 47, 634), the majority of Jung's specific citations of Kabbalistic symbols and ideas are of the writings of Knorr Von Rosenroth, whose *Kabbalah Denudata,* published in 1684, is a Latin translation of passages from the *Zohar,* other Kabbalistic writings, and essays on the meaning of the Kabbalah (Scholem, 1974). Knorr's work was the most important non-Hebrew reference on the Kabbalah until the close of the 19th century and was the major source on the Kabbalah for non-Jewish scholars at least up to that time. Knorr, writing after the advent and dissemination of the Lurianic Kabbalah, includes (among many other things) Latin translations of portions of the *Zohar,* Cordovero's *Pardes Rimmonim,* a detailed explanation of the Kabbalistic tree after Luria, and even some of the writings of Luria himself.

Jung had "visions" inspired by the symbolism of the Kabbalist Moses Cordovero (Jung, 1961, pp. 293–295), and Cordovero's *Pardes Rimmonim* is cited in the bibliography of *Mysterium Coniunctionis,* but the only actual reference is in a single footnote, and this is cited through Knorr (Jung, 1955–1956/1963, p. 22). Although Jung was clearly aware of the work of Gershom Scholem, who began attending the Eranos conferences after World War II, he appears not to have read Scholem's writings closely prior to 1954. Otherwise, Jung would have undoubtedly been familiar with certain doctrines of the Lurianic Kabbalah, such as the Breaking of the Vessels and *Tikkun,* prior to the date he acknowledged in his letter to Evans in February of that year. Jung carried on a correspondence with a number of students who had firsthand knowledge of Kabbalistic texts and even acknowledged to R. J. Zwi Werblosky that he had received a copy of the Kabbalist R. Gikatila's text on dreams (Jung, 1973, vol. 2, p. 122), but the overwhelming evidence in both the *Mysterium* and the *Letters* is that Jung derived his working knowledge of the Kabbalah from Knorr Von Rosenroth, references to the Kabbalah in the writings of such alchemists as Dorn, and an occasional perusal of the French and German literature on the Kabbalah extant before the field was thoroughly transformed by Scholem.

Jung's limited familiarity with Kabbalistic texts and ideas in no way prevented him from commenting profoundly and in some detail on certain Kabbalistic symbols, such as the *Sefirot,* of which he was aware. The major Kabbalistic ideas that concerned Jung were those that had clear parallel formations in Gnosticism and alchemy: the notion of a spark of divine light contained within humanity; the concept of Primordial Adam, who contains within himself in *coincidentia opposatorum* the various conflicting tendencies within the human spirit; and the theory of divine unifications, particularly the unifications of good and evil and masculine and feminine.

In spite of an occasional reference to Luria, absent from any detailed consideration in Jung's major works are the symbols of *Tzimtzum* (Divine Contraction), *Shevirah* (the Breaking of the Vessels), and *Tikkun ha-Olam* (the Restoration of the World), which are unique to the Lurianic Kabbalah. It is true, however, that just as these Lurianic concepts were implicit in the Kabbalah that preceded Luria (e.g., the *Zohar*), they are, as we will see, also implicit in the alchemical writings that borrowed so heavily from the earlier Kabbalah. Had Jung considered these symbols prior to 1954, they would have been of invaluable service to him, not only in his attempt to grasp the spiritual and psychological nature of alchemy but also in the expression of his own psychology of the self.

Years later, when Jung took a second look at Gnosticism through the eyes of a more fully developed archetypal psychology, he reversed himself and interpreted it in a manner that is far more friendly to the world and the individual, and, as I argue, far more Kabbalistic than Gnostic.

Jung's Interpretation of Gnosticism

Jung eventually interpreted the Gnostic myths, including the origin of the cosmos in the pleroma, the emergence of an ignorant God or demiurge, the creation of a Primordial Man, and the placing of a spark of divinity within individual persons, in completely psychological terms. The Gnostic myths do not, according to Jung, refer to cosmic or even external human events but rather reflect the basic archetypal developments of the human psyche. Jung regarded the pleroma, within which is contained the undifferentiated unity of all opposites and contradictions, as nothing but the primal unconscious from which the human personality will emerge. The "demiurge," whom the Gnostics disparaged as being ignorant of its pleromatic origins, represents the conscious, rational ego, which in its arrogance believes that it, too, is both the creator and master of the human personality. The spark, or scintilla, which is placed in the human soul, represents the possibility of the psyche's reunification with the unconscious, and the primal anthropos *(Adam Kadmon,* or Christ), which is related to this spark, is symbolic of the "self," the achieved unification of a conscious, individuated personality with the full range of oppositions and archetypes in the unconscious mind. "Our aim," Jung wrote, "is to create a wider personality whose centre of gravity does not necessarily coincide with the ego" but rather "in the hypothetical point between conscious and unconscious" (Jung, 1929/1968a, p. 45). Jung saw in the Gnostic (and Kabbalistic) symbol of Primordial Man a symbol of the goal of his own analytical psychology.

Jung's Interpretation of Alchemy

Jung provided a similar if more daring and far-reaching interpretation of alchemy. According to Jung, what the alchemist sees in matter, and understands in his formulas for the transmutation of metals and the derivation of the *prima materia,* "is chiefly the data of his own unconscious which he is projecting into it" (Jung, 1937/1968c, p. 228). For example, the alchemist's efforts to bring about a union of opposites in the laboratory and to perform what is spoken of as a "chymical wedding" are understood by Jung as attempts to forge a unity, for example, between masculine and feminine, or good and evil aspects of the psyche (Jung, 1937/1968c). "The alchemical opus," Jung wrote, "deals in the main not just with chemical experiments as such, but with something resembling psychic processes expressed in pseudochemical language" (Jung, 1944/1968b, p. 242).

In his *Mysterium Coniunctionis,* Jung (1955–1956/1963) provided a catalogue of alchemical symbols that are rich in spiritual and psychological significance. Many of the most significant of these symbols, including the notions of *Adam Kadmon,* the divine spark in humanity, the union of the cosmic King and Queen, and the divine nature of evil (each of which Jung regarded as foundational for his later psychology), were imported into alchemy from the Kabbalah.

The Kabbalah and Alchemy

Jung himself was aware of the strong relationship between the Kabbalah and late alchemy, and he frequently spoke of specific Kabbalistic influences on the alchemists of the 16th century and later. "Directly or indirectly," Jung (1955–1956/1963) wrote in the *Mysterium,* "the Cabala was assimilated into alchemy. Relationships must have existed between them at a very early date, though it is difficult to trace them in the sources" (p. 24; cf. p. 384). Jung pointed out that by the end of the 16th century the alchemists began making direct quotations from the *Zohar*. For example, he provided a quotation from Blasius Vigenerus (1523–1596) comparing the feminine *Sefirah Malchut* with the moon turning its face from the intelligible things of heaven (Jung, 1955–1956/1963, p. 24). He pointed to a number of alchemists, including Khunrath and Dorn, who made extensive use of the Kabbalistic notion of *Adam Kadmon* as early as the 16th century, and stated that works by Reuchlin *(De Arte Kabalistica,* 1517) and Mirandola had made the Kabbalah accessible to non-Jews at that time (Jung, 1955–1956/1963; see also Reuchlin, 1983). Both Vigenerus and Knorr Von Rosenroth, Jung said, attempted to relate the alchemical notion of the *lapis*, or philosopher's stone, to passages in the *Zohar* that interpret biblical verses (Job 38:6, Isaiah 28:16, Genesis 28:22) as making reference to a stone with essential, divine, and transformative powers (Jung, 1955–1956/1963). He also noted that Paracelsus had introduced the sapphire as an "arcanum" into alchemy from the Kabbalah. Two of the alchemists most frequently quoted by Jung (Knorr and Khunrath) wrote treatises on the Kabbalah, and others, such as Dora and Lully, were heavily influenced by Kabbalistic ideas. These authors included a notion of the "sparks," which was to become a key element in the Lurianic Kabbalah, and gave it a Kabbalistic (as opposed to Gnostic) interpretation in their work.

Although Jung clearly recognized the relationship between the Kabbalah and alchemy, he provided us with only part of the story. The spiritual aspects of alchemy, which interested Jung, were to a very large extent Jewish in origin. Even Jung's own *view* of alchemy appears to have its origins in Jewish sources. Maria the Prophetess, the Egyptian Hellenistic Jewess who was regarded by Zosimos (3rd century) to be the founder of alchemy (and by modern scholarship to be among its earliest practitioners), viewed the alchemical work as fundamentally a process through which the adept attain spiritual perfection (Patai, 1994). Maria regarded the various metals in the alchemical work to be analogous to aspects of humanity, hence her famous maxim "Join the male and the female and you will find what is sought" (Patai, 1994, p. 66), an aphorism that could well serve as a motto for much of Jung's own interpretation of alchemy.

Space limitations prevent me from providing anything like a full survey of the Kabbalistic sources of the spiritual side of alchemy. The interested reader is referred to works by Suler (1972) and Patai (1994).

Jung's Understanding of the Kabbalah

Jung brought the same interpretive posture to the Kabbalah that he had brought to Gnosticism and alchemy, but his approach to the Kabbalistic tradition was far less systematic, and his views on this tradition must occasionally be pieced together from his discussions of parallel Gnostic and alchemical ideas. Among the Kabbalistic notions that were of significance to Jung (or are significant from a Jungian perspective) are *Ein-Sof* (the Infinite), *Tzimtzum* (Divine Contraction), *Adam Kadmon* (Primordial Man), *Shevirat ha-Kelim* (the Breaking of the Vessels), *Kellipot* (Shells or Husks), the separation of the King and Queen, *Tikkun ha-Olam* (the Restoration of the World), and *Partzufim* (Visages). I discuss each of these in turn.

Ein-Sof (the Infinite) is the limitless, unknowable, creative source of all being, which is the union of everything and its opposite. Jung had interpreted the Gnostics' *pleroma,* a conception of the divine that is essentially equivalent to the Kabbalists' *Ein-Sof,* as the infinite, unknowable depths of the collective unconscious. For Jung (1955–1956/1963), *Ein-Sof,* like the pleroma, is the chaotic unknown that unites within itself all contrasts and oppositions and which humanity returns to time and again as the wellspring of creativity and desire.

Tzimtzum (Divine Contraction) is, according to the Lurianists, the concealment, negation, and withdrawal of God's presence that "makes room" for the world. The Lurianists invoked this symbol as a vehicle of transition from an infinite God to the finite world. Accordingly, the original act of creation was a negation in which the Infinite contracts and conceals itself from itself in order to bring about a finite realm. Jung made no mention of *Tzimtzum;* however, this notion of self "contraction" and "concealment" can readily be understood psychologically as an archetypal limitation or repression that separates the ego from the unconscious.

Adam Kadmon (Primordial Man) embodies the 10 value archetypes *(Sefirot)* through which the world was created. Jung reflected in detail on this Kabbalistic notion, noting that a cosmic primordial man is a symbol that appears in many of the world's myths of creation. For Jung, *Adam Kadmon* is a symbol of the "self" (Jung, 1955–1956/1963, p. 50), as it unites within itself the full range of values (the *Sefirot)* through which both the world and humankind were created. It is important to note that, for the Kabbalists, *Adam Kadmon* is in a constant state of transformation and renewal and only fully becomes himself subsequent to the "Breaking of the Vessels" and their reconstruction in *Tikkun.* It is thus no wonder that Jung equated *Adam Kadmon* with the alchemists' Mercurius (Jung, 1955–1956/1963, pp. 10, 394; Jung, 1937/1968c, p. 319) and regarded *Adam Kadmon* as an important symbol of psychological transformation (Jung, 1955–1956/1963, p.429).

Shevirat ha-Kelim (the Breaking of the Vessels) is an archetypal event in which the value archetypes were shattered and distributed throughout the cosmos as "sparks." Jung, as we have seen, was fascinated by the Kabbalistic symbols of the Breaking of the Vessels and *Tikkun* (the vessels' "repair") when he chanced on these ideas in 1954. For him, they represented the role that humankind must play in the restoration of the world, the redemption of evil, and the restoration of the self. However, even prior to that time Jung had encountered these notions in their alchemical guises, as the chaos and destruction that must precede the alchemical work, and which Jung understood as prerequisites for the forging of a unified self.

Kelipot (Shells or Husks) entrap the sparks of divine light, prevent them from serving their purpose in creation, and give rise to the negative realm known as the *Sitra Achra*, or "Other Side." According to the Kabbalists, this evil realm is nevertheless part of the divine plenum and must be given its due. The Kabbalistic notion of the "Other Side" has its Jungian equivalent in the archetype of the Shadow. The Kabbalists regarded the Other Side as a necessary part of the divine plan and, like Jung, held that the individual's baser instincts must be integrated into his or her being rather than rejected or repressed. We read in the *Zohar*:

> Mark this! As Job kept evil separate from good and failed to fuse them, he was judged accordingly; first he experienced good, then what was evil, then again good. For man should be cognizant of both good and evil, and turn evil itself into good. This is a deep tenet to faith (Sperling and Simon, 1931–1934, vol. 3, p. 109).

Compare this to Jung's assertion that "A safe foundation is found only when the instinctive premises of the unconscious win the same respect as the views of the conscious mind" (Jung, 1929/1967, p. 48).

The separation of the King and Queen was understood by the Kabbalists to symbolize a split between the masculine and feminine elements of the deity, which itself reflects the disorder and chaos of a broken world. For the Kabbalists, the disharmony of the world is reflected in a separation between male and female, and the world's restoration and repair is symbolized by a wedding between *Tifereth* and *Malchuth*, the masculine and feminine *Sefirot*, known in the Kabbalah as the Holy One and his Bride. Jung, of course, interpreted these ideas psychologically and saw them as symbols of the union between animus and anima, which in the individual psyche is a prerequisite for individuation and psychological growth. Jung explored the Kabbalistic symbols of the divine marriage extensively (Jung, 1955–1956/1963, pp. 23–24, 396, 432–445, see especially p. 442; Jung, 1973, vol. 1, p. 356, vol. 2, p. 292) and, as we shall see, himself had dreams and visions that incorporated these Jewish ideas.

Tikkun ha-Olam (the Restoration of the World) is the process through which humanity repairs the world in the service of a "second creation." According to the Lurianists, one result of the Breaking of the Vessels is the depositing of a hidden divine spark in the soul of each individual and, in the Kabbalistic (but not Gnostic) view, in the heart of all earthly things. For the Kabbalists, the purpose of *Tikkun,* the Restoration of the World, is for individuals to "raise" and redeem the sparks within both themselves and the world, in order that both humankind and the world can actualize their fullest, divine potential. Jung considered the theory of the "sparks," or "scintillae," as they appeared in Gnosticism, the Kabbalah (Jung, 1955–1956/1963, p. 301, n. 26), and alchemy, and concluded that they represented an element of the primordial, archetypal unconscious in man (Jung, 1955–1956/1963, p. 491). Unfortunately, he was apparently unaware of the development of the "sparks" symbol in later Kabbalah and Hasidism, where, in contrast to the Gnostic understanding of the sparks as a vehicle for escape from the world and self (Jung, 1955–1956/1963, p. 48, and p. 48. n. 55), they are understood as an opportunity for the development of the person and the spiritualization of the world. The Hasidim believe that each individual is placed on earth because there are sparks both within his or her own soul and the world that only that individual can redeem. In raising the sparks, male and female are reunited, and creation is completed and perfected.

The *Partzufim* (Visages) are understood by the Lurianists to be a plurality of archetypal personas through which the Primordial Man must evolve in the process of *Tikkun.* For Jung, the notion of the raising of the sparks and the entire process of *Tikkun* would have been ideal symbols for individuation. That the process of *Tikkun* gives rise to, and causes the Primordial Man to embody, archetypal personalities (the Holy Ancient One, the Father, the Mother, the impulsive Male, and the Female), each of which has a role in *Tikkun* and which clearly anticipates Jung's major archetypes, is further proof of the fit between the Lurianic Kabbalah and the Jungian "Self."

The Kabbalah, Gnosis, and Jungian Psychology

Regardless of the direction of influence, it is clear that nearly all of the basic symbols and ideas of Gnosticism are to be found in one form or another in the Kabbalah and vice versa. The notion of an unknowable, infinite godhead that contains within itself a coincidence of metaphysical opposites, the gradual manifestation of the Infinite through an emanation of *logoi* or *Sefirot,* the notion of a cosmic accident giving birth to the manifest world, the distinction between the God of the Bible and the true Infinite, the estrangement of humankind from its true essence, and the entrapment of a divine spark within the individual's material nature are all themes that found their way into both Gnosticism and the Kabbalah.

Yet for all the similarities between Gnostic and Kabbalistic doctrine, certain essential differences emerge that are of ultimate significance for Jungian psychology. The major difference is that Gnosticism has no equivalent concept or symbol for the Kabbalistic notion of *Tikkun ha-Olam,* the Restoration of the World. As we have seen, for the Gnostics (as well as for Jung in the *Septem Sermones*), the goal of spiritual life is not a restoration but an escape from what they regard to be this worthless, evil world. The Gnostic identifies with the divine spark within the self in order to transcend the physical self and the material world.

The Kabbalist holds a radically different view. Although there are also escapist or "Gnostic" trends within the Kabbalah, the majority of Kabbalists hold that the realization of the divine spark both in the person and the material world brings about an elevation, restoration, and spiritualization of the individual and the environment. In Gnosticism, the world is escaped; in the Kabbalah it is elevated and restored. The latter view is one that is much more congenial to Jungian psychology, not only on the obvious principle that for Jungians life in this world, and the world itself, is worthwhile, but also with respect to the (less obvious) psychological interpretation which Jung placed on the Gnostic myths. As Segal (1992) pointed out, the Gnostic ethic, as interpreted by Jung, would, strictly speaking, lead to a complete identification of the subject with the unconscious mind. This is because the Gnostic attempts to escape from the world (which Jung equates with the ego) into a complete identification with the infinite pleroma which, as we have seen, Jung identified with the collective unconscious.

By way of contrast, for the Kabbalists and Jung (and the alchemists as interpreted by Jung), the godhead creates the world and humankind in order to fully realize itself. By analogy, the unconscious mind manifests itself in a conscious, reflective ego in order to complete and know itself as a "self." "The difference" Jung wrote, "between the natural individuation process, which runs its course unconsciously, and the one which is consciously realized is tremendous: in the first case consciousness nowhere intervenes; the end remains as dark as the beginning" (Jung, 1952/1969a, p. 468). For Jung and the alchemists, the world, and its psychological equivalent, the ego, far from being the superfluous, harmful, and lamentable conditions envisioned by the Gnostics, are actually necessary, beneficial, and laudable (Segal, 1992). Both God and humankind must pass through the world and redeem it in order to realize their full essence. This is precisely the view of the Kabbalists, as expressed in their symbol of *Tikkun ha-Olam.* Gnosticism actually advocates the precise opposite of Jungian psychology (Segal, 1992).

It is interesting that the alchemists are far more compatible with Jung (and the Kabbalah) on this crucial point than are the Gnostics. The *raison d'être* of alchemy is the transformation of worldly matter (Segal, 1992), not the escape from it. For Gnosticism the dissolution of the world is an end in itself; for the alchemists it is a precondition for a new creation, just as in the Kabbalah the *Shevirat ha-Kelim,* the Breaking of the Vessels and destruction of earlier worlds, sets the stage for the world's redemption in *Tikkun ha-Olam.*

Jung is more Kabbalistic than Gnostic on a number of other crucial points as well. For example, according to the Gnostics, the demiurge, or creator God, (the God archetype in Jung) is thoroughly evil, whereas for Jung (and the Kabbalah) it represents both good and evil, persona and shadow, a coincidence of opposites. Quispel (cited in Segal, 1992, p. 236) wrote that the

> fundamentally Jungian interpretation, according to which the representation of God, and thus the godhead, encompasses both good and evil, has no analogy in the Gnostic sources. It is not Gnostic at all. One can call it magical, but only magic with a Jewish foundation.

Indeed, Gnosticism preaches a radical dualism of good immateriality and evil matter; whereas for Jung, as for the Kabbalah, good and evil originate (and end) in the same source, are mutually dependent on one another, and are not simply to be identified with spirit and matter. Had Jung been more familiar with the Kabbalah, particularly in its Lurianic form, he would have found a system of mythical thought that was far more compatible with his own psychology than was Gnosticism. In 1954, shortly after his discovery of the Lurianic Kabbalah and after essentially completing *Mysterium Coniunctionis,* Jung all but acknowledged this point of view. In a letter to James Kirsch (16 February 1954) he wrote:

> The Jew has the advantage of having long since anticipated the development of consciousness in his own spiritual history. By this I mean the Lurianic stage of the Kabbalah, the breaking of the vessels and man's help in restoring them. Here the thought emerges for the first time that man must help God to repair the damage wrought by creation. For the first time man's cosmic responsibility is acknowledged (Jung, 1973, vol. 2, p. 155).

For Jung, in contrast to the Gnostics, man is not enjoined to escape the world (and his conscious life within it) but rather is responsible for its repair and restoration. It is this notion of world restoration, what the Kabbalists referred to as *Tikkun ha-Olam,* that most connects Jung to the Jewish mystical tradition and that clearly distinguishes him from Gnosticism.

Jung's Kabbalistic Vision

Jung appears to have had a personal experience of the Kabbalah that went far beyond his scholarly interests. In his *Memories, Dreams, Reflections,* Jung (1961) recorded a series of visions that he described as "the most tremendous things I have ever experienced." The visions occurred in 1944 when Jung, nearing the end of his seventh decade, was stricken with a heart attack and "hung on the edge of death" (p. 289). They involve the divine wedding between *Tifereth* and *Malchuth,* which, in the Kabbalah, are the masculine and feminine divine principles.

Jung described these visions as occurring in a state of wakeful ecstasy, "as though I were floating in space, as though I were safe in the womb of the universe" (p. 293). He further described his experience as one of indescribable "eternal bliss." He reported:

> Everything around me seemed enchanted. At this hour of the night the nurse brought me some food she had warmed. . . . For a time it seemed to me that she was an old Jewish woman, much older than she actually was, and that she was preparing ritual kosher dishes for me. When I looked at her, she seemed to have a blue halo around her head. I myself was, so it seemed, in the Pardes Rimmonim, the garden of pomegranates, and the wedding of Tifereth with Malchuth was taking place. Or else I was Rabbi

> Simon ben Jochai, whose wedding in the afterlife was being celebrated. It was the mystic marriage as it appears in the Cabbalistic tradition. I cannot tell you how wonderful it was. I could only think continually, "Now this is the garden of pomegranates! Now this is the marriage of Malchuth with Tifereth!" I do not know exactly what part I played in it. At bottom it was I myself: I was the marriage. And my beatitude was that of a blissful wedding (Jung, 1961, p. 294).

Jung related that the vision changed and there followed "the Marriage of the Lamb" in Jerusalem, with angels and light. "I myself," he recorded, "was the marriage of the lamb." In a final image Jung found himself in a classical amphitheater situated in a landscape of a verdant chain of hills. "Men and women dancers came on-stage, and upon a flower-decked couch All-father Zeus consummated the mystic marriage, as it is described in the Iliad" (Jung, 1961, p.294). As a result of these experiences, Jung developed the impression that this life is but a "segment of existence." During the visions, past, present, and future fused into one. According to Jung, "the visions and experiences were utterly real; there was nothing subjective about them" (p. 295).

It is remarkable that Jung, in what he described as the most tremendous and "individuating" experience of his life, should find himself in the "garden of pomegranates," an allusion to a Kabbalistic work of that name by Moses Cordovero, and that he should identify himself with the *coniunctio* of *Tifereth* and *Malchuth* as it is described in the Kabbalah. In this vision, which can only be described as Kabbalistic, Jung further identified himself with Rabbi Simeon ben Yochai, who in Jewish tradition is regarded as the author of the *Zohar*. Here, on the brink of death, Jung had a mystical experience in which the truth of the Kabbalistic wedding is equated with the truth of the *hierosgamos,* the divine wedding in Greek mythology. The sexual union of male and female is mystically experienced as the source of both immortality and personal individuation and redemption. According to Jung, such experience involves an "objective cognition" in which all emotional ties, "relationships of desire, tainted by coercion and constraint," are transcended in favor of a real *coniunctio,* a relationship with oneself, others, and the world that is beyond, yet also *behind,* desire. Only after this Kabbalistic experience was Jung able to compose the *Mysterium Coniunctionis* and other major works of his final years (Jung, 1961).

Given Jung's familiarity with Kabbalistic ideas and symbols, the profoundly psychological nature of the Kabbalah, and Jung's own Kabbalistic visions, one might ask why he never developed a sustained inquiry into the Kabbalah as he did with regard to Gnosticism and, especially, alchemy. There are several reasons for this. In the first place, as Jung himself noted, he did not know Hebrew and was unfamiliar with the relevant sources, most of which in his day had been neither translated nor even summarized into languages with which Jung was familiar.

It is more significant that, in spite of Jung's protestations that he was neither metaphysician nor theologian, his major concern in his later works was a psychological revivification of Christianity through a study of its undercurrents, Gnosticism and alchemy, which he understood as the compensatory "shadow" to official religion. Although Jung held that the Kabbalah played a similar role *vis-à-vis* Orthodox Judaism, as a Christian this was of peripheral interest to him. True, there was a Christian Kabbalah (of which Knorr was an example), but to Jung the Kabbalah was essentially Jewish in origin and import.

Finally, and perhaps most significant, Jung maintained a strong ambivalence toward Jews and Judaism, which, at least during a critical point in his career, may have compromised his receptivity to Jewish ideas.

Jung and Judaism

As is well-known, Jung was originally placed by Freud in the unenviable position of playing guarantor that psychoanalysis would not be looked on as a "Jewish national affair." According to Jung, after the two parted ways, Freud accused him of anti-Semitism because Jung could not abide with Freud's "soulless materialism" (Jung, 1973, vol. 1, p. 162). The relationship with Freud appears to have colored Jung's view of Judaism, as Jung's later identification of psychoanalysis as a Jewish psychology inapplicable to Europeans appears to have in part been fueled by his competitiveness with and personal animosity toward Freud (McLynn, 1996; see Jung, 1934/1970).

Although the controversy regarding Jung's personal and professional stance with regard to the Nazis during the 1930s is beyond the scope of this discussion (see Jaffé, 1971, and McLynn, 1996), it is important to recall that during this period Jung expressed certain negative views about "Jewish psychology." In the 1930s, during the rise of Nazi anti-Semitism, Jung chose to highlight what in his view were the differences between Jewish and German psychology (Jung, 1934/1970). His statements were understood by many to be anti-Semitic and as playing directly into the hands of those who would view Jews as a threat to, or parasites on, Germany and other European states.

Jung's observations that the "Jewish race as a whole. . . possesses an unconscious which can be compared with the 'Aryan' only with reserve" and that "the Aryan unconscious has a higher potential than the Jewish" (Jung 1934/1970 p. 166) were seen as reinforcing Nazi ideology (despite a context that could be understood as praising the Jewish mind in other respects). Furthermore, in his polemic against Freud, Jung, as early as 1928, wrote that "it is quite an unpardonable mistake to accept the conclusions of a Jewish psychology as generally valid" (Jung, 1928/1966, p. 148, n. 8, see also Jung 1934/1970, p. 544). In a letter to B. Cohen he later explicitly stated: "In so far as [Freud's] theory is based in certain respects on Jewish premises, it is not valid for non-Jews" (Jung, 1973, vol. 1, p. 154).

It was during the period of Jung's early, and perhaps greatest, involvement with alchemy that he chose to distance the Western/Christian psyche from Judaism. In 1935, Jung wrote to Erich Neumann (who had written to Jung about Judaism) that "analytical psychology has its roots in the Christian middle ages and ultimately in Greek philosophy, with the connecting link being alchemy" (Jung, 1973, vol. 1, p. 206). Given Jung's need in the 1930s to distinguish his Christian/Western psychology from the Jewish psychology of Freud, one wonders whether Jung underemphasized the huge impact of Judaism (via the Kabbalah) on alchemy and thereby on his own thinking. It is not until after World War II that Jung began to make numerous references to the Kabbalah and noted the importance of the Kabbalah for alchemy.

I do not know for a fact that Jung suppressed the Jewish mystical origins of some of his ideas. However, given his polemic against Freud, his characterizations of the Jewish psyche, his desire to distinguish his psychology from "Jewish psychology," and the situation in Europe during the 1930s, he had a powerful motive for doing so. If indeed Jung had consciously or unconsciously suppressed the Jewish mystical sources of some of his ideas, his Kabbalistic visions during his apparently mortal illness in 1944 can be understood (in Jungian terms) as a powerful compensation for that suppression or, more generally, as an atonement for his anti-Jewish writings and sentiments.

It is important to note that Jung's attitude toward Judaism, even in the 1930s, was by no means always pejorative. During that period, Jung steadfastly defended himself against any accusations of anti-Semitism and worked to prevent Jewish psychotherapists from being pushed out of their profession. He defended his right to point out the unique features of Jewish psychology, as he had done, for example, with respect to the Indians and Chinese, and insisted that his views on Jewish psychology long antedated the rise of National Socialism in Germany (Jung 1934/1970), though he seemed to forget his earlier view that on the deepest psychological level it is "impossible to distinguish between an Aryan, Semitic, Hamitic or Mongolian mentality, [as] all human races have a common collective psyche" (Jung, 1928/1966, p. 149, n. 8). Even in his 1934 article, Jung (1934/1970) held that the Jewish mind had a greater consciousness and was more differentiated than the Aryan, and, in a letter to Aaron Roback, held that Jews have an extension into their own subconscious that is rare among non-Jews (Jung, 1973, vol. 1, p. 224).

Although it is clear that Jung regretted even the appearance of having flirted with National Socialism (Jaffé, 1971; McLynn, 1996), he never, as far as I can tell, provided a full and satisfactory accounting of his earlier views on Jewish psychology. His disciple and confidante, Aniele Jaffé (1971), later wrote that Jung's early statements about the Jewish mind "spring from a lack of comprehension of Judaism and Jewish culture which is scarcely intelligible today" (p. 85). In a letter to Jaffé, Gershom Scholem related that after the war Jung was confronted by the Jewish scholar Leo Baeck on these matters, and the two ultimately made peace after Jung's confession that he had "slipped up." This, Scholem related, was sufficient for both Baeck and Scholem to, in effect, forgive Jung and continue their relationship.

I am deeply troubled by Jung's apparent duplicity and opportunism with respect to what he himself termed the "Jewish question." However, none of the above considerations should, in my opinion, prevent us from either appreciating the affinities between the Kabbalah and the position at which Jung eventually arrived, or in noting the influence of Kabbalistic ideas both directly and indirectly (through alchemy) on Jungian psychology. Nor should these considerations prevent us from embarking on the fascinating task of examining the vast Kabbalistic literature that has come to light in the past 60 years from a Jungian perspective and thereby enriching our understanding of both the Kabbalah and our own psyches.

As I have attempted to show, Jung's relationship to the Kabbalah is multi-textured, if somewhat unsettling. The story of Jung and Jewish mysticism is one, I believe, that is only beginning to be told and understood.

CHAPTER 15

Aryeh Maidenbaum

The Shadows Still Linger

In January of 1989, in preparation for the first international conference held on the subject of C. G. Jung and anti-Semitism, I traveled to Zurich to conduct a series of filmed and taped interviews with a number of first generation Jungians. Joining me in this project were close friends and colleagues Stephen Martin (co-editor of *Lingering Shadows: Jungians, Freudians and Anti-Semitism* and former president of the Philadelphia Association of Jungian Analysts); Robert Hinshaw (former member of the Curatorium of the Jung Institute of Zurich and publisher of Daimon Books) and Peter Amman, Jungian Analyst from Geneva (who, with his considerable experience in the world of film before becoming a Jungian analyst, was in charge of our technical arrangements). All three helped me during the course of the interviews with comments, corrections of fact, and pertinent follow-up questions. All of us were graduates of the C. G. Jung Institute of Zurich, committed to Jung's psychology and ideas in our professional and personal lives and active in the professional Jungian world.

During the course of our interviews, one of the leading Jungians we spoke to was C. A. Meier—personally chosen by Jung to be the first president of the Jung Institute in Zurich, and a man who during much of his life was closer to Jung than any other person. At one point, Meier remarked that this question came up regularly—be it in Switzerland, other parts of Europe or the U.S. Still, he observed, no matter how thoroughly this conference will explore the issue, no matter how many articles or books would appear in print on this topic, Meier predicted:

> We won't change a thing. It will come up again...more legends about St. Jung will be created out of the blue—out of the fantasy—the shadow fantasies of these people. There must be a devil someplace, you know. And to the Freudians, of course, it's Jung. That's clear enough so you always have a scapegoat. Good to have a scapegoat.

With the passage of time, I have come to understand that Meier was right; the topic will not go away. Perhaps the primary reason why it keeps resurfacing is that there is no clear, definitive answer. Unfortunately, yet consistent with the complexity one would expect in the personality and life of as large a figure as Jung embodied, the issue remains very much alive.

Nevertheless, while Meier correctly identified a piece of the collective Freudian shadow as continually labeling Jung anti-Semitic in order to discredit his immense contributions to the field of psychology, he did not take into account the fact that a number of Jung's own comments on Jews and Judaism still troubled many in the Jungian world, including many internationally recognized Jungian analysts, authors and historians as well as the general public that attended Jungian programs.

Ironically, as it has turned out, Jungian analysts themselves as well as a great number of individuals interested in the relevancy of the psychology and ideas of Jung to their personal lives, have been the most affected by this issue. For, notwithstanding the fact that this well-attended, first international conference (co-sponsored by The C. G. Jung Foundation of New York, The Postgraduate Center for Mental Health, the Union of American Hebrew Congregations and The New School for Social Research) did not prove to be the final, definitive discussion surrounding this controversy, it nevertheless became the beacon from which a great deal of light was shed on the question posed: Was C. G. Jung anti-Semitic?

From this conference, held at the New School for Social Research in April of 1989, emerged *Lingering Shadows: Jungians, Freudians and Anti-Semitism*, a source book that included many of the leading papers of the conference as well as an extensive bibliography and all known writings and comments of Jung about Jews and Judaism. Additionally, a host of articles focusing on this theme began appearing in Jungian journals around the world; Jungian groups in the United States began openly holding seminars and public programs on the topic and (for the first time) the International Association for Analytical Psychology (IAAP) presented a workshop on "Jung and Anti-Semitism" at its eleventh International Conference (held in Paris in 1989)—a workshop that, interestingly enough, turned out to be the most well-attended of the conference, as several hundred Jungian analysts from around the world participated.

Nevertheless, though for different reasons, just as Meier had anticipated it would, the heat surrounding this controversy remained, and indeed remains, very much alive though unfortunately *Lingering Shadows* has gone out of print. The fact that it was out of print, combined with new material written subsequent to the publication of *Lingering Shadows*; the reaction of the Jungian community at large (see Jerome Bernstein, "Report to the Delegates of the XII International Congress") to this subject, and the realization that interviews I had recorded but chose not to use earlier might be of interest, provided me with the impetus to once again address this issue. In revisiting this material, I have come to understand that the subject of how to reconcile the brilliance of Jung's psychology with his less-than-exemplary public pronouncements about Jews and Judaism, represents a painful place that many of us in the Jungian community need to continue addressing through our work with the general public. Like it or not, the subject keeps resurfacing, and at the very least, a book on this topic must always be in print, despite the fact that most of us prefer ignoring rather than revisiting this controversial issue.

Interestingly enough, as I think back and reflect on the first public Jungian conference, the most succinct observation on the difficulties Jungians face in addressing this issue came from Dr. Mortimer Ostow, internationally noted Professor of Pastoral Psychiatry, and Visiting Professor at the Jewish Theological Seminary. Dr. Ostow, a Freudian-trained psychiatrist who served as a respondent at the New York conference, perceptively commented that he didn't understand why Jungians themselves had such a difficult time accepting the fact that Carl Jung was a man with "a head of gold and feet of clay." Perhaps, for the Jungian community at large, the time has come to accept this as a given—indeed, a description that Jung personally would have approved.

In interpreting fairy tales from a Jungian perspective, one must always bear in mind the folk saying that "the man without a shadow is the devil." Jung, as all who knew him well personally would attest, certainly had a shadow. Personally, this observation strikes a chord and reminds me of Jung's warning that "what the ego idealizes, the Self must tear down." Jung would not have wanted us to idealize him—the compensatory aspect of having to tear him down psychologically is a price he should not have to pay. For Jung was neither the devil many of his detractors have made him out to be, nor a saint, innocent of bias and prejudice as one would expect from such a giant in the field of depth psychology.

I was fortunate enough to have begun my Jungian studies and analyses in 1971. During the course of the next decade, first in Israel and later in Zurich, I was able to work with a number of leading Jungian analysts who had studied with, and in some cases analyzed with, Jung himself. These individuals—especially Jungian analyst Dr. Rivkah Schaerf Kluger, who lived in Haifa, Israel and with whom I worked for five and a half years while I was pursuing my Ph.D., and Dr. Rene Malamud, my analyst, mentor, and dear friend—are very important to me. All had in common an immense love and respect for Jung personally. Part of the difficulty I have faced in dealing with the question of whether or not Jung was anti-Semitic has been compounded by my reverence for them.

Thanks to my Jungian analyses on three continents (in Israel, Switzerland, and New York), what I have been able to reconnect to through Jung's psychology and ideas has been an appreciation of my Judaism and my own heritage. For example, during the course of my analysis with her, Rivkah Kluger often mentioned, quoting Jung himself, that one of the goals of analysis for a Jewish person was to make a Jew a better Jew. Paradoxically, while my Jungian work has enabled me to do just that, for years I have had to struggle with the personally troubling question of whether or not this man himself may or may not have been anti-Semitic.

Prior to entering Jungian analysis, my rebellion toward the Orthodox Jewish world I was raised in had been to totally turn from my past and upbringing and deny anything that even reminded me of religion. I stopped going to synagogue, stopped praying, and gave up any semblance of eating kosher food. I wanted, for once, to be just like everybody else and not have to carry the burden (as Isaiah declared) of being "not like all the nations." Yet, paradoxically, I found myself in the strange situation of questioning Jung's view toward Jews at the same time as his psychology was providing me with the ability to maintain a newly-found and much-appreciated connection to my Jewish roots.

Jewish tradition holds that each generation is connected with previous generations; we do not exist independently of our predecessors, which echoes Jung's views on the structure of archetypes and their connection to the unconscious. And so, on both Jewish and Jungian levels, I realized I had to examine for myself if there was any truth to the accusation that Jung was anti-Semitic in his personal life and psychology. It was important to come to a decision as to what I believe and feel about the question—a question that touched upon the very heart and soul of my personal and professional life.

In struggling with this question, the task I found most difficult of all was confronting the possibility of disappointing my mentors or displeasing my friends. Moreover, the question was further complicated by the fear of what I might find. Trained as an historian before entering the field of Jungian psychology, I was aware of the fact that one can never be certain of what one finds when undertaking a serious scholarly effort. What if I came to the conclusion that Jung was indeed anti-Semitic? How could I then, in good conscience, remain a Jungian Analyst, let alone serve as director of a major Jungian educational organization?

In this vein, an example that came to mind from the Jewish world, and which I found applicable to my early role in being a catalyst in the Jungian world for exploring the issue of Jung and anti-Semitism, was found in drawing a parallel between following the authority of the Rabbi and/or respecting the wisdom and authority of the analyst or revered teacher, in this case, Jung. For in the Talmud, there is a question posed as to when one listens to and when one disregards the words of one's Rabbi.

Rabbi Shlomo Riskin, noted Jewish leader now living in Israel, once remarked that "one of the thorniest problems facing anyone who takes both religion and humanistic liberalism seriously is whether adherence to tradition means adherence to the authority of the carriers of that tradition. Are we to bow to previous generations without question, piously relying on the homily that 'since we don't even come up to their shoelaces, who are we to second guess the greats?'" Thus, the question posed in the Talmud is indeed relevant: What does one do when told by one's Rabbi that right is left and left is right? This was the question I posed for myself—what would I do or believe if I came to the conclusion that Jung was anti-Semitic in contrast to what I had been assured by my analysts, that it was impossible that Jung was an anti-Semite. In the end, I remembered the conclusion reached in this Talmudic discussion: one must do and believe what one knows is right, even if it flies in the face of authority. I needed to find out for myself. This attitude, raising the issue to consciousness, rather than relegating it to the unconscious, would be true to Jung's psychology and ideas.

The issue came alive even more dramatically when one of the leading analysts in the Jungian world addressed me at a national Jungian meeting in Los Angeles in front of a group of colleagues and publicly chastised me for holding such a conference declaring that "since I didn't come up to Jung's shoelaces, how could I dare present such a public program which might question Jung in some way?"

Ironically, what I had learned from my Jungian analysis, and drawn on from my Jewish studies, helped me stay true to my own spirit, which in this case meant going ahead with the conference despite pressure to the contrary from some of the powers that be. I became even more determined to continue exploring this topic, publicly and privately, until I was personally satisfied that I had the information I needed to reach an honest and informed position. To do anything less, I would have had difficulty facing myself as both an individual and a Jew. The conference turned out to be a most important one for me, personally, and I believe for the Jungian community as well—one I have never regretted undertaking.

In the process of my explorations, the filmed interviews we held with some of those first-generation Jungian analysts proved pivotal for me. Three, especially C. A. Meier, Aniela Jaffé and Siegmund Hurwitz, were most valuable. Of the three, Hurwitz and Jaffé were Jewish while the third, Meier, had been one of my analysts in Zurich. All three allowed themselves to be vulnerable and subjected to intense—one might even say invasive—personal questioning and filmed interviews, and added to my understanding of Jung in a most profound way. In return, I promised myself that as long as any were still living, these interviews would remain private. It is only now, after the three have passed away, that I feel free enough to share some of these interactions with a wider audience.

C. A. Meier

The first of these figures, Carl Alfred Meier (known as and referred to in the Jungian world as C. A. Meier), is the most problematic individual of the three for me to deal with. An internationally famous and prominent Swiss psychiatrist, Meier was (especially during the 1930s and 1940s, a period when Jung made some his most controversial pronouncements regarding Jews and Judaism) personally and professionally closer to Jung than any other man.

C. A. Meier was clearly one of the leading Jungians of his time and so recognized by Jung who, in 1948, handpicked him to be the first President of the C. G. Jung Institute in Zurich. Additionally, the following year, in 1949, upon Jung's retirement from the Professorship of an endowed Chair at the Swiss Federal Institute (ETH) in Zurich (a venerable institution specializing in scientific work and comparable to MIT in the United States), C. A. Meier was Jung's chosen successor to fill this position. A prolific writer and scholar, Meier was considered by many to be one of Jung' most brilliant disciples.

From 1933–1943, Meier served as General Secretary for the International Society for Medical Psychotherapy while Jung was President—a position Jung has been soundly criticized for accepting. By accepting the presidency at a time when Jewish practitioners were prohibited from practicing in Germany and stripped of membership in the German psychoanalytic society, Jung left himself open to the charge of collaborating with Nazi aims. From his perspective, Jung insisted he was helping his colleagues from within—a claim partly substantiated by the fact that he enabled his Jewish colleagues to enroll as individual members of the society despite being denied access to their home, German professional organization. Meier served Jung as chief editor of the society's journal, the *Zentralblatt*, which was published in Leipzig and where an extremely damaging editorial appeared in the December 1933 issue praising Nazi ideology.

The *Zentralblatt* was theoretically under Jung's (and, by extension, Meier's) control but Jung and Meier, throughout their lives, steadfastly denied advance knowledge of this piece and insisted it was inserted without their permission by Dr. Matthias Göring—who happened to be a cousin of the infamous Hermann Göring, confidant of Hitler and commander in chief of the Luftwaffe in the Third Reich. While the blame for this especially provocative editorial has generally been laid at Jung's feet, Meier, as seen in an excerpt from our interview, insisted that Jung was blameless. When asked to describe his relationship with Jung at the time as well as Jung's role in the production of the *Zentralblatt*, Meier responds:

> Well, the personal relationship, of course, consisted mostly of analytical sessions throughout the years, but then when . . . he was elected President of the International Society—he accepted on condition that I was going to be General Secretary of the International Society [and] simultaneously . . . the editor of the *Zentralblatt* and that kept us of course in constant contact throughout the years. So that is about what you ought to know.

And, when pressed about Jung's role in the editorial that appeared over his name, Meier's answer was:

> Well, that editorial, strangely enough, it appeared without either Jung or myself knowing about it. We had—I had—always received

> all of the galley proofs and the page proofs, etc. and carefully read them and corrected them, purified them, for anti-Semitic, etc. but this appeared without us having seen anything of it before, before it was in the *Zentralblatt*.

Though the journal, as mentioned before, was printed in Leipzig, Germany, C. A. Meier, in Zurich, was editor in chief and theoretically in charge of content. According to Meier (although there is disagreement among scholars on this—see Jay Sherry's article, "Jung, Anti-Semitism and the Weimar Years," for example), the insertion of this editorial was done without Jung's permission. In general, as Meier states, one should absolve Jung of responsibility for any articles that might have appeared in the *Zentralblatt* that might have been anti-Semitic in content:

> I would say that Jung, as I told you before, didn't really care for the *Zentralblatt* as a matter of fact. He left all the dirty work to me and so I would have had to do something but then I was in no position, only being the General Secretary. I mean I couldn't do a thing really and the most important thing of course was the survival of the *Zentralblatt*. I mean through that we still had some kind of a possibility to control what was going to be published. I had refused many anti-Semitic articles and manuscripts that were sent to me—I mean there were some anti-Semitic things, etc. which I simply did not accept. . . . But for the rest, Jung didn't, couldn't really be part of.

In this context, Meier states that one of the tasks Jung assigned him to was to "purify" the Nazi propaganda from anti-Semitic content. This is borne out by a letter Jung sent to Matthias Göring in November of 1937 stating that:

> Dr. Meier has drawn my attention to your short review of Rosenberg's book. For anyone who knows Jewish history and in particular Hasidism, Rosenberg's assertion that the Jews despise mysticism is a highly regrettable error. I would therefore suggest that we pass over this book in silence. I cannot allow my name to be associated with such lapses (Jung, *Letters*, volume 1, p. 238).

Moreover, although Jewish contributions were prohibited, Meier, while he did not remember the name of the contributor, pointed out in our interview, that without the knowledge of his German colleagues, he was able to insert an article by a Jew into the *Zentralblatt*. In an interesting footnote to history, it turns out that the author, in a 1937 piece in the *Zentralblatt*, was none other than Victor Frankl.

One cannot help but ask why Jung and Meier stayed connected to both the journal and the International Society at a time when the very existence of Jews was threatened by the Nazis. From the perspective of hindsight, history, and contemporary culture, it is clear they should have resigned. However, in order to present a full picture, there is much merit in what Meier, Hurwitz, and Jaffé all agree on: one has to understand the times. This is not to condone Meier and Jung but rather to help understand their mindset. It is apparent that they really believed they were helping Jewish colleagues, though the naiveté of this position ultimately became clear over time, as Meier acknowledges:

> I would say that with the word naiveté, you touched upon something very important. Jung was naive, as a matter of fact, particularly when he came to, shall we say, political things. He hated these collective things in general, so he even agreed to accept this post in order to be able to do something helpful which is very difficult . . . because if you know Jung, you would sign this statement that he always was looking for the healing aspect of any disturbing neurosis or psychosis or whatever it be, and he always tried to help the patient or cure the patient, etc. . . . and so, he accepted this German movement as a disease, as the collective disease which maybe even had a chance to do something good to the German nation. . . . But of course, he was rather naive as you said, correctly. But still he had a hope.

The naiveté of Jung quite possibly manifested itself both in his trust of and his confidence that he could handle Matthias Göring—a stance that apparently backfired. While Meier refers to Göring as basically a "decent fellow," Göring's allegiance to the Nazi hierarchy transcended any decency he might have had. Both Jung and Meier were of the opinion that they could manipulate Göring. For when asked if Jung hadn't anticipated the danger of Göring using him in some ways, Meier's opinion was: "I don't think there was any such danger. I mean, Göring was a relatively weak person whereas Jung was a bulldozer—he didn't have to fear anything."

In retrospect, it is clear that both Jung and Meier were naive; the user was used, as can be seen in the editorial that was inserted in the *Zentralblatt* advocating the racial superiority of Aryans. However, even allowing for the difficulties of the time, and accepting Jung's disclaimer that he never advocated cultural or racial superiority, only "differences," upon publication of an editorial he insisted he did not write, Jung should have resigned both the Presidency and the *Zentralblatt* journal. One cannot help but wonder if Jung, caught in his own shadow issue of feeling unappreciated by the psychoanalytical world, saw the presidency as an opportunity to correct this. In effect, one might say he was a victim of his own inflation that he could easily handle Göring and the Nazi machine that was, in effect, overseeing the psychoanalytical professional world. For, in the final analysis, Jung was used and his reputation indelibly tarnished for an ultimately ill-advised political foray in his acceptance of the presidency of the General Medical Society for Psychotherapy.

The interviews with Meier were the most difficult as well as the most meaningful ones for me personally. I had been in touch with Meier prior to the "official" interview but was not comfortable with what might emerge—for him as well as myself. Still, in the end, through my meetings with Meier, I came to understand Jung better. I was made all the more aware of, and remembered, Jung's dictum that "the trouble with the unconscious is that it is 'un-conscious.'" I came to understand that ascribing motivations to people, especially one as great as Jung, is complex, tricky, and not as simple a task as it may seem. Jung's various political activities in the 1930s were no doubt some combination of good will, the need for ego gratification, and political naiveté on a large plane. Combine this with his almost larger-than-life shadow and it is easy to understand why the charges that he was anti-Semitic have persisted.

Notwithstanding Jung's explanation that he was accepting the presidency for the purpose of helping from within, there is little doubt that advancing his own theories was an important factor for him. For, having broken with Freud some two decades earlier, Jung had been labeled anti-Semitic by Freud, relegated to the role of rebel and dismissed from the inner circle. By the 1930s, Jung found himself pushed from the position of "Crown Prince" (which he had been called by Freud himself prior to the break) to that of outsider in the burgeoning new field of psychoanalysis clearly controlled by Freud and his followers. Indeed, in another part of the interview, Meier acknowledges as much:

> Maybe that Jung [at this time of his life]. . . suffered from the impression that he was not sufficiently accepted—his ideas were not sufficiently accepted in the world—so he had a sort of, a kind of minority complex in that respect and when the Germans started to condemn Freud he had a hope that maybe now, Jungian ideas may have a better chance. . . . no question but that was

very sick. But it all comes from this idea that maybe something could become of it.

In short, Meier validated my own thoughts that, notwithstanding the fact that consciously, Jung believed he was helping his Jewish colleagues, the shadow of power and recognition in the field were in all likelihood motivations that had to be taken into account. His admission, difficult to extract, left no doubt:"Yes, correct, I mean as much as it was devaluating Freud, they might value Jung so much more, you know? That came into it no doubt." And when pushed to describe Jung's Shadow, he readily agreed that Jung's own description, "the greater the light, the greater the shadow," certainly applied to Jung himself: "Well he did . . . [have]. . . a gigantic one since he was a giant."

Among the many honored positions Meier held was the presidency of the Psychological Club of Zurich, a club formed by Jung's analysands and followers, which met monthly and was said to have been inspired by Jung's feeling that many of those who were attracted to his psychology needed to socialize with others as well as continually introvert. The Club met regularly, and aside from the social aspect of the meetings, lectures were presented by the members as well as at times by Jung himself.

During the period of the 1930s and 1940s, an unofficial policy was adopted by the Executive Committee of the Club limiting Jewish members to 10% of the club, although up to 25% could be guests (i.e., attend lectures) at any one time. In 1944, this policy was actually put into writing with Meier as one of three signatories to the agreement, the others being Toni Wolff and Linda Fierz David (whose grandfather is said to have been Jewish).

When I first came across this document, one I eventually made public to the chagrin of many, I found it troubling on several counts. As a Jew, I was deeply offended. As a Jungian, I was disappointed that in a psychological club ostensibly dedicated to openness and exploration of the psyche as its goal, Jews, surely with Jung's knowledge, were singled out and relegated to the role of outsiders. But, perhaps, most importantly, as an individual who had been in analysis with Meier for a considerable period, and had a warm feeling for him personally, I was disturbed.

I had always accepted at face value Meier's and Rivkah Kluger's defense of Jung's attitude toward Jews. Both had assured me that they personally knew Jung and that he could never have been anti-Semitic. Now, faced with the fact that I personally knew Meier and prior to this never would have believed it possible for him to be a party to restricting Jews, I found myself doubting and angry at myself for being naive and confused.

I knew, loved, and wholeheartedly respected Rivkah Kluger. Rivkah was a brilliant scholar, and an outstanding and internationally-recognized Jungian analyst known especially for her expertise in Near Eastern religions in general but Judaism in particular. There were few people who had played a more important role in my life and I had no reason in the world to doubt her statement. Clearly, something was amiss, for Rivkah (herself Swiss, but in all aspects committed to and proud of her Jewish heritage) knew Meier and Jung personally and professionally for many years. Additionally, Rivkah had pictures of both Jung and Toni Wolff prominently displayed in her consulting room (the room where I had been in analysis each week) and she had encouraged me to work with Meier in Zurich.

Through numerous, highly personal conversations with Meier, as well as continued meetings with him over the years until he died at the age of 90, I was able to grasp the fact that part of what was transpiring was a broader, perhaps unconscious cultural bias—one that both he and Jung shared in common. Knowing Meier personally, I believe, helped me understand Jung's attitudes better as well.

Still, it is apparent that Jung underwent a profound personal change in his understanding of "the Jewish Question." The Holocaust came as a harsh reminder to him of the dangers of his own as well as the collective's shadow. Indeed, insofar as National Socialism of the 1930s was concerned, it was a movement Jung underestimated, took too lightly and naively believed would turn positive because of his own positive attitude toward the unconscious. Nevertheless, he did himself and the Jungian community at large a disservice by not speaking or writing about the injustice done to Jews more publicly. Private statements, even to Jewish leaders, that he "slipped up," were not enough, and criticism of him in this context is deserved.

What always impressed me about Meier was his zest for life and sense of humor. Indeed, at the very start of our first interview, knowing I had come across this document and was going to confront him about this in the presence of three other Jungian analysts, the following exchange took place:

"Dr. Meier, I wanted just to begin by thanking you for being willing to. . . ."

"Not at all. I hope it is going to be a pleasure."

Or, when I asked him about the Jewish quota, he openly offered the fact that it had informally been in effect for many years, indeed, from the early 1930s onward and well before the document was dated. When I asked why then had it been put to paper in 1944, he asked to see the document as he had no recollection of it. When I showed it to him, his response, almost to himself was, "Oh, we put it in writing? How Swiss of us!"

Meier was himself, as he always was. Apologies were not part and parcel of his makeup, even when he knew he was wrong. I came to understand that, as many had told me, he and Jung had much in common, physically as well as emotionally, from their earthy sense of humor to their physical size, from their political naiveté to an incredible stubbornness they shared. Indeed, similarly to Meier, from all the interviews, it emerged that Jung was too proud to publicly admit any mistakes he had made in judgment, timing or opinion though privately he was clearly able to acknowledge mistakes, changes in his point of view, and shortcomings of his own.

In Meier's case, as well, despite my relentless attempts to get him to admit the Jewish quota was wrong, he insisted on his position that I work harder on understanding the times. He simply would not openly admit it was a mistake though, privately, he did confide in me that in retrospect it could be seen as an "ugly thing."

Looking back, I am realistic enough to understand that during this same period Jewish quotas existed in leading universities of the United States, including Harvard, Yale, and many others. Somehow, in retrospect, that did not bother me as much as finding out it existed in the Psychological Club fostered by Jung. Perhaps it is because in the U.S. these quotas had been made public and condemned by the institutions themselves while the Club was in denial. Indeed, the reactions of most Club members I spoke to was to either justify the quota as a means of protecting Jung when the Nazis invaded Switzerland or, to say it was a policy aimed at foreigners in general as they wanted to keep the Swiss nature of the Club.

Neither reason holds water, so to speak, nor does any attempt to deny Jung's personal knowledge and acceptance of this quota. Throughout the 1930s and the early 1940s, when the danger of a German invasion was real and possibly immanent, the policy was an unwritten one and implemented informally and unofficially. By mid-1944, when it was finally put to paper, the greatest danger had passed.

The second reason offered, that it was meant to keep the Swiss nature of the Club rings a bit hollow and would be better understood, even accepted gladly, had the limitation been on "foreigners" or "non Swiss" rather than specifically singling out Jews. One need not go far to understand that to many, even in the recent past, the term foreigners is synonymous with Jews, i.e., the real outsiders in the community.

Finally, as all those interviewed agreed, Jung himself certainly knew about it, indeed insisted the Club waive restrictions when it came to including such members as Rivkah Kluger, Aniela Jaffé and Siegmund Hurwitz, strongly offering to guarantee they would be accepted no matter the percentages then in force. Indeed, when asked directly whether or not Jung knew about the quotas in effect, Meier (one of the signatories) responded without equivocation: "Of course."

For me, this was both a collective wound as well as a personal hurt because of Meier's involvement. Why Toni Wolff, who is pretty much accepted as being the prime mover behind the quota, felt the way she did, I will leave to others who might know better. Why Linda Fierz David, whose grandfather was Jewish, would be a party to this might well have to do with a personal denial of her own roots and history. In any case, to my mind, it is a sad commentary on her own life and analysis.

In Meier's case, and by extension Jung's own issues with the German psychotherapy society as well as the Club, I am satisfied that conscious anti-Semitism is not an accusation that rings true. Both Jung and Meier, for their own complex unconscious reasons, were participants and actors in events that can understandably be viewed by others as anti-Semitic. Yet, when the full picture is examined, I believe neither Jung nor Meier were anti-Semitic on a conscious level.

Both Jung and Meier struggled to understand their own and their collective's shadow. A long list of Jewish analysands and students who knew both Jung and Meier intimately attest to their compassion and care for them on an individual level, though many of us are disappointed that Jung especially could not publicly own some of this shadow material—material that, for most Jewish individuals, is painful and sensitive. In many ways, most of us are more upset at his silence after the fact than his insensitivity at the time. To err is human; not to correct it when you know it was wrong makes two mistakes.

Erich Neumann, who loved Jung dearly, was very disappointed that Jung remained publicly silent while Jews were being murdered throughout Europe. Try as he might, Neumann could not get Jung to speak out. Meier's first response to this was that Jung

> …hated international politics or anything of the sort. I would say [however] he could indeed have said something but he thought it was of no use anyhow. These things took place anyhow and nobody could interfere at all. Nobody could. Not even somebody

> like Jung. Nobody could. It was a mass movement that there were no brakes to.

However, when pressed further, Meier readily agreed that the silence itself was wrong:

> Silence can be a crime. A sin. I agree but that was not his [Jung's] cup of tea, this sort of thing [but]. . . I would say that it was simply impossible to speak of anti-Semitism with [regarding] Jung. Impossible, in spite of things he may have said that sounded like it, but when it comes to the real importance of Jewish psychology and Jewish history and so forth, I know of nobody who took it that seriously as Jung did.

Siegmund Hurwitz

The differences between C. A. Meier and Siegmund Hurwitz could not have been greater. In almost all ways, the two were polar opposites. Physically, Meier was tall and robust in stature, while Dr. Hurwitz was short and slight. Their personality differences were just as great. While Meier was an imposing individual who took charge, smoked cigars throughout sessions and generally dominated the scene, Siegmund Hurwitz was a quiet, gentle, and humble individual who took every question seriously. In contrast to Meier's interviews, which proved to be difficult and challenging, we all found Dr. Hurwitz easy to be with, delightful to speak to and one of the sweetest individuals any of us had met in the Jungian professional world.

Dr. Siegmund Hurwitz ("Siggy," as he was called by those close to him) was a deeply committed Jew, fluent in Hebrew and other ancient languages and familiar with Jewish tradition, history, and culture. Dr. Hurwitz was close to Jung—personally and professionally—and received his analytical training from Jung, Toni Wolff, and Marie-Louise von Franz. He was considered an outstanding scholar of Jewish mysticism, and a highly respected author of a number of articles and books, including *Lilith—The First Eve: Historical and Psychological Aspects of the Dark Feminine*. Indeed, it was common knowledge that Jung often consulted with Dr. Hurwitz when he needed help understanding ancient texts. He was also Jung's dentist, and he related to us that he and Jung had a barter arrangement where Dr. Hurwitz provided the dentistry and Jung the analysis: "I myself had not to pay because Jung was also my patient so I think I didn't send him a bill for treatment."

Among his many other accomplishments, Dr. Hurwitz should be remembered for being the person most responsible for having the Analytical Club's Jewish quota abolished. As Dr. Hurwitz recalls it:

> In 1945, I became a guest member in the Club without any difficulties. Five years later, Jung and Toni Wolff encouraged me to become an "ordinary" member. Until then, I had never heard anything about restrictions or limitations for Jewish members so I sent my request to Toni Wolff. . . . Several days later, I heard a rumor in the Club that there were some limitations and restrictions against Jewish members. I immediately wrote to Toni Wolff and withdrew my request and told her that I don't like to be a member in a society with restrictions against Jews. Then I had a long discussion with Jung about this matter. Jung defended his view—a point of view that said it is not a discrimination, but more a differentiation, but I couldn't accept his point of view. Three or four weeks later, these restrictions were canceled so I could enter as an "ordinary member."

It is important to remember that this quota was a secret one, and while a sizable number of Club members undoubtedly knew about the policy, only the Executive Committee was privy to the document itself. Indeed, neither Siegmund Hurwitz nor Aniela Jaffé had ever seen it in writing, and both were shaken up when we showed it to them. The reality of what had been expressed as a vague policy hit home and stung when seen on paper. It was painful for all of us who had to witness that first moment of recognition.

Ironically, while he would not join the Club with such restrictions, far from being angry at Jung, Hurwitz at first defended the policy as one meant to protect Jung. He pointed out that 1944, the year the document was dated, "was also a very dangerous time here. . . . we all were very upset that [the] invasion of the Nazis could come here." Nevertheless, there could be no such explanation for why the policy had been in effect throughout the 1930s, well before the war had begun. Ultimately, Dr. Hurwitz had to acknowledge that an imminent Nazi invasion was not the primary motivation for the quota. Rather, as Jung had implied when first confronted, the fear was not from the Germans but the Jews. For, apparently, rumor had it that the Jungian Analytical Club in London had split due to an influx of Jewish Jungians who had come to England to escape the Nazis. Dr. Hurwitz recollected:

> Yes, I have only once discussed this problem with Jung, and he told me that this problem was also in the London Club of Analytical Psychology and there came many Jewish analysts and the Club was split then. I don't remember exactly the fact. I was also not so much interested in that but Jung was afraid that many [Jewish] analysts come here and dominate the Club. . . . If too much [*sic*] were to come, they would dominate the Club and Jung was afraid the Club would change—they would change the Club in their own way, like in London. The problem was acute in London, so told me Jung. When a lot of Jewish analysts came to London and applied for membership in the London Club. . . it became an explosive situation and the Club was split and he was afraid that the same would happen here.

Speaking of the London Club, throughout the years there has been gossip and rumors accusing Jung of overt anti-Semitism. Some of the accusations display a viciousness that even those who question Jung find offensive. He has been accused of running cults, of being a Nazi himself, of meeting with Hitler and more. One of the more outlandish (yet often given credibility) statements Jung is alleged to have made was to no less a person than noted English psychiatrist Michael Fordham. According to this source, Jung is quoted as having said to Dr. Fordham that "Jews are different. They should even wear different clothes." When this supposed comment of Jung's was related to Dr. Hurwitz, his reply was, "I have heard of that. He [supposedly]. . . said that to Dr. Fordham. But I can't imagine that Jung was so stupid to say such things. I don't believe that at all."

What impressed me about Siegmund Hurwitz was his acceptance and lack of anger about this whole question. If anything, what quickly became evident in the discussions with him was the hurt and sadness at this situation. His position came not from the lack of courage at standing up for his Jewishness as can be seen in his refusal to join such a Club, but, rather, from a deeper level of understanding at how the unconscious works. When he was asked the question as to why he wasn't more upset at this policy, since it was not a social club but rather a "Psychological Club," Dr. Hurwitz responded, "You are quite right, but psychologists are people like others. They have their own shadow and very often, a very dark shadow and we must live with that. We must accept that. Even Jung had his shadow."

Interestingly enough, it appears that converted Jews were readily accepted without question and, notwithstanding rumors to the contrary, did not count against the Jewish quota. In fact, Dr. Hurwitz told us, "baptized Jews" were accepted immediately and one even became President of the Club. Ironically, however, speaking of shadows, one of the three signatories to the document limiting Jewish membership, and someone who I had been told was an active proponent of limiting Jewish membership, was Linda Fierz David, whose grandfather, Hurwitz told us, was Jewish. "Yes. Yes," Dr. Hurwitz said, "The grandfather . . . came from Galicia. His name was Morritz Izchak Grossman and the grandson . . . I met him last year for the first time [and] he told me it was a wonderful idea that in his family is . . . Jewish blood."

The question of Jung's shadow and its relation to the accusations of anti-Semitism was one of the most significant topics of our discussions. Hurwitz, when asked if he and Jung ever discussed the accusations of anti-Semitism that were being directed toward him, replied, "Yes. We discussed these problems but only later, not in the beginning of the analysis." Hurwitz, clearly knowing Jung and experiencing no hint of anti-Semitism at all from Jung personally, was more concerned with the timing and content of some of Jung's pronouncements.

Jung's lack of sensitivity to time and place, for example, can be seen in his 1934 article on "The State of Psychotherapy Today," which appeared in the *Zentralblatt*. In it, Jung discussed the differences between what he called the Jewish psychology and the Germanic psychology. Much of this article offended his Jewish followers, many of whom have said they spoke to Jung about this highly controversial piece. Hurwitz, too, was taken aback by some of Jung's comments and remarked that he was not alone in this feeling.

> I discussed these problems also with my friends, the late Erich Neumann, the late Gerhard Adler, James Kirsch . . . [and others] and we all discussed the article Jung sent to the *Zentralblatt*. . . . Jung published there an article and we all had long discussions. . . . I spoke with Jung personally about this problem so no letters are between us. . . . It was [about] the problem of the German-Jewish differences. . . . but when Jung wrote this article, I found it was a great fault of Jung at that time because in 1934, the Jewish people were in great danger—a dangerous situation, and that was the fault of Jung to discuss it at that time.

Nevertheless, timing was not Hurwitz's only criticism; Jung's content left much to be desired. However, Hurwitz refused to accept a linkage between Jung's views and any possible anti-Semitism. Rather, he felt Jung had a right or even obligation to examine similarities and/or differences in different collectives, but that Jung was just poorly informed about Judaism at that stage of his life.

> He changed, naturally, his point of view. He did not know much about Judaism but in the later years he was very much interested in Kabbalah and he bought books [on the topic]. . . . I brought him together with [Gershom] Scholem and I helped him with Kabbalistic texts.

Dr. Hurwitz, in his discussions with us, related in detail his conversation with Jung about the 1934 article. Jung's own comment as to the significance of his 1934 views on German and Jewish psychology are fascinating; as Hurwitz related it:

> Yes, I discussed that problem [the 1934 article] only in 1950. Then I read for the first time his article and we had a long discussion. I said, Jung, I did not agree. And he said to me, "You know, today, I would not write this article in this way. I have written in my long life many books, and I have also written nonsense, and that was nonsense." And, unfortunately, that was not printed as a footnote in the collected works, what he said to me.

In the final analysis, Dr. Hurwitz was adamant in his defense of Jung despite the controversial public statements and articles of Jung during the 1930s. In this opinion, Hurwitz was joined by every leading Jewish Jungian analyst that I am aware of. Many were disappointed in what they saw as insensitivity to the plight of Jews collectively and had hoped he would speak out. They understood that, especially during the early years prior to the War, Jung was both caught in some of his own shadow wars with Freud as well as limited in his knowledge of the Jewish religion and Judaism as a culture.

Jung's leading Jewish students clearly believed it was impossible to consider Jung anti-Semitic on a personal level given all he had done for them personally as well as for others they had heard of. As Siegmund Hurwitz relates it, "He had helped many [Jewish] persons I know—analysts—and they hadn't to pay any charges. They had no money. For instance, Aneila Jaffé."

Aniela Jaffé

Aniela Jaffé herself confirms Siegmund Hurwitz's report that throughout his life Jung personally helped her and other Jewish colleagues. Aniela not only paid Jung no fee for her analysis, but shared with us the following story that took place when she was ill and in need of a holiday but could not afford to take one.

> He gave me a large sum of money so that I could go to the mountains. . . . And then [he said] . . . I give you money and please go to the best, the best hotel in a wonderful Swiss place . . . and I spent three weeks and it was a great help to me, to my health.

Aniela Jaffé, unlike most all of those close to Jung in Zurich, was not Swiss by birth. Born and raised as a Jew in Berlin, Germany, she studied psychology at the University of Hamburg and escaped to Switzerland shortly before World War II began. In Zurich, she began working with (and later for) Jung and ultimately became his most important collaborator through her editing of his *Collected Letters* and autobiographical book *Memories, Dreams, Reflections.* Author of *The Myth of Meaning* and highly respected Jungian analyst in her own right, her loyalty to Jung was legendary.

Among the articles and books Aniela Jaffé wrote was "C. G. Jung and National Socialism," published in *From the Life and Work of C. G. Jung* in 1970. Aniela, as she was known to most all who knew her, wrote this piece as an attempt to answer the constant accusations surrounding Jung's alleged anti-Semitism. Published less than a decade after Jung's death in 1961, it was considered the definitive response to the charges that Jung was a Nazi, and/or anti-Semitic. However, with the passage of time, and the uncovering of new information, including, but not limited to, the Club's Jewish quota, Aniela's work was not enough to calm the troubled waters surrounding Jung's reputation. The "Lingering Shadows" conference, and especially the interview we conducted with her, proved painful to witness as she had a difficult time comprehending why this topic kept resurfacing.

Practically blind and not physically well at the time, she deserves special commendation for subjecting herself to questions that alternately angered and saddened her. Indeed, it was her devotion to Jung and the understanding that we were not there to accuse Jung but rather to gather information that allowed her to participate. We are all grateful for her trust in us. My hope is that, while she may not have been happy with everything I have written as a result of the interviews and subsequent conferences and book, she would accept the fact that Jung himself would have approved, his cause being consciousness.

Aniela first met Jung in 1936 and began analyzing with him regularly in 1938 when, as she relates it, he realized how important her work with him was. As she was a refugee from Germany with no money and little income, "he [Jung] didn't ask for any fee," she told us. One of the topics that came up early in her analysis was the difficult question of Jung's attitude toward the collective, i.e. German vs. Jewish archetypes.

> First he spoke about the difference between Jewish people and German people but that was not at all critical because you see every Jew knows there is a difference and then the end of the session was very interesting. He took my hand . . . and put his hand side by side and he showed me the similarity between our hands so there is a difference but there is also, from a human standpoint, a similarity. . . .

In fact, to support this position, Aniela quoted from Freud's famous letter to Karl Abraham telling him, "don't forget that really it is easier for you to follow my thoughts than for Jung, since . . . the racial relationship brings you close to my constitution, whereas he, being a Christian and the son of a pastor, can only find his way to me against great inner resistances." Aniela accepted as fact that Jung wrote about these cultural and archetypal differences without malice and in the name of psychological explorations. Despite being openly identified with Judaism herself, even events that discriminated against her, (for example, not being admitted to the Psychological Club because she was Jewish, and being told so by no less an authority than Toni Wolff) did not turn her against Jung or Jungians. In this regard, it is important to note that during the interview she relates how she and other Jewish individuals were at one time kept from becoming members of the Club but that Jung interceded on their behalf:

> [We] had difficulties to become members of the Club and I didn't care very much. I followed the lectures, so I am not a member? But one day it was in town . . . and a Swiss lady wanted to become a member and Jung said, I heard it, "If you accept this lady," and I don't say her name, "and don't accept Rivkah [Kluger] and Aniela, I'll resign from the Club forever. Straight out. . . . I'll resign from the Club." That was Jung. I'm sure he didn't know about this letter.

The letter Aniela was referring to was the secret document limiting Jewish membership in the Club—a paper she had seen for the first time two days earlier. Notwithstanding the fact that Toni Wolff and Meier had signed this document, since Jung's name was not on it, she refused to believe that Jung knew about it. Aneila was a very special person but it is obvious that the love she had for Jung caused her to be in a state of denial when it came to Jung's knowledge and acceptance of this policy. For, as we have seen, not only did everyone we interviewed readily and openly agree that Jung was aware of this policy, but Aniela herself heard Jung discuss and acknowledge it in the context of her own admission to the Club.

It is safe to say that Jung had a special relationship with her—a protective father figure is what comes to mind. Because of this, it seems to me, Aniela was able to compartmentalize this issue and dismiss the conflict from consciousness. This is not to say Jung was anti-Semitic. Rather, for Aniela, it was clear that other people's questioning of some of Jung's actions and writings was personally very upsetting. Her reaction and comments during the interview with her attested to this. For example, her response to a question that some of Jung's attitudes toward Jews might have been colored by his relationship with Freud brought the following response:

> Now, I tell you something. May I interrupt you? I cannot hear these things which you ask. . . [there] are things that are much more interesting. And let me tell you something about him that I find—he was very friendly to me. He wrote his biography [with me]. He had a Jewish student, me. He could have chosen somebody else but the most interesting thing for me is how he stood for Jewish religion. This is something, you see? This is much more important than Jung and Freud. You see? I cannot hear it any more. Always the same questions, and always the same nonsense.

Or, further on in the interview, when asked whether or not other Jewish analysts such as James Kirsch or Gerhard Adler, who were also close to Jung, had ever discussed the issue of Jung and anti-Semitism with her (as they had with Dr. Hurwitz, for example), she responded, "No. There was no doubt he was not. No, Jung was not anti-Semitic and I must emphasize it and . . . [ask] you not to repeat this question. It's nonsense . . . he made some errors but otherwise he was not, never did we discuss it. No doubt. No doubt."

Nevertheless, Aniela Jaffé was wise enough to know that not all of Jung's actions or pronouncements were to be defended. She, possibly even more than most others, due to her close working relationship with him, saw his fallibility. As she pointed out:

> I told you, he made mistakes. He said even that the difference between [Jewish] people and German people should not be wiped or hidden. It was good for the science [i.e. to explore this]. It was nonsense but . . . the difference for him was not less worth but difference. . . . But if you read my article [i.e. "Jung and National Socialism"] I wrote many quotations on a number of quotations where Jung spoke nonsense but he wasn't anti-Semitic. I said in my article at this moment, a dangerous moment, he should have been silent about this problem and not write about it.

Conclusion

Notwithstanding Aniela Jaffé's emotional reactions, there is no doubt among any of those who knew him intimately concerning Jung and the issue of anti-Semitism. They had no question in their minds. For those close to Jung, including his Jewish followers, Jung was not personally anti-Semitic. In this respect, C. A. Meier, Siegmund Hurwitz and Aniela Jaffé all were in agreement.

Still, as Meier predicted, the issue will not disappear; questions will continually be asked as material in the body of Jung's work (especially his early writings) practically jumps out and invites such a question. When one reads of "racial differences," or of "less developed cultures," and the like, one cannot help but wonder if its author had an agenda. When one hears of Jung assuming the presidency of an international society that allows all its German Jewish members to be excluded from its local society and editorials that appear under his name advocating Aryan superiority, the question of anti-Semitism and Jung begs to be asked.

Nevertheless, as I have come to realize, Jung's life and work must be examined in its totality rather than taken in only one context. By all accounts, the younger Jung of the 1930s was not the same person as the older, wiser Jung, more in touch with his own shadow and sobered by the Holocaust and its horrors. It seems to me, moreover, that in this regard, C. A. Meier understood the issue best, for it was an issue that he himself faced in light of the Analytical Psychology Club's Jewish quota.

Nothing summarizes Jung's shadow issue—and, in a sense, Meier's position, as well—more than the following analysis by Meier (who was not Jewish):

> Well, I have known very few people who are capable of accepting our shadows. Most know how to protect it . . . and this may well have been also in the case of Jung. The shadow problem is a fact—it is a simple fact. You have to cope with it somehow or another, whether we are Jewish or Gentile, makes no difference whatsoever, when it comes to this anti-Semitic shadow which exists among us all over the world. . . .
>
> We have to come to terms with it, particularly when we deal with our unconscious in an analytic way and to some extent we are certainly capable of doing so when it comes to the personal realm only, whereas the collective realm is ever so much more powerful—more shall we say kind of innate. It cannot very well be done away with, so there remains some proportional shadow of anti-Semitic shadow within every one of the Gentiles as well and we have to simply admit it—this was the case with Jung as well.
>
> Whereas when it came to the personal shadow and that sort of thing, then I know of nobody who has so deeply and seriously dealt with the Jewish psychology as Jung did."

What Meier is courageously pointing out is that (when it came to Jews) Jung's shadow was connected to the collective, archetypal level of Christian Switzerland, where anti-Semitism was a part of the culture, as well as Jung's own personal experience as the son of a pastor. While not condoning or in any way agreeing with what Jung said or did during his early career, one must understand that Jung was totally focused on approaching the world from the perspective of the psyche—personal and collective. And, as it concerned Jung and, by extension, Meier, in the issue of the Club's Jewish quota, being raised a Christian (we must also remember that Jung's father was a minister) meant that, as Meier pointed out, one of the shadow aspects of his collective was anti-Semitism—conscious and unconscious.

Regarding this shadow, Meier was honest and straightforward:

> In my own case, I have learned it . . . and [am still learning it] . . . by talking and discussing with Jewish friends. I'm grateful for that and for [learning about] . . . any possible anti-Semitism I might have suffered from without knowing. I knew nothing about Jews until very late. The place in which I grew up, Schaffhausen, had only three Jews. . . . Nobody knew what Jewish meant as a matter of fact.

When asked if the same thing held true for Jung as well, Meier responded:

> Oh, Absolutely. No question about that. No doubt. He [Jung] was forced to deal with Judaism by his patients only; for no other reason, and he did so and he dealt with it very, very, seriously, indeed. More so than anybody else I know.

In the end, while it is not a pretty picture, it seems to me that Jung was not *consciously* anti-Semitic. Nevertheless, one must sift through all the material to realize this and understand that Jung himself did undergo change in the course of his life. Jung, in the earlier period of his life, was not the same Jung as later. Indeed, it seems clear he would have been the first to acknowledge this. Unfortunately, for Jung's reputation (and Jungians today) due to a combination of his own pride, defensiveness relating to his own anger vis-à-vis Freud and his Jewish followers, opportunism, and (in Jung's own words) "Swiss woodenheadedness," Jung refused to publicly acknowledge this change. In this context, however, in private, it appears that Jung did come to understand his own shadow issues surrounding the so-called "Jewish question." Having spoken to many of his students, analysands, and others in Jung's inner circle, it seems to me that any anti-Semitism that can be attributed to Jung (and in his early career there clearly exists enough of his writings to make such a case) should be attributed to a cultural, unconscious prejudice on his part and not what one would define as consciously anti-Semitic.

Finally, in this regard, it is important to remember that, as Hurwitz and Jaffé have attested, Jung himself disowned some of his earlier writings, especially (but not limited to) the controversial 1934 piece entitled "The State of Psychotherapy Today." Jung's own admission to a number of his closer students and disciples that some of his earlier views were nonsense represents an acknowledgment that deserves admiration, as does Jung's psychology and ideas and (especially) Jung, himself—the man with a golden mind and feet of clay.

Appendix A
Significant Words and Events
Revised and Updated by Jay Sherry

Originally compiled by Michael Vannoy Adams & Jay Sherry

1875

Jung is born on July 26, 1875.

1897

"In 1877 the noble Zöllner published his scientific tracts in Germany, and fought for the spiritualist cause in a series of seven volumes. But his was "a voice crying in the wilderness." Mortally wounded in his struggle against the Judaization of science and society, this high-minded man died in 1882, broken in body and spirit. To be sure, his friends, the renowned physicist Wilhelm Weber, the philosopher Fechner, the mathematician Schubner, and Ulrici, continued to promote Zöllner's cause, while the stubborn Wundt, the slippery Carl Ludwig, and the spiteful DuBois-Reymond defamed this cause throughout a Germany in moral decline. All in vain—the Berlin Jew came out on top. The little group of the faithful melted away" (C. G. Jung, "Some Thoughts on Psychology," in *The Zofingia Lectures* Bollingen Series XX:A [Princeton: Princeton University Press, 1983], p. 35).

1906

Jung initiates a correspondence with Freud by sending him a copy of *Diagnostic Association Studies.*

1907

Freud and Jung meet for the first time when Jung visits Vienna.

1908

Freud to Abraham, May 3, 1908:

"Please be tolerant and do not forget that it is really easier for you than it is for Jung to follow my ideas, for in the first place you are completely independent, and then you are closer to my intellectual constitution because of racial kinship, while he as a Christian and a pastor's son finds his way to me only against great inner resistances. His association with us is the more valuable for that. I nearly said that it was only by his appearance on the scene that psychoanalysis escaped the danger of becoming a Jewish national affair."

Abraham to Freud, May 11, 1908:

"I freely admit that I find it easier to go along with you rather than with Jung. I, too, have always felt this intellectual kinship. After all, our Talmudic way of thinking cannot disappear just like that." (Gerhard Adler quotes Jung as saying: "The Talmudists go to Freud, the Cabbalists come to me." "Analytical Psychology and the Principle of Complementarity," in Joseph B. Wheelwright, ed., *The Analytic Process*, p. 114.)

Freud to Abraham, July 20, 1908:

"On the whole it is easier for us Jews, as we lack the mystical element." (See also David Bakan, *Sigmund Freud and the Jewish Mystical Tradition.*)

Freud to Abraham, July 13, 1908:

"May I say that it is consanguineous Jewish traits that attract me to you? We understand each other....

". . . I nurse a suspicion that the suppressed anti-Semitism of the Swiss that spares me is deflected in reinforced form upon you. But I think that we, as Jews, if we wish to join in, must develop a bit of masochism, be ready to suffer some wrong. Otherwise there is no hitting it off. Rest assured that, if my name were Oberhuber, in spite of everything my innovations would have met with far less resistance."

Freud to Abraham, December 26, 1908:

"Our Aryan comrades are really completely indispensable to us, otherwise psychoanalysis would succumb to anti-Semitism."

1909

Freud and Jung travel to the United States to deliver lectures at Clark University and to receive honorary doctorates.

1910

The Second International Psychoanalytic Congress is held in Nuremberg on March 30–31. Freud proposes Jung as president of the International Psychoanalytic Association. Viennese analysts hold a protest meeting, and Freud addresses the group. In *Sigmund Freud: His Personality, His Teaching, and His School* (New York: Dodd, Mead, 1914), Fritz Wittels quotes Freud as follows: " 'Most of you are Jews, and therefore you are incompetent to win friends for the new teaching. Jews must be content with the modest role of preparing the ground. It is absolutely essential that I should form ties in the world of general science. I am getting on in years, and am weary of being perpetually attacked. We are all in danger.' Seizing his coat by the lapels, he said, 'They won't even leave me a coat to my back. The Swiss will save us—will save me, and all of you as well'" (p. 140). Jung is elected president.

Freud to Ferenczi, April 24, 1910:

Commenting on an assertion that the emphasis on sexuality in psychoanalytic theory merely reflects the sensuality of Vienna, Freud says: "There one hears just the argument I tried to avoid by making Zurich the center. Viennese sensuality is not to be found anywhere else! Between the lines you can read further that we Viennese are not only swine but also Jews. But that does not appear in print."

1912

Jung delivers lectures at Fordham University and publishes *Transformations and Symbols of the Libido* (now *Symbols of Transformation*). These mark his intellectual divergence from Freud.

"Let us keep in mind that Christ's teaching separates man from his family without consideration, and in the talk with Nicodemus we saw the specific endeavor of Christ to procure activation of the incest libido. Both tendencies serve the same goal—the liberation of man; the Jew from his extraordinary fixation to the family, which does not imply higher development, but greater weakness and more uncontrolled incestuous feeling, produced the compensation of the compulsory ceremonial of the cult and the religious fear of the incomprehensible Jehovah." (C. G. Jung, *The Psychology of the Unconscious*, English translation of *Transformation and Symbols of the Libido* by Beatrice M. Hinkle [New York: Dodd, Mead & Co., 1946], p. 454).

Freud forms the Committee, with Ferenczi, Abraham, Jones, Sachs, and Rank as members. In *The Life and Work of Sigmund Freud*, Jones says: "I became, of course, aware, somewhat to my astonishment, of how extraordinarily suspicious Jews could be of the faintest sign of anti-Semitism and of how many remarks or actions could be interpreted in that sense. The members most sensitive were Ferenczi and Sachs; Abraham and Rank were less so. Freud himself was pretty sensitive in this respect" (2: 163). Jones also says: "A Gentile would have said that Freud had few overt Jewish characteristics, a fondness for relating Jewish jokes and anecdotes being perhaps the most prominent one. But he felt himself to be Jewish to the core, and it evidently meant a great deal to him. He had the common Jewish sensitiveness to the slightest hint of anti-Semitism and he made very few friends who were not Jews. He objected strongly to the idea of their being unpopular or in any way inferior, and had evidently suffered much from school days onward, and especially at the University, from the anti-Semitism that pervaded Vienna. It put an end forever to the phase of German nationalistic enthusiasm through which he passed in early years" (1: 22). (See also Jones, "The Psychology of the Jewish Question," *Miscellaneous Essays* I: 284-300).

Freud to Ferenczi, July 28, 1912

Freud acknowledges that he has failed to unite "Jews and goyim in the service of psychoanalysis." He says: "They separate themselves like oil and water."

Freud to Rank, August 18, 1912:

Freud says that he had wanted to accomplish the "integration of Jews and anti-Semites on the soil of psychoanalysis."

1913

Freud proposes to Jung that they end personal relations, and Jung agrees. They maintain professional relations until 1914.

Freud to Abraham, May 13, 1913:

Freud says that the publication of *Totem and Taboo* "will serve to cut us off cleanly from all Aryan religiousness."

In *The Life and Work of Sigmund Freud*, Jones says: "Maeder wrote to Ferenczi that the scientific differences between the Viennese and the Swiss resulted from the former being Jews and the latter 'Aryans.' Freud advised Ferenczi to answer on the following lines [Freud to Ferenczi, June 8, 1913]. 'Certainly there are great differences between the Jewish and the Aryan spirit [*Geist*]. We can observe that every day. Hence there would assuredly be here and there differences in outlook on life and art. But there should not be such a thing as Aryan or Jewish science. Results in science must be identical, though the presentation of them may vary. If these differences mirror themselves in the apprehension of objective relationships in science there must be something wrong' " (2: 149).

1914

Jung resigns as president of the International Psychoanalytic Association. He and Freud end professional relations.

Freud publishes *On the History of the Psychoanalytic Movement* and says of Jung that "he seemed ready to enter into a friendly relationship with me and for my sake to give up certain racial prejudices which he had previously permitted himself" (*Standard Edition* 114: 43).

1918

Jung publishes "The Role of the Unconscious," in which he distinguishes between Jewish and Germanic (or "Aryan") psychology (*CW* 10: 3-28):

"Christianity split the Germanic barbarian into an upper and a lower half, and enabled him, by repressing the dark side, to domesticate the brighter half and fit it for civilization. But the lower, darker half still awaits redemption and a second spell of domestication. Until then, it will remain associated with the vestiges of the prehistoric age, with the collective unconscious, which is subject to a peculiar and ever-increasing activation. As the Christian view of the world loses its authority, the more menacingly will the 'blond beast' be heard prowling about in its underground prison, ready at any moment to burst out with devastating consequences. When this happens in the individual it brings about a psychological revolution, but it can also take a social form.

"In my opinion this problem does not exist for the Jews. The Jew already had the culture of the ancient world and on top of that has taken over the culture of the nations amongst whom he dwells. He has two cultures, paradoxical as that may sound. He is domesticated to a higher degree than we are, but he is badly at a loss for that quality in man which roots him to the earth and draws new strength from below. This chthonic quality is found in dangerous concentration in the Germanic peoples. Naturally the Aryan European has not noticed any signs of this for a very long time, but perhaps he is beginning to notice it in the present war; and again, perhaps not. The Jew has too little of this quality—where has he his own earth underfoot? The mystery of earth is no joke and no paradox. . . .

"The soil of every country holds some such mystery. We have an unconscious reflection of this in the psyche: just as there is a relationship of mind to body, so there is a relationship of body to earth. I hope the reader will pardon my figurative way of speaking, and will try to grasp what I mean. It is not easy to describe, definite though it is. There are people—quite a number of them—who live outside and above their bodies, who float like bodiless shadows above their earth, their earthy component, which is their body. Others live wholly in their bodies. As a rule, the Jew lives in amicable relationship with the earth, but without feeling the power of the chthonic. His receptivity to this seems to have weakened with time. This may explain the specific need of the Jew to reduce everything to its material beginnings; he needs these beginnings in order to counterbalance the dangerous ascendency of his two cultures. A little bit of primitivity does not hurt him; on the contrary, I can understand very well that Freud's and Adler's reduction of everything psychic to primitive sexual wishes and power-drives has something about it that is beneficial and satisfying to the Jew, because it is a form of simplification. For this reason, Freud is perhaps right to close his eyes to my objections. But these specifically Jewish doctrines are thoroughly unsatisfying to the Germanic mentality; we still have a genuine barbarian in us who is not to be trifled with, and whose manifestation is no comfort for us and not a pleasant way of passing the time. Would that people could learn the lesson of this war! The fact is, our unconscious is not to be got at with over-ingenious and grotesque interpretations. The psychotherapist with a Jewish background awakens in the Germanic psyche not those wistful and whimsical residues from the time of David, but the barbarian of yesterday, a being for whom matters suddenly become *serious* in the most unpleasant way. This annoying peculiarity of the barbarian was also apparent to Nietzsche—no doubt from personal experience—which is why he thought highly of the Jewish mentality and preached about dancing and flying and not taking things seriously. But he overlooked the fact that it is not the barbarian in us who takes things seriously—-they become serious for him. He is gripped by the daemon. And who took things more seriously than Nietzsche himself?

"It seems to me that we should take the problem of the unconscious very seriously indeed. The tremendous compulsion towards goodness and the immense moral force of Christianity are not merely an argument in the latter's favor, they are also a proof of the strength of its suppressed and repressed counterpart—the anti-Christian, barbarian element. The existence within us of something that can turn against us, that can become a serious matter for us, I regard not merely as a dangerous peculiarity, but as a valuable and congenial asset as well. It is a still untouched fortune, an uncorrupted treasure, a sign of youthfulness, an earnest of rebirth. Nevertheless, to value the unconscious exclusively for the sake of its positive qualities and to regard it as a source of revelation would be fundamentally wrong" (pp. 12–14).

1926

Freud delivers an address to the B'nai B'rith:

"That you were Jews could only be agreeable to me; for I was myself a Jew, and it had always seemed to me not only unworthy but positively senseless to deny the fact. What bound me to Jewry was (I am ashamed to admit) neither faith nor national pride, for I have always been an unbeliever and was brought up without any religion though not without a respect for what are called the 'ethical' standards of human civilization. Whenever I felt an inclination to national enthusiasm I strove to suppress it as being harmful and wrong, alarmed by the warning examples of the peoples among whom we Jews live. But plenty of other things remained over to make the attraction of Jewry and Jews irresistible—many obscure emotional forces, which were the more powerful the less they could be expressed in words, as well as a clear consciousness of inner identity, the safe privacy of a common mental construction" (*Standard Edition* 20: 273–274).

1928

Jung publishes *The Relations between the Ego and the Unconscious* and discusses the collective psyche in terms of racial differences (*CW* 7: 121–241):

"Thus it is a quite unpardonable mistake to accept the conclusions of a Jewish psychology as generally valid.* Nobody would dream of taking Chinese or Indian psychology as binding upon ourselves. The cheap accusation of anti-Semitism that has been levelled at me on the ground of this criticism is about as intelligent as accusing me of an anti-Chinese prejudice. No doubt, on an earlier and deeper level of psychic development, where it is still impossible to distinguish between an Aryan, Semitic, Hamitic, or Mongolian mentality, all human races have a common collective psyche. But with the beginning of racial differentiation essential differences are developed in the collective psyche as well. For this reason we cannot transplant the spirit of a foreign race *in globo* into our own mentality without sensible injury to the latter, a fact which does not, however, deter sundry natures of feeble instinct from affecting Indian philosophy and the like" (152 n.). **So ist es ein ganz unverzeihlicher Irrtum, wenn wir die Ergebnisse einer jüdischen Psychologie für allgemeingültig halten!* This sentence is more accurately translated: "Thus it is an unpardonable error when we accept the conclusions of a Jewish psychology as generally valid!" (*Die Beziehungen Zwischen dem Ich und dem Unbewussten* [Darmstadt: Reichl Verlag, 1928], p. 54.)

1930

Jung becomes honorary vice-president of the General Medical Society for Psychotherapy.

Freud writes a preface for the Hebrew translation of *Totem and Taboo*:

"No reader of [the Hebrew version of] this book will find it easy to put himself in the emotional position of an author who is ignorant of the language of holy writ, who is completely estranged from the religion of his fathers—as well as from every other religion—and who cannot take a share in nationalist ideals, but who has yet never repudiated his people, who feels that he is in his essential nature a Jew and who has no desire to alter that nature. If the question were put to him: 'since you have abandoned all these common characteristics of your countrymen, what is there left to you that is Jewish?' he would reply: 'A very great deal, and probably its very essence.' He could not now express that essence clearly in words; but some day, no doubt, it will become accessible to the scientific mind" (*Standard Edition* 13: xv).

1932

Jung travels to Egypt and Palestine.

1933

Hitler is named Chancellor of Germany.

Ernst Kretschmer resigns as president of the General Medical Society for Psychotherapy. Jung agrees to serve as president on condition that the organization be renamed the International General Medical Society for Psychotherapy and that it be reconstituted to enable Jewish psychotherapists barred from the German national section to join the international society directly as individual members with equal rights. In an editorial in the society's journal, Jung writes: "The differences which actually do exist between Germanic and Jewish psychology and which have long been known to every intelligent person are no longer to be glossed over, and this can only be beneficial to science. . . . At the same time I should like to state expressly that this implies no depreciation of Semitic psychology, any more than it is a depreciation of the Chinese to speak of the peculiar psychology of the Oriental" (*CW* 10: 533–534).

Jung gives an interview on Radio Berlin and discusses the importance of consciously responsible individuals as leaders of collective movements (*C. G. Jung Speaking*, pp. 59–66):

"The self-development of the individual is especially necessary in our time. When the individual is unconscious of himself, the collective movement too lacks a clear sense of purpose. Only the self-development of the individual, which I consider to be the supreme goal of all psychological endeavor, can produce consciously responsible spokesmen and leaders of the collective movement. As Hitler said recently, the leader must be able to be alone and must have the courage to go his own way. But if he doesn't know himself, how is he to lead others? That is why the true leader is always one who has the courage to be himself, and can look not only others in the eye but above all himself" (p. 64).

"Times of mass movement are always times of leadership. Every movement culminates organically in a leader, who embodies in his whole being the meaning and purpose of the popular movement. He is an incarnation of the nation's psyche and its mouthpiece. He is the spearhead of the phalanx of the whole people in motion. The need of the whole always calls forth a leader, regardless of the form a state may take. . . . It is perfectly natural that a leader should stand at the head of an elite, which in earlier centuries was formed by the nobility. The nobility believe by the law of the nature in the blood and exclusiveness of the race" (p. 65).

In "Carl Gustav Jung and the Jews: The Real Story," *Journal of Psychology and Judaism* 6, no. 2 (Spring/Summer 1982): 113–143, James Kirsch relates the following anecdote:

"During his stay in Berlin in May, 1933, Jung was invited to see Dr. Goebbels, the infamous minister of propaganda. Jung went and the following conversation occurred:

Goebbels: You wanted to see me, Dr. Jung.
Jung: No. You wanted to see me.
Goebbels: No. You wanted to see me.

"Jung turned around and left Goebbels' office—and vomited!!! From there he came to my house for lunch where my wife had prepared an ocean fish. He ate with excellent appetite!" (p. 135).

1934

Jung publishes "The State of Psychotherapy Today" and again distinguishes between Jewish and Germanic psychology (*CW* 10: 157–173):

"Freud and Adler have beheld very clearly the shadow that accompanies us all. The Jews have this peculiarity in common with women; being physically weaker, they have to aim at the chinks in the armour of their adversary, and thanks to this technique which has been forced on them through the centuries, the Jews themselves are best protected where others are most vulnerable. Because, again, of their civilization, more than twice as ancient as ours, they are vastly more conscious than we of human weaknesses, of the shadow-side of things, and hence in this respect much less vulnerable than we are. Thanks to their experience of an old culture, they are able, while fully conscious of their frailties, to live on friendly and even tolerant terms with them, whereas we are still too young not to have 'illusions' about ourselves. Moreover, we have been entrusted by fate with the task of creating a civilization—and indeed we have need of it—and for this 'illusions' in the form of one-sided ideals, convictions, plans, etc. are indispensable. As a member of a race with a three-thousand-year-old civilization, the Jew, like the cultured Chinese, has a wider area of psychological consciousness than we. Consequently it is *in general* less dangerous for the Jew to put a negative value on his unconscious. The 'Aryan' unconscious, on the other hand, contains explosive forces and seeds of a future yet to be born, and these may not be devalued as nursery romanticism without psychic danger. The still youthful Germanic peoples are fully capable of creating new cultural forms that still lie dormant in the darkness of the unconscious of every individual—seeds bursting with energy and capable of mighty expansion. The Jew, who is something of a nomad, has never yet created a cultural form of his own and as far as we can see never will, since all his instincts and talents require a more or less civilized nation to act as host for their development.

"The Jewish race as a whole—at least this is my experience—possesses an unconscious which can be compared with the 'Aryan' only with reserve. Creative individuals apart, the average Jew is far too conscious and differentiated to go about pregnant with the tensions of unborn futures. The 'Aryan' unconscious has a higher potential than the Jewish; that is both the advantage and the disadvantage of a youthfulness not yet fully weaned from barbarism. In my opinion it has been a grave error in medical psychology up till now to apply Jewish categories—which are not even binding on all Jews—indiscriminately to Germanic and Slavic Christendom. Because of this the most precious secret of the Germanic peoples—their creative and intuitive depth of soul—has been explained as a morass of banal infantilism, while my own warning voice has for decades been suspected of anti-Semitism. This suspicion emanated from Freud. He did not understand the Germanic psyche any more than did his Germanic followers. Has the formidable phenomenon of National Socialism, on which the whole world gazes with astonished eyes, taught them better? Where was that unparalleled tension and energy while as yet no National Socialism existed? Deep in the Germanic psyche, in a pit that is anything but a garbage-bin of unrealizable infantile wishes and unresolved family resentments. A movement that grips a whole nation must have matured in every individual as well. That is why I say that the Germanic unconscious contains tensions and potentialities which medical psychology must consider in its evaluation of the unconscious. Its business is not with neuroses but with human beings—that, in fact, is the grand privilege of medical psychology: to treat the whole man and not an artificially segregated function. And that is why its scope must be widened to reveal to the physician's gaze not just the pathological aberrations of a disturbed psychic development, but the creative powers of the psyche labouring at the future; not just a dreary fragment but the meaningful whole" (pp. 165–166).

Jung publishes "A Rejoinder to Dr. Bally" (*CW* 10: 535–544):

"About three years ago I was elected honorary [vice-] president of the General Medical Society for Psychotherapy. When, owing to the political upheaval, Professor Kretschmer resigned from the presidency, and the Society like so many other scientific organizations in Germany received a profound shock, some leading members pressed me—I may say, fervently—to take the chair. This, I would expressly emphasize, was the presidency not of the *German* but of the *International* Society. . . . Thus a moral conflict arose for me as it would for any decent man in this situation. Should I, as a prudent neutral, withdraw into security this side of the frontier and wash my hands in innocence, or should I—as I was well aware—risk my skin and expose myself to the inevitable misunderstandings which no one escapes who, from higher necessity, has to make a pact with the existing political powers in Germany? Should I sacrifice the interests of science, loyalty to colleagues, the friendship which attaches me to some German physicians, and the living link with the humanities afforded by a common language—sacrifice all this to egotistic comfort and my different political sentiments?" (pp. 535–536).

"If the doctors of Petersburg [*sic*] or Moscow had sought my help I would have acceded without hesitation, because I am concerned with human beings and not with Bolsheviks—and if I was then inevitably branded a Bolshevik it would have bothered me just as little" (p. 539).

"Admittedly I was incautious, so incautious as to do the very thing most open to misunderstanding at the present moment: I have tabled the Jewish question. This I did deliberately. My esteemed critic appears to have forgotten that the first rule of psychotherapy is to talk in the greatest detail about all the things that are the most ticklish and dangerous, and the most misunderstood. The Jewish problem is a regular complex, a festering wound, and no responsible doctor could bring himself to apply methods of medical hush-hush in this matter.

"As to the difference between Jewish and 'Aryan-Germanic-Christian-European' psychology, it can of course hardly be seen in the individual products of science as a whole. But we are not so much concerned with these as with the fundamental fact that in psychology the object of knowledge is at the same time the organ of knowledge, which is true of no other science. It has therefore been doubted in all sincerity whether psychology is possible as a science at all. In keeping with this doubt I suggested years ago that every psychological theory should be criticized in the first instance as a subjective confession. For, if the organ of knowledge is its own object, we have every reason to examine the nature of that organ very closely indeed, since the subjective premise is at once the object of knowledge which is therefore limited from the start. This subjective premise is identical with our psychic idiosyncrasy. The idiosyncrasy is conditioned (1) by the individual, (2) by the family, (3) by the nation, race, climate, locality, and history.

"I have in my time been accused of 'Swiss wooden-headedness.' Not that I have anything against possessing the national vices of the Swiss; I am also quite ready to suppose that I am a bigoted Swiss in every respect. I am perfectly content to let my psychological confession, my so-called 'theories,' be criticized as a product of Swiss wooden-headedness or queer-headedness, as betraying the sinister influence of my theological and medical forbears, and, in general, of our Christian and German heritage, as exemplified for instance by Schiller and Meister Eckhart. I am not affronted when people call me 'Teutonically confused,' 'mystical,' 'moralistic,' etc. I am proud of my subjective premises, I love the Swiss earth in them, I am grateful to my theological forbears for having passed on to me the Christian premise, and I also admit my so-called 'father complex': I do not want to knuckle under to any 'fathers' and never shall (see 'queer-headedness').

"May it not therefore be said that there is a Jewish psychology too, which admits the prejudice of its blood and its history? And may it not be asked wherein lie the peculiar differences between an essentially Jewish and an essentially Christian outlook? Can it really be maintained that I alone among psychologists have a special organ of knowledge with a subjective bias, whereas the Jew is apparently insulted to the core if one assumes him to be a Jew? Presumably he would not have one assume that his insights are the products of a mere cipher, or that his brain emerged only today from the featureless ocean of non-history. I must confess my total inability to understand why it should be a crime to speak of 'Jewish' psychology.

". . . Are we really to believe that a tribe which has wandered through history for several thousand years as 'God's chosen people' was not put up to such an idea by some quite special psychological peculiarity? If no differences exist, how do we recognize Jews at all?

". . . All branches of mankind unite in one stem—yes, but what is a stem without separate branches? Why this ridiculous touchiness when anybody dares to say anything about the psychological difference between Jews and Christians? Every child knows that differences exist.

"It seems to be generally assumed that in tabling the discussion of ethnological differences my sole purpose was to blurt out my 'notorious' anti-Semitism. Apparently no one believes that I—and others—might also have something good and appreciative to say. . . .

"I express no value-judgments, nor do I intend any veiled ones. I have been engaged for many years on the problem of imponderable differences which everybody knows and nobody can really define. . . .

"Consequently I am amused to find myself cast in the role of the nitwit who is unable to spot a single difference between Jews and Christians. . . . I would like to bring the parties together round a conference-table, so that they could at last get to know and acknowledge their differences. Very often this sort of knowledge is the way to understanding" (pp. 539-542).

"But, my public will object, why raise the Jewish problem today of all days and in Germany of all places? Pardon me, I raised it long ago, as anybody knows who is acquainted with the literature. I did not speak about it only since the revolution; I have been officially campaigning for criticism of subjective psychological premises as a necessary reform in psychology ever since 1913. This has nothing to do with the form of the German state. If I am to be exploited for political ends, there's nothing I can do to stop it. Or can anyone stop anything he pleases in Germany? It is rather late in the day for my critical attitude to attract attention only now, and it is, alas, characteristic that it should be construed in such a way as to suggest that Nazism alone has lent wings to my criticism. It is, I frankly admit, a highly unfortunate and disconcerting coincidence that my scientific programme should, without any assistance of mine and against my express wish, have been lined up with a political manifesto. But an event of this kind, although regrettable in itself, often has the consequence of ventilating problems which would otherwise be sedulously avoided" (p. 543).

Jung to W. M. Kranefeldt, February 9, 1934:

". . . As is known, one cannot do anything against stupidity, but in this instance the Aryan people can point out that with Freud and Adler specifically Jewish points of view are publicly preached, and as can be proven likewise, points of view that have an essentially corrosive character. If the proclamation of this Jewish gospel is agreeable to the government, then so be it. Otherwise there is also the possibility that this would not be agreeable to the government. . . ." (the portion of a letter published by the auction house of I. A. Stargard, Marburg, Germany, Catalogue No. 608, and reprinted in the *International Review of Psycho-Analysis* 4 [1977]: 377).

Jung to A. Pupato, March 2, 1934:

"The question I broached regarding the peculiarities of Jewish psychology does not presuppose any intention on my part to depreciate Jews, but is merely an attempt to single out and formulate the mental idiosyncrasies that distinguish Jews from other people. No sensible person will deny that such differences exist, any more than he will deny that there are essential differences in the mental attitude of Germans and Frenchmen. . . . Again, nobody with any experience of the world will deny that the psychology of an American differs in a characteristic and unmistakable way from that of an Englishman. . . . To point out this difference cannot possibly, in my humble opinion, be in itself an insult to the Jews so long as one refrains from value judgments. If anyone seeking to pin down my peculiarities should remark that this or that is specifically Swiss, or peasant-like, or Christian, I just wouldn't know what I should get peeved about, and I would be able to admit such differences without turning a hair. I have never understood why, for instance, a Chinese should be insulted when a European asserts that the Chinese mentality differs from the European mentality. . . .

"It is my opinion that the peculiarity of the Jews might explain why they are an absolutely essential symbiotic element in our population. If there actually were no differences between them and other people, there would be nothing to distinguish them at all. . . . It must after all be supposed that a people which has kept itself more or less unadulterated for several thousand years and clung onto its belief in being 'chosen' is psychologically different in some way from the relatively young Germanic peoples whose culture is scarcely more than a thousand years old.

"It is true that I fight Freud's psychology because of its dogmatic claim to sole validity. The monotony of Freudian explanations obliterates the wealth of differences that do indeed exist. I am persuaded that I am not doing another person a favour by tarring him with the brush of my subjective assumptions. If I want a proper knowledge of his nature I must ascertain where and to what extent he is different from me. Then only is it possible for me to know him really objectively. I would consider it most fortunate if, for example, Germany and France took the trouble to understand each other better and could appreciate and acknowledge each other's characteristic values. But the way things are, each explains the other in terms of the assumptions of its own psychology, as you can convince yourself daily by reading the French and German newspapers.

"That people in some respects are also all alike is by this time a familiar fact, but it leads to no misunderstandings. These come from the differences, which should therefore be a worthy subject of investigation."

Jung to B. Cohen, March 26, 1934:

"Your criticism of my lack of knowledge in things Jewish is quite justified. I don't understand Hebrew. But you seem to impute a political attitude to me which in reality I do not possess. I am absolutely not an opponent of the Jews even though I am an opponent of Freud's. I criticize him because of his materialistic and intellectualistic and—last but not least—irreligious attitude and not because he is a Jew. In so far as his theory is based in certain respects on Jewish premises, it is not valid for non-Jews. Nor do I deny my Protestant prejudice. Had Freud been more tolerant of the ideas of others I would still be standing at his side today. I consider his intolerance—and it is this that repels me—a personal idiosyncrasy."

Jung to Max Guggenheim, March 28, 1934:

"As a psychotherapist I cannot be indifferent to the future of psychotherapy. Its development in Germany will also be crucial for us. Freud once told me, very rightly: 'The fate of psychotherapy will be decided in Germany.' To begin with it was doomed to absolute perdition because it was considered wholly Jewish. I have broken this prejudice by my intervention and have made life possible not only for the so-called Aryan psychotherapists but for the Jewish ones as well. What with the hue and cry against me it has been completely forgotten that by far the greatest number of psychotherapists in Germany are Jews. People do not know, nor is it said in public, that I have intervened personally with the regime on behalf of certain Jewish psychotherapists. If the Jews start railing at me this is shortsighted in the extreme and I hope you will do what you can to combat this idiotic attitude. The existence of The Society for Psychotherapy, which has very many Jewish members, is now assured, also the membership of Jewish doctors. Actually the Jews should be thankful to me for that, but it seems that the—as you say—paranoid attitude prevents them from seeing clearly. . . . The understandable opposition of the Jews to the Hitler regime now makes it quits: everything German is outlawed, regardless of whether people are involved who are entirely innocent politically. . . . I find that shortsighted too."

Jung to E. Belt von Speyer, April 13, 1934:

"I have fallen foul of contemporary history. From abroad one can hardly have anything to do with Germany without becoming politically suspect on one side or the other. People now think I am a blood-boltered anti-Semite because I have helped the German doctors to consolidate their Psychotherapeutic Society and because I have said there are certain differences between Jewish and so-called Aryan psychology which are mainly due to the fact that the Jews have a cultural history that is 2,000 years older than the so-called Aryan. There has been a terrific shindy over this."

Jung to James Kirsch, May 26, 1934:

"We can also record the satisfying fact that at my suggestion a special provision was adopted whereby German Jewish doctors can individually join the International Society. They have thus become members with equal rights.

"I need hardly go into the other rumours. It is a downright lie to quote me as saying that Jews are dishonest in analysis. Anyone who believes I could say anything so idiotic must think me extraordinarily stupid. Neither have I addressed Hitler over the radio or in any other manner, nor have I made any political statements.

"With regard to my opinion that the Jews so far as we can see do not create a cultural form of their own, this opinion is based on (1) historical data, (2) the fact that the specific cultural achievement of the Jew is most clearly developed within a host culture, where he very frequently becomes its actual carrier or its promoter. This task is so specific and demanding that it is hardly conceivable how any individual Jewish culture could arise alongside it. Since very specific conditions do in fact exist in Palestine, I have inserted a cautious 'so far as we can see' in my sentence. I would in no wise deny the possibility that something specific is being created there, but so far I do not know it. I simply cannot discover anything anti-Semitic in this opinion.

"Coming to your suggestion that I should write a special work on this question, this has already been anticipated, as I have proposed a correspondence with Dr. Neumann, who has worked with me and is now also in Palestine, that will deal with all controversial questions. So far I have heard nothing from him.

"The Jewish Christ-complex is a very remarkable affair. As you know, I completely agree with you in this matter. The existence of this complex makes for a somewhat hysterical attitude of mind which has become especially noticeable to me during the present anti-Christian attacks upon myself. The mere fact that I speak of a difference between Jewish and Christian psychology suffices to allow anyone to voice the prejudice that I am an anti-Semite. . . . This hypersensitivity is simply pathological and makes every discussion practically impossible. As you know, Freud previously accused me of anti-Semitism because I could not abide his soulless materialism. The Jew directly solicits anti-Semitism with his readiness to scent out anti-Semitism everywhere. I cannot see why the Jew, unlike any so-called Christian, is incapable of assuming that he is being criticized personally when one has an opinion about him. Why must it always be assumed that one wants to damn the Jewish people? Surely the individual is not the people? I regard this as an inadmissible method of silencing one's adversary. In the great majority of cases I have got along very well with my Jewish patients and colleagues. It happens with other people, too, that I have had to criticize the individual, but they do not ascribe it to the fact that they are English, American or French. However, there is one exception worth mentioning, and that is the German. It has happened more than once that when I criticized a German he immediately concluded that I hate the Germans. . . .

" . . . You ought to know me sufficiently well to realize that an unindividual stupidity like anti-Semitism cannot be laid at my door. You know well enough how very much I take the human being as a personality and how I continually endeavour to lift him out of his collective condition and make him an individual. This, as you know, is possible only if he acknowledges his peculiarity which has been forced on him by fate. No one who is a Jew can become a human being without *knowing* that he is a Jew, since this is the basis from which he can reach out towards a higher humanity. This holds good for all nations and races. Nationalism—disagreeable as it is—is therefore a *sine qua non*, but the individual must not remain stuck in it. On the other hand, in so far as he is a particle in the mass he must not raise himself above it either. As a human being I am a European, as an atom in the mass I am a Swiss bourgeois, domiciled at Seestrasse 228, Küsnacht near Zurich."

Jung to Gerhard Adler, June 9, 1934:

"Best thanks for your detailed letter, the tenor of which I find completely acceptable. I have pointed out in several places in my article that Freud does not appear to me as the typical exponent of the Jewish attitude to the unconscious. In fact I expressly state that his view of it is not binding for all Jews. Nevertheless there is something typically Jewish about his attitude, which I can document with your own words: 'When a Jew forgets his roots, he is doubly and triply in danger of mechanization and intellectualization.' With these words you have laid your finger on exactly what is typically Jewish. It is typically Jewish that Freud can forget his roots to such an extent. It is typically Jewish that the Jews can utterly forget that they are Jews despite the fact that they know they are Jews. That is what is suspicious about Freud's attitude and not his materialistic, rationalistic view of the world alone. Freud cannot be held responsible for the latter. In this respect he is simply a typical exponent of the expiring 19th century, just like Haeckel, Dubois-Reymond, or that *Kraft und Stoff* ass Büchner. These people, however, are not as completely rootless as the Jewish rationalist, for which reason they are also much more naive and therefore less dangerous. So when I criticize Freud's Jewishness I am not criticizing the *Jews* but rather that damnable capacity of the Jew, as exemplified by Freud, to deny his own nature. Actually you should be glad that I think so rigorously, for then I speak in the interests of all Jews who want to find their way back to their own nature. I think the religious Jews of our time should summon up the courage to distinguish themselves clearly from Freud, because they need to prove that spirit is stronger than blood. But the prejudice that whoever criticizes Freud is criticizing the Jews always demonstrates to us that blood is thicker than spirit, and in this respect anti-Semitism has in all conscience learnt much from the Jewish prejudice.

"As to my assertion that the Jews have not created a 'cultural form' of their own, please note that I did not say 'culture.' I expressly stated that the Jews have a culture nearly 3,000 years old, but one can have a culture without possessing a cultural form of one's own. For instance, Switzerland has a culture but no cultural form. It has still to be proved conclusively that the Jews have ever created a cultural form of their own. At any rate they haven't in the last 2,000 years. It is also difficult to see how a relatively small folk ranging from India through Europe to America would be in a position to create such a form. I came across the same objection in a letter from a Jew a few days ago. Considering the proverbial intelligence of the Jews it has always seemed to me incomprehensible that they can no longer see the simplest truths because they are blinded by hypersensitivity. Blood is undoubtedly thicker than spirit, but, as you very rightly say, it is a tremendous danger for the Jew to get lost in the viscosity of sheer materialism."

Jung to C. E. Benda, June 19, 1934:

"I wonder what can have caused you to misconstrue my article to the point where you consider it necessary to defend Jewish culture against me. No one is more deeply convinced than I that the Jews are a people with a culture. Between culture and cultural form there is, as we know, an essential difference. The Swiss, for instance, are a people with a culture but no cultural form of their own. For this, as you rightly remark, certain conditions are needed, such as the size of a people, its ties to the soil, etc. In my opinion the Bible is not a cultural form but a document.

"A people with no ties to the soil, having neither land nor homeland, is commonly called nomadic. If you will submit these two points to which you took exception to unprejudiced scrutiny, you will probably come to the conclusion that there is no unjustified criticism in them. Had I said of the Jews what I said of the Germans in the same article, there might have been some cause for excitement, since 'barbarism' comes close to a value judgment.

"That psychoanalysis is, so to speak, a Jewish national affair is not my invention but Freud's. When I wrote my book *Wandlungen und Symbole der Libido* [*Symbols of Transformation*] and deviated at one point from orthodox theory, Freud suddenly accused me of anti-Semitism. From this I must conclude that I had somehow trespassed against the Jews. This prejudice has stuck to me ever since and has been repeated by all Freudians, thereby confirming every time that psychoanalysis is in fact a Jewish psychology which nobody else can criticize without making himself guilty of anti-Semitism."

1935

Jung delivers a series of lectures at the Tavistock Clinic in London (*CW* 18: 1–182):

"Who would have thought in 1900 that it would be possible thirty years later for such things to happen in Germany as are happening today? Would you have believed that a whole nation of highly intelligent and cultivated people could be seized by the fascinating power of an archetype? I saw it coming, and I can understand it because I know the power of the collective unconscious. But on the surface it looks simply incredible. Even my personal friends are under that fascination, and when I am in Germany, I believe it myself, I understand it all, I know it has to be as it is. One cannot resist it. It gets you below the belt and not in your mind, your brain just counts for nothing, your sympathetic system is gripped. It is a power that fascinates people from within, it is the collective unconscious which is activated, it is an archetype which is common to them all that has come to life. . . . We cannot be children about it, having intellectual and reasonable ideas and saying: this should not be. That is just childish. This is real history, this is what really happens to man and has always happened, and it is far more important than our personal little woes and our personal convictions. I know highly educated Germans who were just as reasonable as I think I am or as you think you are. But a wave went over them and just washed their reason away, and when you talk to them you have to admit that they could not do anything about it. An incomprehensible fate has seized them, and you cannot say it is right, or it is wrong. It has nothing to do with rational judgment, it is just history" (p. 164).

Jung to Erich Neumann, December 22, 1935:

"The 'cultivated Jew' is always on the way to becoming a 'non-Jew.' You are quite right: the way does not go from good to better, but dips down first to the historical data. I usually point out to most of my Jewish patients that it stands to reason they are Jews. I wouldn't do this had I not so often seen Jews who imagined they were something else. For them 'Jewishness' is a species of personal insult.

". . . . I find your very positive conviction that the soil of Palestine is essential for Jewish individuation most valuable. How does this square with the fact that Jews in general have lived *much* longer in other countries than in Palestine? Even Moses Maimonides preferred Cairo Fostat although he had the opportunity of living in Jerusalem.

"Is it the case that the Jew is so accustomed to being a non-Jew that he needs the Palestinian soil *in concreto* to be reminded of his Jewishness? I can scarcely feel my way into a psyche that has not grown up on any soil."

1936

The Berlin Psychoanalytic Institute ceases to exist as an independent entity.

The German Institute for Psychological Research and Psychotherapy (popularly known as the Göring Institute) opens in Berlin.

Jung prepares a press release for a trip to the United States (*CW* 18: 564-565):

"I make this statement in order to disillusion any attempt to claim me for any particular political party. I have some reason for it, since my name has been repeatedly drawn into the political discussion, which is, as you best know, in a feverish condition actually. It happened chiefly on account of the fact that I am interested in the undeniable differences in national and racial psychology, which chiefly account for a series of most fatal misunderstandings and practical mistakes in international dealings as well as in internal social frictions. In a politically poisoned and overheated atmosphere the sane and dispassionate scientific discussion of such delicate, yet most important problems has become well-nigh impossible. To discuss such matters in public would be about as successful as if the director of a lunatic asylum were to set out to discuss the particular delusions of his patients in the midst of them" (pp. 564–565).

Jung to Abraham Aaron Roback, September 29, 1936:

"Concerning my so-called 'Nazi affiliation' there has been quite an unnecessary noise about it. I am no Nazi, as a matter of fact I am quite unpolitical. German psychotherapists asked me to help them to maintain their professional organization, as there was an immediate danger that psychotherapy in Germany would be wiped out of existence. It was considered as 'Jewish science' and therefore highly suspect. Those German doctors were my friends and only a coward would leave his friends when they are in dire need of help. Not only did I set up their organization again but I made it clear that psychotherapy is an honest-to-God attempt and moreover I made it possible for Jewish German doctors, being excluded from professional organizations, to become immediate members of the International Society at least. But nobody mentions the fact that so many perfectly innocent existences could have been completely crushed if I had not stepped in.

"It is true that I have insisted upon the *difference* between Jewish and Christian psychology since 1917, but Jewish authors have done the same long ago as well as recently. I am no anti-Semite."

Jung to Roback, December 19, 1936:

"Unfortunately the political events in Germany have made it quite impossible to say anything reasonable about the most interesting difference between Jewish and non-Jewish psychology. The disinterested discussion of this most interesting difference is well-nigh impossible in our time of a new barbary. One risks being labelled as anti-Semite or pro-Semite without being heard at all."

Jung publishes "Wotan" and proposes an archetypal explanation for Nazism (*CW* 10: 179–193):

"We are always convinced that the modern world is a reasonable world, basing our opinion on economic, political, and psychological factors. But if we may forget for a moment that we are living in the year of Our Lord 1936, and, laying aside our well-meaning, all-too-human reasonableness, may burden God or the gods with the responsibility for contemporary events instead of man, we would find Wotan quite suitable as a causal hypothesis. In fact I venture the heretical suggestion that the unfathomable depths of Wotan's character explain more of National Socialism than all three reasonable factors put together" (p. 184).

"The impressive thing about the German phenomenon is that one man, who is obviously 'possessed,' has infected a whole nation to such an extent that everything is set in motion and has started rolling on its course towards perdition.

" It seems to me that Wotan hits the mark as an hypothesis. . . . He is a fundamental attribute of the German psyche, an irrational psychic factor. . . . Despite their crankiness, the Wotan-worshippers seem to have judged things more correctly than the worshippers of reason. Apparently everyone had forgotten that Wotan is a Germanic datum of first importance, the truest expression and unsurpassed personification of a fundamental quality that is particularly characteristic of the Germans. . . . The emphasis on the Germanic race (vulgarly called 'Aryan'), the Germanic heritage, blood and soil, the Wagalaweia songs, the ride of the Valkyries, Jesus as a blond and blue-eyed hero, the Greek mother of St. Paul, the devil as an international Alberich in Jewish or Masonic guise, the Nordic aurora borealis as the light of civilization, the inferior Mediterranean races—all this is the indispensable scenery for the drama that is taking place and at bottom they all mean the same thing: a god has taken possession of the Germans . . ." (pp. 185-186).

"It is above all the Germans who have an opportunity, perhaps unique in history, to look into their own hearts and to learn what those perils of the soul were from which Christianity tried to rescue mankind. Germany is a land of spiritual catastrophes, where nature never makes more than a pretence of peace with world-ruling reason. . . . Because the behaviour of a race takes on its specific character from its underlying images we can speak of an archetype 'Wotan.' As an autonomous psychic factor, Wotan produces effects in the collective life of a people. . . . It is only from time to time that individuals fall under the irresistible influence of this unconscious factor" (p. 187).

"All human control comes to an end when the individual is caught in a mass movement. Then the archetypes begin to function. . . . But what a so-called Führer does with a mass movement can plainly be seen if we turn our eyes to the north or south of our country" (pp. 189–190).

1937

Jung to J. Wilhelm Hauer, June 7, 1937:

"I myself have personally treated very many Jews and know their psychology in its deepest recesses, so I can recognize the relation of their racial psychology to their religion, but it would be quite beyond me to relate Islam or the ancient Egyptian religion to its devotees as I lack any intimate knowledge of Arab and Egyptian psychology."

In October, Jung gives a seminar at the Göring Institute.

Jung to M. H. Göring, November 16, 1937:

"Dr. Meier has drawn my attention to your short review of Rosenberg's book. For anyone who knows Jewish history, and in particular Hasidism, Rosenberg's assertion that the Jews despise mysticism is a highly regrettable error. I would therefore suggest that we pass over this book in silence. I cannot allow my name to be associated with such lapses."

1938

In *Jung, His Life and Work: A Biographical Memoir*, Barbara Hannah describes a cooperative effort by Swiss Jews and Jungians to convince Austrian Jews, including Freud, to leave after the Anschluss:

"Franz Riklin, Jr.—at that time nearing thirty and just starting his medical career—was chosen by some exceedingly rich Swiss Jews to go into Austria at *once*, with a very large sum of money, to do all that he could to persuade leading Jews to leave the country before the Nazis had time to start persecuting them. Franz said he was largely chosen for this work because of his exceedingly Teutonic appearance: no one would suspect him of any connection with the Jews. He also was a very resourceful young man who would obviously be adept at throwing dust in the eyes of the Nazis and at persuading the Jews to take advantage of the opportunity. In general he was *exceedingly* successful in carrying out this mission, but in one place, where he perhaps most wanted to succeed, he failed entirely.

"Before he left Zurich, his father, Franz Riklin, Sr., had pressed him to try above all to persuade Freud to leave Austria and to take advantage of the most unusual facilities which he could offer. His father had known Freud very well in the old days. Both he and Alfons Maeder had left the Freudian group at the same time as Jung, but none of that counted anymore in comparison with Dr. Riklin's very human wish to see his old friend in safety.

"Franz Jr. went to see Freud as soon as he got to Vienna and explained the situation to him. He was bitterly disappointed when Freud answered: 'I refuse to be beholden to my enemies.' Franz had been a very young child when Freud visited his parents, but he remembered him well. He did his best to persuade Freud that neither his father nor Jung felt any enmity toward him; on the contrary, he said, they really only wanted to know that he was safe. He also pointed out that there was no need for Freud to stay in Switzerland, for once there he could travel wherever he liked. It was all to no avail. Freud merely repeated that he would accept no favors from his enemies. The Freuds were very friendly to Franz himself; he was much too young to have been involved in the quarrel. They even asked him to dinner before he left Vienna, but nothing he could say was able to shake Freud's iron determination.

"This was a great disappointment to young Franz, for he knew how much it would disappoint his father, who was counting on him to bring Freud back with him. He knew that Jung, of whom he had always been particularly fond, would also be very sorry. The latter, however, had known Freud better than the Riklins. He was sad but not surprised. When reproached, as he sometimes was, for not doing more to help Freud leave Austria, Jung always replied: 'He would not take help from me under any circumstances'" (pp. 254–255).

In *Quadrant* 20, no. 2 (1987): 73–74, Robert S. McCully provides another version of the event:

"Sometime in the middle 1960s, Franz Riklin, Jr., came to the United States on an invited lecture tour, and when he came to New York, he spoke to the psychiatric faculty at Cornell University Medical College—The New York Hospital—on the topic of depression. At the time I was an associate professor there, and was asked by the departmental chairman to act as host to Dr. Riklin, and to see to his entertainment following his presentation. We spent the afternoon together talking a good deal about Jung, the man, since I was also at the time a senior analytical trainee at the New York C. G. Jung Institute. Later we had dinner together, and the charge was an honor and a pleasure for me.

"Dr. Riklin described the details of his journey from Zurich to Vienna on Freud's behalf. Both his father and Jung combined five thousand dollars of their own funds, which they wished to give to Freud so that he, a sick man soon to die, could get out of Vienna and to England. Riklin told me that he was chosen because he was young and quite Nordic in appearance, and his mission into Nazi territory could be a dangerous one. He had the cash in a money belt. After arriving in Vienna he went to the Freud residence. While it may have been the case, he did not mention to me any other aim attached to his journey, other than to present the monies to Freud. Miss Hannah writes that wealthy Swiss Jews got together monies to take to Austria to help leading Jews get out of the country. It could have been so, but he did not include that in his report on his adventure to me. I got the distinct impression that his father and Jung provided the money from their own funds, and I am certain the amount was five thousand each. It would be a bit different for history if the monies were personally from Riklin, Sr., and Jung than from wealthy Jews in Switzerland as Miss Hannah presents it.

"Riklin, Jr., then said to me he knocked on the door, and it was answered, opened cautiously part way by Freud's daughter Anna. Riklin, Sr., had known Freud well in the old days. Dr. Riklin explained to Miss Freud that he had come from Zurich on behalf of his father and Jung in order to make a present of some monies to her father. She did not ask young Riklin into the house and simply said she would speak to her father. She returned to the door and said her father would not receive him. Young Riklin again pleaded his cause, hoping to provide the aid to her father that brought him there. The door was about half open as he spoke to Anna, when Freud himself stepped to the door saying, 'I refuse to be beholden to my enemies.' Riklin virtually begged him to take the gift, while Freud only repeated he would accept no favors from enemies. Riklin said he was met with such hostility that he departed, returning to Switzerland with the unaccepted monies."

The Vienna Psychoanalytic Institute is dissolved.

Freud leaves Austria for England.

Jung to Erich Neumann, December 19, 1938:

"I am right in the thick of it and every day I follow the Palestine question in the newspapers and often think of my friends there who have to live in this chaos. Unfortunately I foresaw all too clearly what was coming when I was in Palestine in 1932. I also foresaw bad things for Germany, actually very bad, but now that they have come to pass they seem unbelievable. Everyone here is profoundly shaken by what is happening in Germany. I have very much to do with Jewish refugees and am continually occupied in bringing all my Jewish acquaintances to safety in England and America. In this way I am in ceaseless touch with contemporary events.

"I am very interested in what you have told me about your plans for work. Your experiences exactly parallel those I have had in Europe for many years. But I think you should be very cautious in judging your specifically Jewish experiences. Though it is true that there are specifically Jewish traits about this development, it is at the same time a general one which is also to be found among Christians. It is a general and identical revolution of minds. The specifically Christian or Jewish traits are only of secondary importance. Thus the patient you want to know about is a pure Jew with a Catholic upbringing, but I could never with absolute certainty characterize his symbolism—insofar as I have presented it—as Jewish although certain nuances occasionally seem so. When I compare his material with mine or with that of other academically trained patients one is struck only by the astonishing similarities, while the differences are insignificant. The difference between a typically Protestant and a Jewish psychology is particularly small where the contemporary problem is concerned. The whole problem is of such overwhelming importance for humanity that individual and racial differences play a minor role. All the same, I can very well imagine that for Jews living in Palestine the direct influence of the surroundings brings out the chthonic and ancient Jewish element in a much more pregnant form. It seems to me that what is specifically Jewish or specifically Christian could be most easily discovered in the way the unconscious material is assimilated by the subject. In my experience the resistance of the Jew seems to be more obstinate and as a result the attempt at defence is much more vehement. This is no more than a subjective impression."

1939

Jung publishes an interview in which he diagnoses the dictators (*C. G. Jung Speaking*, pp. 115–135):

"Few foreigners respond at all, yet apparently every German in Germany does. It is because Hitler is the mirror of every German's unconscious, but of course he mirrors nothing from a non-German. He is the loudspeaker which magnifies the inaudible whispers of the German soul until they can be heard by the German's unconscious ear.

"He is the first man to tell every German what he has been thinking and feeling all along in his unconscious about German fate, especially since the defeat in the World War, and the one characteristic which colors every German soul is the typically German inferiority complex . . ." (p. 118).

"In a way, the position of the Germans is remarkably like that of the Jews of old. Since their defeat in the World War they have awaited a Messiah, a Savior. That is characteristic of people with an inferiority complex. The Jews got their inferiority complex from geographical and political factors. They lived in a part of the world which was a parade ground for conquerors from both sides, and after their return from their first exile to Babylon, when they were threatened with extinction by the Romans, they invented the solacing idea of a Messiah who was going to bring all the Jews together into a nation once more and save them.

"And the Germans got their inferiority complex from comparable causes. They came up out of the Danube valley too late, and founded the beginnings of their nation long after the French and the English were well on their way to nationhood. They got too late to the scramble for colonies, and for the foundation of empire. Then, when they did get together and make a united nation, they looked around them and saw the British, the French, and others with rich colonies. . . .

"This was the *original* source of the German inferiority complex which has determined so much of their political thought and action and which is certainly decisive of their whole policy today. It is impossible, you see, to talk about Hitler without talking about his people, because Hitler is only the German people" (p. 122).

"If he is not their true Messiah, he is like one of the Old Testament prophets: his mission is to unite his people and lead them to the Promised Land. This explains why the Nazis have to combat every form of religion besides their own idolatrous brand" (p. 123).

"As a physician, I have not only to analyze and diagnose, but to recommend treatment.

"We have been talking nearly all the while about Hitler and the Germans, because they are so incomparably the most important of the dictator phenomena at the moment. It is for this, then, that I must propose a therapy" (p. 131).

"So I say, in this situation, the only way to save Democracy in the West—and by the West I mean America too—is not to try to stop Hitler. . . . You can only hope to influence the direction of his expansion.

"I say let him go East. Turn his attention away from the West, or rather, encourage him to keep it turned away. Let him go to Russia. That is the logical *cure* for Hitler" (p. 132).

"Our interest in it is simply that it will save the West. Nobody has ever bitten into Russia without regretting it. It's not very palatable food. It might take the Germans a hundred years to finish that meal. Meanwhile we should be safe, and by we, I mean all of Western civilization" (p. 133).

Jung has a dream at the time of the Hitler-Stalin pact.

E. A. Bennet records this version of the dream on March 29, 1946, after visiting Jung:

"He was in a vast field with, in the distance, buildings like barracks. The place was filled with hordes of buffalos (i.e., Germans). He was on a mound, and Hitler was on another mound. He felt that as long as he fixed his gaze on Hitler all would be well. Then he saw a cloud of dust in the distance, and horsemen—Cossacks—rounding up the buffalos and driving them out of the field. Then he woke up and was glad, for he knew that Germany would be beaten by Russia. This, he said, was a collective dream, and very important" (*Meetings with Jung*, p. 14).

Esther Harding records another version of the dream on June 8, 1948, after visiting Jung:

"He found himself in a castle, all the walls and buildings of which were made of trinitrotoluene (dynamite). Hitler came in and was treated as divine. Hitler stood on a mound as for a review. C. G. was placed on a corresponding mound. Then the parade ground began to fill with buffalo or yak steers, which crowded into the enclosed space from one end. The herd was filled with nervous tension and moved about restlessly. Then he saw that one cow was alone, apparently sick. Hitler was concerned about this cow and asked C. G. what he thought of it. C. G. said, 'It is obviously very sick.' At this point, Cossacks rode in at the back and began to drive the herd off. He awoke and felt, 'It is all right'" (*C. G. Jung Speaking*, p. 181).

In the account that Harding provides, Jung interprets the dream as follows: "He emphasized that Hitler was treated as *divine*. Consequently, he felt, we had to view him like that, that Hitler is not to be taken primarily as a human man, but as an instrument of 'divine' forces, as Judas, or, still better, as the Antichrist must be. That the castle was built of trinitrotoluene meant that it would blow up and be destroyed because of its own explosive quality. The herds of cattle are the instincts, the primitive, pre-human forces let loose in the German unconscious. They are not even domestic cattle, but buffalo or yaks, very primitive indeed. They are all male, as is the Nazi ideology: all the values of relationship, of the person or individual, are completely repressed; the feminine element is sick unto death, and so we get the sick cow. Hitler turns to C. G. for advice, but he limits his comment to the diagnosis, 'The cow is very sick.' At this, as though the recognition of the ailment released something, the Cossacks burst in. Even before that, the herd had been disturbed and nervous, as indeed the male animal is if separated too long or too completely from its complement, the female. The Cossacks are, of course, Russians. From that, C. G. said, he deduced that Russia—more barbaric than Germany, but also more directly primitive, and therefore of sounder instinct—would break in and cause the overthrow of Germany" (*C. G. Jung Speaking*, pp. 181–182). (See also Jay Sherry, "Jung, the Jews, and Hitler," *Spring* 1986, pp. 170–174).

In *Jung, His Life and Work*, Hannah comments on the dream as follows:

"We were all home again and Jung was at Bollingen when the news of the unholy alliance of Germany with Russia burst upon a horrified Europe. Jung was further disturbed by a most indigestible dream which he had immediately afterward. He dreamed that Hitler was 'the devil's Christ,' the Anti-Christ, but that nevertheless, as such, he was the *instrument of God*. He told me it took him a long time and much effort before he was able to accept this idea. Although Jung had been occupied with the idea of the dark side of God since his childhood, it was still many years before he finally faced the problem in *Answer to Job*, and the idea that a dangerous madman like Hitler could be the instrument of God was still far from his consciousness when he had this dream" (pp. 264-265).

Freud publishes *Moses and Monotheism* and discusses differences between Jews and non-Jews (*Standard Edition* 23: 1–137):

"The poor Jewish people, who with their habitual stubbornness continued to disavow the father's murder, atoned heavily for it in the course of time. They were constantly met with the reproach 'You killed our God!' And this reproach is true, if it is correctly translated. If it is brought into relation with the history of religions, it runs: 'You will not *admit* that you murdered God (the primal picture of God, the primal father, and his later reincarnations).' There should be an addition declaring: 'We did the same thing, to be sure, but we have *admitted* it and since then we have been absolved.' Not all the reproaches with which anti-semitism persecutes the descendants of the Jewish people can appeal to a similar justification. A phenomenon of such intensity and permanence as the people's hatred of the Jews must of course have more than one ground. It is possible to find a whole number of grounds, some of them clearly derived from reality, which call for no interpretation, and others, lying deeper and derived from hidden sources, which might be regarded as the specific reasons. Of the former, the reproach of being aliens is perhaps the weakest, since in many places dominated by anti-semitism today the Jews were among the oldest portions of the population or had even been there before the present inhabitants. This applies, for instance, to the city of Cologne, to which the Jews came with the Romans, before it was occupied by the Germans. Other grounds for hating the Jews are stronger—thus, the circumstances that they live for the most part as minorities among other peoples, for the communal feeling of groups requires, in order to complete it, hostility towards some extraneous minority, and the numerical weakness of this excluded minority encourages its suppression. There are, however, two other characteristics of the Jews which are quite unforgivable. First is the fact that in some respects they are different from their 'host' nations. They are not fundamentally different, for they are not Asiatics of a foreign race, as their enemies maintain, but composed for the most part of remnants of the Mediterranean peoples and heirs of the Mediterranean civilization. But they are none the less different, often in an indefinable way different, especially from the Nordic peoples, and the intolerance of groups is often, strangely enough, exhibited more strongly against small differences than against fundamental ones. The other point has a still greater effect: namely, that they defy all oppression, that the most cruel persecutions have not succeeded in exterminating them, and, indeed, that on the contrary they show a capacity for holding their own in commercial life and, where they are admitted, for making valuable contributions to every form of cultural activity.

"The deeper motives for hatred of the Jews are rooted in the remotest past ages; they operate from the unconscious of the peoples, and I am prepared to find that at first they will not seem credible. I venture to assert that jealousy of the people which declared itself the first-born, favourite child of God the Father, has not yet been surmounted among other peoples even today: it is as though they had thought there was truth in the claim. Further, among the customs by which the Jews made themselves separate, that of circumcision has made a disagreeable, uncanny impression, which is to be explained, no doubt, by its recalling the dreaded castration and along with it a portion of the primaeval past which is gladly forgotten. And finally, as the latest motive in this series, we must not forget that all those peoples who excel today in their hatred of Jews became Christians only in late historic times, often driven to it by bloody coercion. It might be said that they are all 'mis-baptized.' They have been left, under a thin veneer of Christianity, what their ancestors were, who worshipped a barbarous polytheism. They have not got over a grudge against the new religion which was imposed on them; but they have displaced the grudge on to the source from which Christianity reached them. The fact that the Gospels tell a story which is set among Jews, and in fact deals only with Jews, has made this displacement easy for them. Their hatred of Jews is at bottom a hatred of Christians, and we need not be surprised that in the German National-Socialist revolution this intimate relation between the two monotheist religions finds such a clear expression in the hostile treatment of both of them" (pp. 90–92).

"We may start from a character-trait of the Jews which dominates their relation to others. There is no doubt that they have a particularly high opinion of themselves, that they regard themselves as more distinguished, of higher standing, as superior to other peoples—from whom they are also distinguished by many of their customs. At the same time they are inspired by a peculiar confidence in life, such as is derived from the secret ownership of some precious possession, a kind of optimism: pious people would call it trust in God.

"We know the reason for this behaviour and what their secret treasure is. They really regard themselves as God's chosen people, they believe that they stand especially close to him; and this makes them proud and confident. Trustworthy reports tell us that they behaved in Hellenistic times just as they do to-day, so that the complete Jew was already there; and the Greeks, among whom and alongside of whom they lived, reacted to the Jewish characteristics in the same way as their 'hosts' do today" (pp. 105–106).

Freud dies on September 13, 1939.

1940

In *Jung, His Life and Work*, Hannah recounts the following incident:

"Here we learned what had caused the Jungs to take their grandchildren and daughter-in-law so suddenly to the mountains. He had been telephoned from a very high place in Bern, late the night before, and asked to leave Zurich immediately. The Swiss authorities had learned that Jung's name was on the Nazi blacklist and they did not want the Germans to have an opportunity to capture him. . . . That morning, moreover, he had been called by a friend in the High Command of the army who said that Switzerland was almost sure to be attacked that very day" (p. 269).

1944

Jung suffers a heart attack and while recuperating experiences a number of ecstatic visions (*Memories, Dreams, Reflections,* pp. 293-294):

"Toward evening I would fall asleep, and my sleep would last until about midnight. Then I would come to myself and lie awake for about an hour, but in an utterly transformed state. It was as if I were in an ecstasy. I felt as though I were floating in space, as though I were safe in the womb of the universe—in a tremendous void, but filled with the highest possible feeling of happiness. 'This is eternal bliss,' I thought. 'This cannot be described; it is far too wonderful!'

"Everything around me seemed enchanted. At this hour of the night the nurse brought me some food she had warmed—for only then was I able to take any, and I ate with appetite. For a time it seemed to me that she was an old Jewish woman, much older than she actually was, and that she was preparing ritual kosher dishes for me. When I looked at her, she seemed to have a blue halo around her head. I myself was, so it seemed, in the Pardes Rimmonim, the garden of pomegranates, and the wedding of Tifereth with Malchuth was taking place. Or else I was Rabbi Simon ben Jochai, whose wedding in the afterlife was being celebrated. It was the mystic marriage as it appears in the Cabbalistic tradition. I cannot tell you how wonderful it was. I could only think continually, 'Now this is the garden of pomegranates! Now this is the marriage of Malchuth with Tifereth!' I do not know exactly what part I played in it. At bottom it was I myself: I was the marriage. And my beatitude was that of a blissful wedding.

"Gradually the garden of pomegranates faded away and changed. There followed the Marriage of the Lamb, in a Jerusalem festively bedecked. I cannot describe what it was like in detail. These were ineffable states of joy. Angels were present, and light. I myself was the 'Marriage of the Lamb.'

"That, too, vanished, and there came a new image, the last vision. I walked up a wide valley to the end, where a gentle chain of hills began. The valley ended in a classical amphitheater. It was magnificently situated in the green landscape. And there, in this theater, the *hierosgamos* was being celebrated. Men and women dancers came onstage, and upon a flower-decked couch All-father Zeus and Hera consummated the mystic marriage, as it is described in the *Iliad*."

1945

Jung publishes "After the Catastrophe," in which he addresses the issues of collective guilt, inferiority, and hysteria in relation to the archetype of the shadow (*CW* 10: 194–217):

"While I was working on this article I noticed how churned up one still is in one's own psyche, and how difficult it is to reach anything approaching a moderate and relatively calm point of view in the midst of one's emotions. No doubt we should be cold-blooded and superior; but we are, on the whole, much more deeply involved in the recent events in Germany than we like to admit. . . . I must confess that no article has ever given me so much trouble, from a moral as well as a human point of view. I had not realized how much I myself was affected. There are others, I am sure, who will share this feeling with me. This inner identity or *participation mystique* with events in Germany has caused me to experience afresh how painfully wide is the scope of the psychological concept of *collective guilt*. So when I approach this problem it is certainly not with any feelings of cold-blooded superiority, but rather with an avowed sense of inferiority" (pp. 194–195).

"If only people could realize what an enrichment it is to find one's own guilt, what a sense of honour and spiritual dignity! But nowhere does there seem to be a glimmering of this insight. Instead, we hear only of attempts to shift the blame on to others—'no one will admit to having been a Nazi.' The Germans were never wholly indifferent to the impression they made on the outside world. They resented disapproval and hated even to be criticized. Inferiority feelings make people touchy and lead to compensatory efforts to impress. . . . Inferiority feelings are usually a sign of inferior feeling—which is not just a play on words. All the intellectual and technological achievements in the world cannot make up for inferiority in the matter of feeling. The pseudo-scientific race-theories with which it was dolled up did not make the extermination of the Jews any more acceptable. . ." (p. 202).

"A more accurate diagnosis of Hitler's condition would be *pseudologia phantastica*, that form of hysteria which is characterized by a peculiar talent for believing one's own lies. . . . Hitler's theatrical, obviously hysterical gestures struck all foreigners (with a few amazing exceptions) as purely ridiculous. When I saw him with my own eyes, he suggested a psychic scarecrow (with a broomstick for an outstretched arm) rather than a human being. . . . But the German people would never have been taken in and carried away so completely if this figure had not been a reflected image of the collective German hysteria. It is not without serious misgivings that one ventures to pin the label of 'psychopathic inferiority' on to a whole nation, and yet, heaven knows, it is the only explanation which could in any way account for the effect this scarecrow had on the masses" (pp. 203–204).

"But we must not forget that we are judging from today, from a knowledge of the events which led to the catastrophe. Our judgment would certainly be very different had our information stopped short at 1933 or 1934. At that time, in Germany as well as in Italy, there were not a few things that appeared plausible and seemed to speak in favour of the regime. An undeniable piece of evidence in this respect was the disappearance of the unemployed, who used to tramp the German high-roads in the hundreds of thousands. After the stagnation and decay of the post-war years, the refreshing wind that blew through the two countries was a tempting sign of hope" (p. 205).

"We must all open our eyes to the shadow who looms behind contemporary man. . . . As to what should be done about this terrifying apparition, everyone must work this out for himself. It is indeed no small matter to know of one's own guilt and one's own evil, and there is certainly nothing to be gained by losing sight of one's shadow. When we are conscious of our guilt we are in a more favourable position—we can at least hope to change and improve ourselves. As we know, anything that remains in the unconscious is incorrigible; psychological corrections can be made only in consciousness. Consciousness of guilt can therefore act as a powerful moral stimulus. In every treatment of neurosis the discovery of the shadow is indispensable, otherwise nothing changes" (pp. 215–216).

"The question remains: How am I to live with this shadow? What attitude is required if I am to be able to live in spite of evil?" (p. 217).

1946

Jung gives a talk, "The Fight with the Shadow," on a British Broadcasting Corporation program (*CW* 10: 218–226):

"Hitler was the exponent of a 'new order,' and that is the real reason why practically every German fell for him. . . . Like the rest of the world, they did not understand wherein Hitler's significance lay, that he symbolized something in every individual. He was the most prodigious personification of all human inferiorities. He was an utterly incapable, unadapted, irresponsible, psychopathic personality, full of empty, infantile fantasies, but cursed with the keen intuition of a rat or a guttersnipe. He represented the shadow, the inferior part of everybody's personality, in an overwhelming degree, and this was another reason why they fell for him.

"But what could they have done? In Hitler, every German should have seen his own shadow, his own worst danger. It is everybody's allotted fate to become conscious of and learn to deal with this shadow. But how could the Germans be expected to understand this, when nobody in the world can understand such a simple truth?" (p. 223).

In the epilogue to *Essays on Contemporary Events*, Jung characterizes Nazism as a mass psychosis (*CW* 10: 227–243):

"When Hitler seized power it became quite evident to me that a mass psychosis was boiling up in Germany. But I could not help telling myself that this was after all Germany, a civilized European nation with a sense of morality and discipline. Hence the ultimate outcome of this unmistakable mass movement still seemed to me uncertain, just as the figure of the Führer at first struck me as being merely ambivalent. It is true that in July 1933, when I gave a series of lectures in Berlin, I received an extremely unfavourable impression both of the behaviour of the Party and of the person of Goebbels. But I did not wish to assume from the start that these symptoms were decisive, for I knew other people of unquestionable idealism who sought to prove to me that these things were unavoidable abuses such as are customary in any great revolution. It was indeed not at all easy for a foreigner to form a clear judgment at that time. Like many of my contemporaries, I had my doubts" (p. 236).

"National Socialism was one of those psychological mass phenomena, one of those outbreaks of the collective unconscious about which I had been speaking for nearly twenty years. The driving forces of a psychological mass movement are essentially archetypal. Every archetype contains the lowest and the highest, evil and good, and is therefore capable of producing diametrically opposite results. Hence it is impossible to make out at the start whether it will prove to be positive or negative. My medical attitude towards such things counselled me to wait, for it is an attitude that allows no hasty judgments, does not always know from the start what is better, and is willing to give things 'a fair trial.' Far from wishing to give the beleaguered consciousness its death-blow, it tries to strengthen its powers of resistance through insight, so that the evil that is hidden in every archetype shall not seize hold of the individual and drag him to destruction. The therapist's aim is to bring the positive, valuable, and living quality of the archetype—which will sooner or later be integrated into consciousness in any case—into reality, and at the same time to obstruct as far as possible its damaging and pernicious tendencies. It is part of the doctor's professional equipment to be able to summon up a certain amount of optimism even in the most unlikely circumstances, with a view to saving everything that it is still possible to save. He cannot afford to let himself be too much impressed by the real or apparent hopelessness of a situation, even if this means exposing himself to danger. Moreover, it should not be forgotten that Germany, up till the National Socialist era, was one of the most differentiated and highly civilized countries on earth, besides being, for us Swiss, a spiritual background to which we were bound by ties of blood, language, and friendship" (p. 237).

1948

The state of Israel is founded.

Jung writes a memorandum, "Techniques of Attitude Change Conducive to World Peace," in response to a request from UNESCO (*CW* 18: 606–613):

"Hitler's enormous psychological effect was based upon his highly ingenious method of playing on the well-known national inferiority complex of the Germans, of which he himself was the most outstanding example" (p. 607).

1949

Jung gives an interview in response to articles in the *Saturday Review of Literature* in which he is accused of being pro-Nazi and anti-Semitic (*C. G. Jung Speaking*, pp. 192–200):

"It must be clear to anyone who has read any of my books that I never have been a Nazi sympathizer and I never have been anti-Semitic, and no amount of misquotation, mistranslation, or rearrangement of what I have written can alter the record of my true point of view" (p. 193).

"During this fateful time the Nazis played double with my name. On the one hand, my name was placed on their blacklist on account of various things I had written which they could not swallow, as, for instance my lecture on the 'Theory of Complexes,' held in Bad Nauheim in May 1934, in which I paid tribute to Freud. Still later, my Swiss publisher received news that my books were banned and destroyed. On the other hand, the Nazis were only too pleased to publicize my name, as a Swiss feather in their caps, in an effort to prop their waning reputation in the eyes of the world. Many false and conflicting rumors were circulated about me: that I was anti-Semitic, that I was a Jew, that I was Hitler's doctor, etc., etc." (pp. 198–199).

1957

Jung to Edith Schroder, April [?] 1957:

". . . I must remark that many important things could be said about the theme you propose, 'The Significance of Freud's Jewish Descent for the Origin, Content, and Acceptance of Psychoanalysis,' if only the problem could be treated on a very high level. Racial theories and the like would be a most unsatisfactory foundation, quite apart from the futility of such speculations. For a real understanding of the Jewish component in Freud's outlook a thorough knowledge would be needed of the specifically Jewish assumptions in regard to history, culture and religion. Since Freud calls for an extremely serious assessment on all these levels, one would have to take a deep plunge into the history of the Jewish mind. This would carry us beyond Jewish orthodoxy into the subterranean workings of Hasidism (e.g., the sects of Sabbatai Zwi), and then into the intricacies of the Kabbalah, which still remains unexplored psychologically. The Mediterranean man, to whom the Jews also belong, is not exclusively characterized and moulded by Christianity and the Kabbalah, but still carries within him a living heritage of paganism which could not be stamped out by the Christian Reformation.

"I had the privilege of knowing Freud personally and have realized that one must take all these facts into consideration in order to gain a real understanding of psychoanalysis in its Freudian form.

"I do not know how far you are acquainted with these various sources, but I can assure you that I myself could carry out such a task only in collaboration with a Jewish scholar since unfortunately I have no knowledge of Hebrew.

"In view of the blood-bespattered shadow that hangs over the so-called 'Aryan understanding of the Jew,' any assessment that fell below the level of these—as it may seem to you—high-falutin conditions would be nothing but a regrettable misunderstanding, especially on German soil.

"Despite the blatant misjudgment I have suffered at Freud's hands, I cannot fail to recognize, even in the teeth of my resentment, his significance as a cultural critic and psychological pioneer. A true assessment of Freud's achievement would take us far afield, into dark areas of the mind which concern not only the Jew but European man in general, and which I have sought to illuminate in my writings. Without Freud's 'psychoanalysis' I wouldn't have had a clue."

1961

Jung dies on June 5, 1961.

1963

Gershom Scholem to Aniela Jaffé, May 7, 1963:

"In the summer of 1947 Leo Baeck was in Jerusalem. I had then just received for the first time an invitation to the Eranos meeting in Ascona, evidently at Jung's suggestion, and I asked Baeck whether I should accept it, as I had heard and read many protests about Jung's behavior in the Nazi period. Baeck said: 'You must go, absolutely!' and in the course of our conversation told me the following story. He too had been put off by Jung's reputation resulting from those well-known articles in the years 1933-34, precisely because he knew Jung very well from the Darmstadt meetings of the School of Wisdom and would never have credited him with any Nazi and anti-Semitic sentiments. When, after his release from Theresienstadt, he returned to Switzerland for the first time (I think it was 1946), he therefore did not call on Jung in Zurich. But it came to Jung's ears that he was in the city and Jung sent a message begging him to visit him, which he, Baeck, declined because of those happenings. Whereupon Jung came to his hotel and they had an extremely lively talk lasting two hours, during which Baeck reproached him with all the things he had heard. Jung defended himself by an appeal to the special conditions in Germany but at the same time confessed to him: 'Well, I slipped up'—probably referring to the Nazis and his expectation that something great might after all emerge. This remark, 'I slipped up,' which Baeck repeated to me several times, remains vividly in my memory. Baeck said that in this talk they cleared up everything that had come between them and that they parted from one another reconciled again. Because of this explanation of Baeck's I accepted the invitation to Eranos when it came a second time."

Appendix B
Report to the Delegates of the XIIth Congress of the International Association for Analytical Psychology

The following report was delivered on August 21, 1992

During the XIth Congress in Paris in August 1989, a two-day workshop on Jung and Anti-Semitism was held. I was Chairman of the Workshop proceedings. I am today, as Chairman of that workshop, presenting to this Congress a report on a follow-up to that workshop with which I was charged in Paris. The details will reveal themselves below.

During the first day of the workshop it was revealed in a presentation given by Dr. Aryeh Maidenbaum, that The Psychology Club of Zurich had an official policy of limiting membership to those of the Jewish faith to 10 percent.

The very last comment at the conclusion of the two-day Paris workshop was made by Dr. John Beebe of San Francisco who stated his conviction that seeking some act of atonement from the Psychology Club of Zurich regarding the quota put on Jewish membership in the club during the period from the 1930s to 1950 is essential for moving forward and for healing. His suggestion was met with approbation by those in attendance.

Accordingly, after caucusing with Tom Kirsch, President, and other members of the Executive Committee of the IAAP, and receiving their informal concurrence, on November 6, 1989, I wrote the President of the Psychology Club of Zurich, Dr. Alfred Ribi the following letter:

November 6, 1989
Dr. med. Alfred Ribi, President
The Psychology Club of Zurich
Rebstr. 19
8703 Erlenbach
Switzerland

Dear Dr. Ribi:

As you may be aware, the XIth International Congress of the IAAP was held between August 28 and September 2, 1989, in Paris, France. On August 31st and September 1st, a Workshop entitled Jung and Anti-Semitism was held as part of the Congress program. I was Chairman of that Workshop.

Although there were three workshops which ran concurrently, the workshop on Jung and anti-Semitism was far and away the most heavily attended, each of the two workshops having to be moved to larger rooms to accommodate a standing room attendance. There were over 150 attendees at the first day of the workshop and nearly 250 at the second. I mention the heavy attendance to give you some notion of the importance attached to this topic by the international analytic community.

I have enclosed my introductory notes for the opening of the workshop. These remarks will give you some idea of the history and genesis of the workshop that was recently held in Paris and another meeting, entitled, "Lingering Shadows," which was held at the C. G. Jung Foundation in New York in March of this year.

One of the facts that was reported at the Paris workshop was that the Analytical Psychology Club of Zurich imposed a secret quota (10%) on the maximum number of Jews who may hold membership in the Club at any one time. This quota was enforced unofficially since the thirties, was formalized in 1944 and remained on the record until 1950 when, finally, it was rescinded. I have enclosed a copy of a paper by Dr. Aryeh Maidenbaum, Executive Director of the C. G. Jung Foundation of New York who did the research on this question (along with another analyst, Dr. Steve Martin, of Philadelphia, Pennsylvania) which documents this history.

There was considerable discussion of this issue during both days of the Paris workshop. Indeed, one attending analyst was so disturbed by this revelation that she declared that she would have to consider resigning from the IAAP because of Jung's complicity in such an onerous policy on the part of the Club.

It is noteworthy that the final comment made at the close of the second day of the workshop was one by John Beebe, M.D., a San Francisco analyst. He observed that, from the Jewish perspective, atonement for a sin is essential, both for the healing of the one injured by the act and for the perpetrator of the act itself. We noted that, as far as anyone knew, the Analytical Psychology Club of Zurich has never offered any statement of regret or any other act of atonement for such an injurious policy. He suggested that the present Club make some such expression. After consultation with various people who were present, it was decided that as Chairman of the workshop, I would convey the sentiments of those in attendance and would forward a formal request for some expression of atonement by the Club. (I wish to be clear that this request is from the attendees of the two-day workshop and is not the result of formal action by the IAAP.)

As I have written this, I have been reminded of Joseph Campbell's observation that the word "atonement," structurally is composed of the words, "at-one-ment." Symbolically, I think that Dr. Beebe's suggestion provides an opportunity to begin a process of healing which has been long overdue.

Should you wish additional information concerning the Paris workshop or the Lingering Shadows program held in New York earlier this year, I will be glad to forward papers, backup research material, etc. for your edification.

The proceedings of the Paris Congress will be published next year in a book. I am in the process of preparing material on the workshop for forwarding to the editor of that volume. It would be both appropriate and timely to have some response to this formal request to the Analytical Psychology Club of Zurich which emanated from the workshop to include in that package of material which I will forward to the editor.

If I can be of assistance, please don't hesitate to contact me.

Sincerely yours,
Jerome Bernstein, M.A.P.C., NCPsyA.
Chairman, Workshop on Jung and Anti-Semitism
XIth Congress of the IAAP
cc: John Beebe

Dr. Ribi responded on November 21, 1989. However, since Dr. Ribi has forbidden me to publish his end of the correspondence between us, I will read my responses to his communications which for the most part will reveal the nature of his responses to my letters to him.

In his response to me of November 21, 1989, Dr. Ribi stated that since only the Executive Committee voted secretly on the quota and the general membership was not informed of the vote, that the general membership then and present Club membership couldn't be responsible for it. He went on to say that the Club was appointing an historian to research this period in its history, including the imposition of a Jewish quota and that he would let me know the results of their efforts.

I responded to his November 21st letter on December 27, 1989, thanking him for his response and stated that I would be looking forward to hearing from him on the results of their research over the next few months.

After hearing nothing further from Dr. Ribi after my December 27, 1989 letter to him, I again wrote Dr. Ribi on April 5, 1991, nearly a year and a half later.

April 5, 1991
Dr. med. Alfred Ribi, President
The Psychology Club of Zurich
Rebstr. 19
8703 Erlenbach
Switzerland

Dear Dr. Ribi:

You will recall, I presume, our correspondence around November of 1989 in the wake of the XIth meeting of the IAAP in Paris and the workshop which took place there entitled, "Jung and Anti-Semitism." You informed me that the general members during the period of 1944-50 were not informed about the establishment of a Jewish quota for the Club and therefore did not vote on it. On the basis of this information, neither the Club then, nor the present club can be held responsible for that action.

You also informed me that an historian would investigate the whole history of the club, including the quota incident, and that you would keep me informed of the findings. I am writing to find out how that research is going and what information has been uncovered since our last correspondence.

Also, the proceedings of the workshop are being published in a book along with the proceedings of a conference entitled, "Lingering Shadows," by the C. G. Jung Foundation of New York. The conference at the Jung Foundation dealt with a similar topic and preceded the Paris Conference by six months. I have proposed to include exact copies of the correspondence between you and me in November of 1989 as part of the proceedings of the Paris Workshop. The publisher has requested your written consent to have your letter to me published as part of the book. If you would be kind enough to do so and to mail back your written consent to me at the above address by EXPRESS MAIL, I would be most grateful....

Sincerely yours,

Jerome S. Bernstein, M.A.P.C., NCPsyA.
Chairman, Workshop on Jung and Anti-Semitism
XIth Congress of the IAAP

Dr. Ribi responded to my letter on April 9, 1991. I responded to him on June 26, 1991 as follows:

June 26, 1991
Dr. med. Alfred Ribi, President
The Psychology Club of Zurich
Rebstr. 19
8703 Erlenbach
Switzerland

Dear Dr. Ribi:

I received your express letter to me of April 9, 1991, and in consideration of your request did not release for publication our correspondence after the International Congress in Paris about the workshop "Jung and Anti-Semitism." Pursuant to your letter, I did include in my report of the congress proceedings your feeling that our correspondence was an "afterthought" of the congress and therefore should not be included.

When you wrote that I "preferred" to discuss the role of the Club without your input, you seem to imply that I was trying to stage some kind of outcome of the workshop. That observation seems to me gratuitous about me—we've never met—and without basis in knowledge or fact. Indeed, I did not know about the revelations about the Jewish quota in the Club during that period until just a few days before the Congress, and thus a few days before the workshop itself. No doubt it would have been better to have invited you to sit on the panel on one of the two days and to invite you to discuss the fact of the quota and its history and implications. I wish I had known far enough in advance to have done so. . . .

Since the workshop generated such extreme interest on the part of the attendees—several hundred over two days—and since there was so much interest in the subject, particularly the existence of a Jewish quota which apparently Jung was aware of, your complaint of not having a voice suggests that a follow-up at next year's Congress would be a good idea. It could provide ample opportunity to further explore the subject and to present whatever facts may have been missing from the presentation in Paris. Certainly, your presence on a panel to explain the Club's historical role in this matter could be very helpful in bringing to light other facts that have been overlooked and in resolving whatever shadow issues remain unengaged.

I was particularly disappointed with the last paragraph of your letter which stated that the "history of the club"—which earlier you indicated would shed light on the period in question and the facts surrounding the issue of a Jewish quota—"will take several years" and that you can give me no information about it. That statement feels like there is no genuine interest on your part in pursuing this issue at all and without my persistence might choose to leave it in the realm of the shadow. I hope that is not so.

More disappointing seems to be a dismissal of the sentiment of the hundreds of our colleagues in attendance at the workshop and their overwhelming sentiment that, as John Beebe proposed, there be some kind of feeling gesture of atonement from the Club—at the least a disavowal of the Club from the actions of the Executive committee of that period—surrounding an issue that was wounding to many of its colleagues and to many of our present colleagues, non-Jewish as well as Jewish.

It was and remains my position that anti-Semitism, to whatever extent attributable to Jung himself, and on the part of the Psychology Club of Zurich, resulted in a moral and psychological wound to the Jungian community as a whole. As Jungian analysts we are healers and should be no less concerned about the wounds inflicted on ourselves as well as those inflicted on our patients.

It seems to me important too to recognize that since the Psychology Club of Zurich (as far as we know) was the only Jungian group which had a formal quota limiting Jewish membership, it stands as a symbol of whatever anti-Semitism was present within the larger Jungian community. That Jung himself was a member of this particular Club makes that symbol all the more potent. The fact that these events took place over fifty years ago does not diminish the damage to Jung's name and his work and to our professional community. The persistence and vitriol of the attacks on Jung which exist at the present time attest to that fact. As I wrote in my report of the workshop in the Congress proceedings:

> Only by dissociating itself from this past discriminatory act in its history can the Club finally close the door on this subject. Although it is true that no discriminatory policy has been part of the Club's history since 1950, it is also true that its history during the period 1944–1950 has remained a festering shadow issue for the Club and the Jungian community as a whole. . . The concern here is not just the moral stance of the Club, but

rather the moral stance of the Jungian community at large, both in its own eyes and in the eyes of the world.

Lastly, Dr. Ribi, I would like to assure you of my sincerity in pursuing this topic with you. I am not trying to embarrass you, the Club, nor anyone else. The embarrassment is already there—with the persistent and pernicious view on the part of the non-Jungian community that Jung was not only anti-Semitic, but a Nazi sympathizer as well. (One American psychiatrist compared him to Joseph Mengele!) It seems to me that only a combination of truth, consciousness and humility on all our parts will redeem the wound to Jung's name and work and to our own community. I would like to work with you toward that end and am open to your suggestions.

I have no doubt that the question of what did happen as a follow-up pursuant to the workshop in Paris will come up at the Congress in Chicago next year. I would like to be able to report, jointly with you, that we have done our work and that some healing has taken place to the benefit of us all.

Jerome S. Bernstein, M.A.P.C., NCPsyA.
Chairman, Workshop on Jung and Anti-Semitism
XIth Congress of the IAAP
cc: John Beebe

I received a prompt reply from Dr. Ribi on July 26, 1991. I have spent considerable time trying to figure out how to convey to this assembly the tone and content of his letter to me since I do not have his permission to publish that letter. I can only say that it was scornful, personally insulting, and above all else, contemptuous of the sentiment expressed at the end of the two-day Paris workshop and the idea that there is a wound to be healed. It was a stunning letter.

It was obvious to me that further correspondence between me and Dr. Ribi with respect to my charge from the Paris workshop would not be functional. Dr. Ribi could not seem to grasp that I was acting on the sentiments at the end of the Paris workshop and following through on those sentiments as Chairman of the workshop. All of his responses were as if I were pressing an exclusively personal issue, notwithstanding the fact that I signed all correspondence as Chairman of the Paris Workshop on Jung and Anti-Semitism,

Accordingly I asked Dr. John Beebe of San Francisco to write Dr. Ribi in the wake of Dr. Ribi's July 26, 1991 letter to me. I requested Dr. Beebe to write Dr. Ribi because it was his suggestion at the end of the

Paris workshop to seek some kind of gesture of atonement from the Psychology Club of Zurich, because of the international respect that he commands both professionally and as someone who is balanced and fair, and frankly, because he is not Jewish.

Acceding to my request, Dr. Beebe wrote Dr. Ribi on February 20th of this year:

February 20, 1992
Dr. med. Alfred Ribi
President Psychologischer Club, Zurich
Gemeindestr. 27
8032 Zurich
Switzerland

Dear Dr. Ribi,

I am writing in anticipation of the next Congress of the IAAP, which will entertain a report on my suggestion at the last congress that the Analytical Psychology Club of Zurich may well want to make some statement regretting or disavowing the once-secret official policy of allowing only a quota of Jewish members. It is widely rumored that, in 1950 or so, Jung himself was responsible for the rescinding of this policy, which seems to have been a misguided effort to protect him in the event of Nazi occupation of Switzerland.

It is important that this history be brought out, together with some statement of regret, lest it appear that present-day Jungians stand behind this history and are still unashamed of any institutional anti-Semitism in their past. I hope you can see how embarrassing it will be for the Analytical Psychology Club, and for analytical psychology in general, if this past is simply allowed to be discussed without comment. The issue here is not a defense, or an acceptance of more shadow-projection than is rightful, but a mere acknowledging, with appropriate contrition, that includes the recognition that the actions of a past leadership can never be fully comprehended, from which then we can all move on.

I personally regret having to suggest what anyone else might do. Yet at least one Jewish woman member of the IAAP told me after I made my suggestion that my having done so made it possible for her to continue her membership. You can see how much a simple expression of regret would mean to her.

Sincerely,
John Beebe, M.D.

Dr. Ribi wrote Dr. Beebe on February 28, 1992 that he was not clear under whose auspices Dr Beebe was writing, whether he was extending an invitation to make a formal presentation to the Congress in Chicago, and other questions. He also stated that Dr. Beebe's questions about the Jewish quota have been thoroughly dealt with and Dr. Ribi did not wish to go into the matter since he could only offer a personal impression. Regarding an expression of atonement from the club as requested by Dr. Beebe, Dr. Ribi said that he could not apo1ogize for something he didn't do.

Accordingly, Dr. Beebe turned the matter over to Tom Kirsch as President of the IAAP. Dr. Kirsch did extend an invitation to Dr. Ribi to attend this Congress and participate in the presentation of this report.

On April 22, 1992, Dr. Ribi wrote Tom Kirsch thanking Dr. Kirsch for his invitation to attend the Congress and stated that interviews had been completed of "old members" of the Club and that since Professor C. A. Meier was president of the Club during World War II, to please address him about the role of the Club during that period.

On May 3, 1992, I wrote Professor Meier. The non-repetitive portions of my letter to him read as follows:

> May 3, 1992
> C. A. Meier, Dr. med.
> Steinwiesstr. 37
> Ch-8032 Zurich
> Switzerland
>
> Dear Dr. Meier:
>
> I was Chairman of a workshop entitled Jung and Anti-Semitism at the XIth International Congress in Paris, August 1989. . . .
>
> [B]eginning on November 6, 1989, I entered into correspondence with Dr. Alfred Ribi as President of the Psychology Club of Zurich. Although to date Dr. Ribi and I have exchanged a number of letters, Dr. Ribi has not addressed the request for such a statement from the Club. . . .
>
> Recently Dr. Ribi was informed that I would be giving a report to the XIIth Congress which will take place in August of this year in Chicago, USA, on the results of my efforts with the Club. Dr. Tom Kirsch, President of the IAAP, invited Dr. Ribi to attend and participate in the presentation of that report. If I were giving that report today, I regret to say that I would have to report to the Congress that no statement addressing this issue has been forthcoming from the President of the Club.

Dr. Ribi, in his response to Dr. Kirch's invitation, suggested that you be contacted regarding this matter. I am doing so in the hope that you will be able to assist in providing a statement on behalf of the Psychology Club of Zurich reflecting regret for the Club's action in establishing a "Jewish quota" during the period 1944 thru 1950. I am hoping that with your assistance an ethical wound to our Jewish colleagues, to the Club itself, to Dr. Jung's image, and to our community as a whole can be healed and a piece of undigested shadow within our community can at last be integrated.

It would also be helpful if you could provide any information which would put the historical facts of this tragic period in a more complete light, including the degree of actual enforcement of such a quota and the thinking and feeling expressed at the time it was promulgated and finally terminated.

Any assistance you can provide us in this regard will be greatly appreciated and welcomed. I have enclosed for your information copies of my letters to Dr. Ribi and Dr. Ribi's April 22nd letter to Dr. Kirsch.

Sincerely yours,
Jerome Bernstein, M.A.P.C. NCPsyA.
Chairman, Workshop on Jung and Anti-Semitism
XIth Congress of the IAAP
CC: Thomas Kirsch, M.D.
President, IAAP
John Beebe, M.D.
Jungian Analyst

Professor Meier responded on June 2, 1992. With his permission, I read his response to my letter:

June 2, 1992
Jerome S. Bernstein, MA.
3907 Jocelyn Street, NW.
Washington, D.C. 20015

Dear Colleague:

At long last I find the time to try to answer your letter of May 3rd.

Let me first make a few general statements: I happened to know Jung intimately for more than 30 years and can therefore testify that there was no such thing ever as antisemitism with him. In the contrary, there was always great admiration for the Jews, which

I inherited from him, so that my best friends always have been Jewish. Jung always said that the Jews were the people with the deepest religious genius, and it is not for nothing that a few of his best pupils at that time were Jews, as you certainly know. For this reason alone it is preposterous to discuss Jung's "antisemitism."

Now comes the affair of the Psychological Club. [None] of you younger people could possibly do justice to that "quota" since you did not live in Switzerland at that period. First of all, our country was during that period invaded by Jewish refugees. Lots of them gravitated toward Jung and had had some Jungian analysis in Germany. Myself, I continued giving analysis to quite a number of them gratis, so that it is not for nothing that they also wanted to become Club members. At this time Switzerland was under constant danger of being invaded by the Nazis, and we were all in fear and trembling. I was myself at our frontier as an officer and experienced at two different times the running motors of a German [tank] on the other side. Now on the other hand, the Club, in view of a possible invasion, would have been in danger of dissolution by the Germans as a Jewish community. This we had at all events to prevent, and therefore took that incriminated step. Now, when the war was over, the secret protective measure was simply forgotten, and I was no longer president. Or is that antisemitism?

Myself, I had [through] all this period been editor of the "Zentralblatt". As such, I had to fight the German antisemitism and have consequently successfully repressed publication of antisemitic papers submitted. I even published during that whole period papers of Jewish members of the "International". I also read a paper of a Hungarian Jew during the London Congress, whereupon the German delegation left the room out of protest! Whereupon all the remaining audience burst with laughter! That was shortly before the war.

Sorry to say that I feel no atonement for that step that the Club had to take, since simultaneously it served as protection of these poor Jewish would be members. Although I admire the great amount of work you are giving to this would-be-question of Jung's antisemitism I cannot help feeling that the more public attention you give to it, the more you plant antisemitism on the other hand. Where the hell is that shadow?, analytically speaking. I can only wish for you that you come to the point where you can happily drop the whole damned nonsense.

With kind regards and best wishes

Sincerely yours

This concludes my report on my efforts since the Paris Congress to act on the sentiment of the Paris workshop that some gesture of atonement for the Jewish quota be sought from the Psychology Club of Zurich. In the end, I was not successful in obtaining any expression of atonement from the Psychology Club of Zurich regarding the Jewish quota in the club during the period in question. I have wanted this report to be just that—a report. I felt it not appropriate to interpret, or present new data. If nothing else, this correspondence will be included for the record in the proceedings of the XIIth Congress and will add to the published archives on this period in the history of analytical psychology and its founder C. G. Jung, as well as the Psychology Club of Zurich.

Before closing I would like to make one observation. Not surprisingly, this subject cannot be addressed without projections flying about. One projection I would like to clarify again for the record. My efforts since the Paris workshop have been as chairman of that workshop and a follow-up of sentiments expressed at that workshop. This has not been my personal mission.

It seems that in carrying out this role, I end up with the projection of trying to brand Jung as anti-Semitic. As I stated in the Paris workshop, as documented in the book, *Lingering Shadows*, and in the published proceedings of the Paris Congress, I never subscribed to the viewpoint that Carl Jung was an anti-Semite, although I believe that he indulged in some anti-Semitic behaviors. I am on record as stating that Jung's behavior in this sphere seems to me to have stemmed primarily from a pathologically defective feeling function more than from an endemic attitude of anti-Semitism. That is still my view.

No doubt some more information will be forthcoming in future years regarding this crucial period in the history of analytical psychology now that the door within the Jungian community has been publicly opened. For this we can all take some satisfaction.

Epilogue

After the delivery of my report to the Congress there was some lively discussion, at the conclusion of which the following statement and resolution were adopted by the assembly:

Statement, submitted from the floor, at the Delegates' Assembly

We, the delegates, protest the tone and nature of the response by the leadership of the APC of Zürich to the Chairman of the Workshop on

Anti-Semitism (Paris 1989). We realize that the membership of the APC probably does not know of this response in a manner similar to the manner in which they did not know of the discriminatory policy under discussion. We also realize that the APC is an organization outside of the IAAP although it has been at the center of the Jungian world for a long time.

> RESOLUTION:
> We request that the constituent societies of the IAAP establish and follow a policy of non-discrimination regarding race, religion, ethnic origin, gender, sexual orientation to apply to membership in professional societies, training programs, and events for the public at large sponsored by them.

The resolution was referred by the delegates to the IAAP Executive Committee for inclusion into the IAAP Constitution and By-Laws in the manner specified by the Constitution and By-Laws.

Appendix C
Bibliographic Survey by Jay Sherry

Freud's assertion in *On the History of the Psychoanalytic Movement* (Standard Edition, 14: 43) that Jung had given up "certain racial prejudices" when they undertook their collaboration is the starting point for the case of Jung's alleged anti-Semitism. The literature has taken many forms: letters to the editor, articles, comments made in passing, treatment in psychology books and biographies. The aim of this essay is to provide a chronological survey of the literature not discussed elsewhere in this book.

The first important period occurred in the 1930s after Jung had become president of the International General Medical Society for Psychotherapy. A Swiss psychiatrist, Dr. Gustav Bally, wrote an article for the *Neue Züricher Zeitung* on February 27, 1934 titled "Deutschstämmige Psychotherapie?" in which he challenged Jung's participation in an organization with a large German membership that had embraced the Nazi ideology. Jung responded soon after in the same newspaper with a thorough defense of his actions. This response, "A Rejoiner to Dr. Bally" (*CW* 10, ¶ 1016-34), is essential reading for anyone with an interest in this topic, as is Jung's "The State of Psychotherapy Today" (*CW* 10, ¶ 333-370), the most widely quoted article regarding the controversy. The latter triggered a heavy correspondence and prompted responses from three of Jung's closest Jewish followers in *Judische Rundschau* (Berlin). In number 43 of that publication, (May 29, 1934), James Kirsch disagreed with Jung that Jews were nomads, suggesting rather that they were a restless people and that Jung had mistaken a stereotypical image of the Jews for what is essential to their identity. This view was countered by Erich Neumann in number 48 (June 15, 1934), where he said that

Jung's observations about Jews would be as important as Zionism in their developing a modern identity. In number 61 (August 15, 1934) Gerhard Adler wrote that Jews "must find by way of the inner experience the connection to the chain of ancestors. Jung has shown a way to do that for all people, Jews and non-Jews; where he attacks the Jews he does this insofar as they are negative and uprooted; is he anti-Semitic for this reason?"

After the war the controversy broke out anew in the United States, where there were intellectual scores to settle. The opening shot was fired by Frederic Wertham in a book review in the *New Republic* (December 4, 1944), where he wrote, "Jung has become one of the most important influences on fascist philosophy in Europe" (p. 774). The tempo picked up in the following year when S. S. Feldman wrote a one-page critique of Jung in the *American Journal of Psychiatry* (September 1945, p. 263) in which he contrasted quotations from Jung's prewar and postwar writings to convey a sense of Jung's opportunism.

The controversy became more polarized in 1946 with the appearance of articles defending and condemning Jung. Ernst Harms wrote an informative and balanced account of Jung's conduct in "C. G. Jung—Defender of Freud and the Jews" in the April, 1946 issue of *The Psychiatric Quarterly* (reprinted in *Lingering Shadows: Jungians, Freudians, and Anti-Semitism*). A. D. Parelhoff, Jung's most vociferous critic, published a three-part article, "Dr. Carl G. Jung—Nazi Collaborationist," in *The Protestant* (I: June-July, pp. 22-28; II: August-September, pp. 26-31; III: February-March, 1947, pp. 17-30). In what appears, even to critics of Jung, to be a pathological diatribe with little or no factual support, Parelhoff attributed to Jung every evil imaginable, including the accusation that Jung had sought to establish Hitler as a seer and "had openly allied himself with an already functioning organization of sadistic degenerates and murderers" (1, p. 26). Parelhoff continued his attacks into the 1950s. A letter to the *New Statesman* (London, May 17, 1958) elicited a response from Gerhard Adler, who questioned Parelhoff's sincerity and concluded, "There are many Jews and refugees among us. . . . None of us has ever experienced anything but friendship and active support—also against the Nazis—from Jung. To all of us the ill-founded presentation of Jung as anti-Semite and pro-Nazi is just utter ignorance or, worse, slander" (May 24, 1958, p. 667).

The charges against Jung were kept in the public eye for much of 1949 by two articles by Robert Hillyer in the *Saturday Review of Literature* (June 11 and 18). Their main focus was to condemn the awarding of the Bollingen Prize for Poetry to Ezra Pound, who had been arrested after the war for making pro-fascist radio broadcasts and who was then being held at St. Elizabeth's Hospital, a federal institution for the insane. Jung's name was dragged in because the prize was named after his retreat home on Lake Zurich. Hillyer conjured up a grand conspiracy plot in which the committee represented a sinister clique bent on imposing a new cultural authoritarianism. Hillyer got most of his information from Parelhoff but recalled, "I had one personal contact with Dr. Jung's Nazism. At the luncheon during the Harvard Tercentary of 1936, Dr. Jung, who was seated beside me, deftly introduced the subject of Hitler, developed it with alert warmth, and concluded with the statement that from the high vantage point of Alpine Switzerland Hitler's new order in Germany seemed to offer the one hope of Europe" (June 11, p. 10). A solid discussion and critique of this affair can be found in William McGuire's *Bollingen* (Princeton University Press, 1982, pp. 208-216).

The July 30, 1949, issue of the *Saturday Review of Literature* contained a pair of articles about Jung, one supportive, by Philip Wylie, and the other critical, by Frederic Wertham. Ignoring Jung's positive accomplishments in helping Jewish analysts, Wertham wrote, "I am talking about the Fascism of Carl Gustav Jung. Nobody who knew the facts was surprised when, in 1933, after Hitler came to power, Jung took over the two important positions in psychotherapy . . . . But the Nazis had a difficult job of finding a psychotherapist or psychoanalyst with a big name. Everybody knew that only Jung would lend himself to such a step. For this act was a major political event in the cultural conquest of Central Europe by the Nazis . . . . [Jung] hoisted the swastika banner in a scientific field. . . ." (p. 7).

Wertham continued his attack in the October 1949 issue of the *American Journal of Psychotherapy* in an article entitled "The Road to Rapallo." Repeating many of his previous charges, he opined that "Bollingen has become the symbol of cultural fascism" (p. 587). This prompted a round of letters pro and con in the January and April 1950 issues. Jung himself responded to all this in an interview with Carol Baumann that first appeared in December 1949 and was later published in *C. G. Jung Speaking* (Princeton University Press, 1977, Pp. 192-200).

By the 1960s the controversy was to be found less often in periodicals but was beginning to find itself in the secondary literature. Indicative of this shift was Edward Glover's *Freud or Jung?* (Cleveland: Meridian Books, 1963), much of which had appeared in *Horizon* (nos. 106, 107, and 111). His evaluation of Jung's views on politics (pp. 146-53) misinterprets Jung's analysis of Nazism as an endorsement of it. Alexander and Selesnick's *History of Psychiatry* (New York: Harper and Row) appeared in 1964 and unfortunately repeated the standard one-dimensional account of Jung's alleged anti-Semitism in its appendix B (pp. 407-409).

In conjunction with the centennial of Jung's birth in 1975, several biographies by close followers were released. Laurens van der Post's *Jung and the Story of Our Time* (New York: Pantheon Books) focused on the Wotanic forces in Germany that had attracted Jung's interest (pp. 22-25, 194-199): "Nonetheless, a vulgar mythological use of the personal story of Freud and Jung themselves continues and it is in the mythological abuse of the story of their relationship, I believe, that lies the real explanation of this continuation of the campaign against Jung for having been pro-Nazi and anti-Semitic" (p. 197). Van der Post recommended that people read Aniela Jaffé's article "C. G. Jung and National Socialism," which appears in her book *The Life and Work of C. G. Jung*, recently republished by Daimon Verlag; but this same article provoked a strong reaction from Marie-Louise von Franz in *C. G. Jung: His Myth in Our Time* (New York: Jung Foundation/ G. P. Putnam's Sons, 1975): "I knew Jung personally from 1933 until his death and I never perceived the slightest conscious or unconscious trace of any such [anti-Semitic] attitude. . . . Jung once confessed to Leo Baeck himself: 'I slipped up' (on the slippery ground of politics). Jaffé uses this occasion to speak of a 'shadow' of Jung's which, in her account, was mixed up in the matter. To me this seems to be an opinion taken from thin air" (p. 63).

The renaissance of occultism in the "new age" movements of the 1970s resulted in viewing this controversy from the point of view of Jung's affinity with romanticism and the occult. An article by S. Grossman in the *Journal of European Studies* 9 (1979, pp. 231-259) concludes by saying, "If Jung was interested in racial archetypes, he was even more interested in exploring the archetypes which were common to all of humanity . . . a broader view of Jung's relationship to National Socialism shows it to be the product of his racial supposition, of the romantic tendencies in his psychological theories, of his personal and professional conflict with Freud, and of his wariness of socialism" (p. 255 and 256). In 1977 Dusty Sklar's *Gods and Beasts: The Nazis and the Occult* appeared (reissued as *The Nazis and the Occult* by the Dorset Press in 1989). She asserted that "the reigning attitudes in Germany expressed mystical affinities with which Jung was very much at home . . . His high degree of tolerance for the 'shadow' side of human nature, a necessary complement to reason, may have caused him to cast the Nazis in a romantic light" (p. 139). Her one-sided account is marred with factual errors, including the misidentification of the General Medical Society for Psychotherapy as the "German Medical Society" (p. 135). A more focused investigation of the occult dimension based on solid historical research can be found in James Webb's *The Occult Establishment* (Richard Drew Publishing, Glasgow, 1981). He emphasized Jung's connection with Jacob Wilhelm Hauer, a German historian of religion who lectured at Eranos in 1934 and who founded the German Faith Movement, about which Jung wrote in his Wotan article. Webb concluded by saying, "If his critics have falsely accused Jung of holding 'Nazi views,' this is at least partly because the Zurich psychologist talked in the language of contemporary illuminism, in whose alarming accents certain criminally eccentric politicians in Germany had also been thoroughly schooled" (p. 401).

In 1980, Walter Kaufmann's *Discovering the Mind*, volume 3: *Freud versus Adler and Jung* (McGraw-Hill, New York), was posthumously published. It contains a trenchant critique of Jung as a person and as a theoretician and deserves careful reading. His analysis of Jung's statements about Jews and Nazi Germany is to be found in section 68 (pp. 387-394), where he asserts that "Jung's writings on [Jewish psychology] and, more generally, Jung's attacks on Freud are a wound that we cannot hush up if we want to understand Jung" (p. 393).

The publication of Aldo Carotenuto's *Secret Symmetry*, Morris West's *The World Is Made of Glass*, and D. M. Thomas's *The White Hotel* in the early 1980s led to a renewed public interest in the Freud-Jung relationship. Sabina Spielrein's emergence as a significant participant in the early psychoanalytic movement added a new dimension to this already complex relationship. In the *Voice Literary Supplement* of October 1982, Melvyn Hill used this triangle as the framework for another highly emotional attack on Jung. It is filled with unsubstantiated allegations, such as the claim that "Freud had told Jung that in order for them to work together, Jung would have to make enormous effort to overcome his racial prejudice" (p. 14). Hill reinforces the fantasy image of Jung created by his most extreme critics, who link him personally to Nazi death camps: "The Nazis, in other words, cured Jung of his paranoid transference onto Freud by giving him the chance to act it out. For Jung as for others, Nazism legitimated a relentless, unrelieved envy that led to a barbaric desire to destroy. In fact it was he and his Nazi friends who felt so weak and cowardly that they had to find defenseless victims on whom to prove their invincible strength" (p. 15).

A similarly off-the-mark attack is made in passing by Paul Johnson in *A History of the Jews* (Harper and Row, New York, 1987): "The 'scandal' of Freud and his teachings was an important collateral proof of the Nazi case, since (it was argued) they removed moral guilt from sexual promiscuity and so increased it. Thus Freud enabled Jews to gain greater access to Aryan women. Here, Jung was able to come to Hitler's assistance by drawing a distinction between Freudian-Jewish psychiatry and the rest" (pp. 473-474). This confabulation of psychiatry, psychology, and psychotherapy is common, even in authors who should know better. In *Acts of Will*, his 1985 biography of Otto Rank, E. James Lieberman managed to condense a number of different errors when he wrote that "the Berlin stronghold of psychoanalysis [was] dissolved, to be replaced by Aryan psychiatrists led by Jung" (New York: Free Press, p. 326). Similarly, Robert Lifton wrote in *The Nazi Doctors* that "they had some sympathy for Jungian psychology, particularly at the time of Jung's collaboration with Nazi psychiatry. . . ." (Basic Books: New York, 1986, p. 486). Jeffrey Masson, who gained notoriety in Janet Malcolm's *In the Freud Archives*, published an extended critique of Jung in *Against Therapy* (Atheneum, New York, 1988, pp. 94-112). He concludes with this observation: "With its coercion and disdain for the real traumas that real people experience, there is a deep strain of fascism running through Jung's psychotherapy" (p. 111).

Just as controversy erupted when Jung's name was linked to Pound's in 1949, an article about Martin Heidegger's Nazi affiliation led to a renewed debate about Jung in 1988 in letters to the editor of *The New York Times* (March 15, April 15, May 3, May 21, and June 11). The Lingering Shadows Conference followed a year later and was a major milestone in the history of this controversy. Its impact was extended by the publication of *Lingering Shadows*, which has found its way into the bibliographies of most recent books dealing with Jung (for a detailed description of this conference, see "Instead of Heat, Light," pp. 57–71 in this book). Participation in the conference led Andrew Samuels to explore this issue and resulted in his foreword to a new edition of *Essays on Contemporary Events* (Princeton University Press, 1989), and a chapter in his *Political Psyche* (Routledge, 1993). A masterful treatment of the Nietzschean background of Jung's opinions appeared in 1995 with the publication of Paul Bishop's *The Dionysian Self* (Berlin and New York: Walter de Gruyter). In contrast, Richard Noll's *The Jung Cult* (Princeton University Press, 1994) achieved undeserved acclaim with his thesis that "The claimed evidence of the active, open espousal of anti-Semitism or Nazism by Jung is, in my opinion, less directly compelling (hence the greater controversy over it), and is more fruitfully framed—from the historian's point of view—in its deeper *volkisch* context" (p. 103). His factual errors, exaggerated assertions, and faulty conclusions compromise both this work and his *The Aryan Christ* (New York: Random House, 1997). These shortcomings were addressed in the numerous reviews that appeared but were, unfortunately, confined to Jungian publications. In *Cult Fictions* (Routledge, 1998), Sonu Shamdasani provides the definitive rebuttal of Noll's fallacious account of the founding of the Psychology Club Zurich.

For many academics, the availability of studies such as this one make little difference since their evaluation of Jung is based on inherited prejudice and what can only be described as a deliberate misreading of his work. One recent example of this is Bram Dijkstra's *Evil Sisters* (New York: Knopf, 1996) in which a misrepresentation of the concept of the anima allows him to link quotes from Hitler and Jung (pp. 393–394; see my article "Turning a Blind Eye: Misreading Jung," in *Spring*, 64, Fall/Winter, 1998). A great deal of emotion is still invested in this topic but one can only hope that continued discussion, and a measure of intellectual honesty, will enlighten both Jung's critics and his sympathizers.

References

Adams, Michael Vannoy. *The Multicultural Imagination.* London and New York: Routledge, 1996.

Alexander, Franz, and Sheldon Selesnick. *A History of Psychiatry.* New York: Harper and Row, 1964.

Allen W. Dulles Papers. Seeley Mudd Library at Princeton University, Princeton, New Jersey.

Altizer, T. J. Science and Gnosis in Jung's Psychology. *Centennial Review* 3, 1959: 304.

Bachofen, J. J. *Myth, Religion, and Mother Right: Selected Writings of J. J. Bachofen.* Preface by George Boas. Introduction by Joseph Campbell. Ralph Manheim, trans. Princeton: Princeton University Press, 1973.

Bally, Gustav. "Deutschstämmige Psychotherapie?" *Neue Züricher Zeitung,* 1934.

Bancroft, Mary *Autobiography of a Spy* (New York, William Morrow and Company, 1983).

Bennet, E. A. *Meetings with Jung, 1946-61.* Zurich: Daimon Verlag, 1985.

Bernstein, Jerome S. *Power and Politics: The Psychology of Soviet-American Partnerships.* Boston: Shambhala, 1989.

Bernstein, Matthew David. "Carl Jung and Anti-Semitism: A Historical Approach." Unpublished paper. New York: Columbia University, 1997.

Buber, M. *Eclipse of God.* M. S. Friedman, trans. New York: Harper & Row, 1952.

Carotenuto, Aldo. *A Secret Symmetry: Sabina Spielrein between Jung and Freud*. Translated by Arno Pomerans, John Shepley, and Krishna Winston. New York: Pantheon Books, 1982.

Cocks, Geoffrey. *Psychotherapy in the Third Reich: The Göring Institute*. Oxford & New York: Oxford University Press, 1985.

Dalal, Farhad. "Jung: A Racist." *British Journal of Psychotherapy* 4, no. 3 (1988).

Douglas, Mary. *Purity and Danger*. New York: Frederick A. Praeger, 1966.

Dourley, J. P. "In the Shadow of the Monotheisms: Jung's Conversations with Buber and White." In J. Ryce-Menuhin, ed., *Jung and the Monotheisms*. London: Routledge, 1994.

Elior, R. *The Paradoxical Ascent to God: The Kabbalistic Theosophy of Habad Hasidim*. J. M. Green, trans. Albany: State University of New York Press, 1993.

Ellenberger, Henri. *The Discovery of the Unconscious: The History and Evolution of Dynamic Psychiatry*. New York: Basic Books, 1970.

Erlenmeyer, Arvid, et al. "Destructiveness in the Tension between Myth and History," in *The Archetype of the Shadow in a Split World*. Proceedings of the Tenth International Congress for Analytical Psychology, Berlin, 1986.

Feldkeller, Paul. "Geist der Psychotherapie," *Deutsche Allgemeine Zeitung*, October 5, 1937; REM 2954.

Feldman, S. S. "Dr. C. G. Jung and National Socialism." *American Journal of Psychiatry*, September, 1945.

Field, Geoffrey. *Evangelist of Race*. New York: Columbia University Press, 1981.

Filoramo, G. *A History of Gnosticism*. A. Alcock, trans. Cambridge, England: Basil Blackwell, 1990.

Freud, Sigmund. *On the History of the Psychoanalytic Movement. Standard Edition* vol. 14.

———. *The Standard Edition of the Complete Psychological Works of Sigmund Freud*. Edited and translated by James Strachey. 24 vols. London: Hogarth, 1957.

Freud, Sigmund, and Karl Abraham. *A Psycho-Analytic Dialogue: The Letters of Sigmund Freud and Karl Abraham*, 1907-1926. New York: Basic Books, 1965.

Frey-Rohn, Liliane. *From Freud to Jung: A Comparative Study of the Psychology of the Unconscious*. Boston and London: Shambhala Publications, 1990.

Gager, John G. *The Origins of Anti-Semitism.* New York: Oxford University Press, 1983.

Gay, Peter. *Freud: A Life for Our Time.* New York: Norton, 1988.

Giegerich, Wolfgang. "Postscript to Cocks." *Spring,* 1979.

Glover, Edward. *Freud or Jung?* Cleveland: Meridian Books, 1963.

Gosset, Thomas. *Race.* New York: Oxford University Press, 1997.

Groesbeck, J. "A Jungian Answer to: 'Yaweh as Freud.'" *American Imago,* Fall, 1982.

Grossman, S. "C. G. Jung and National Socialism." *Journal of European Studies* 9, 1979.

Hannah, Barbara. *Jung, His Life and Work: A Biographical Memoir.* New York: G. P. Putnam's Sons, 1976. Boston: Shambhala Publications, 1991.

Harms, Ernest. "Carl Gustav Jung—Defender of Freud and the Jews." *Psychiatric Quarterly,* April 1946.

Haymond, Robert. "On Carl Gustav Jung: Psycho-Social Basis of Morality during the Nazi Era." *Journal of Psychology and Judaism* 6, no. 2, 1982.

Hesse, Herman. *The Journey to the East.* New York: Noonday Press, 1969.

Hill, Melvyn. "Women, Jews, and Madness." *Voice Literary Supplement,* October 11, 1982.

Idel, Moshe. *Kabbalah: New Perspectives.* New Haven, CT: Yale University Press, 1988.

———. *Hassidism: Between Ecstasy and Magic.* Albany: State University of New York Press, 1995.

Irving, Alexander. "The Freud/Jung Relationship: The Other Side of Oedipus and Countertransference." *American Psychologist,* Spring, 1982.

Jacobs, L. "The Uplifting of the Sparks in Later Jewish Mysticism." In A. Green, ed., *Jewish Spirituality: From the Sixteenth-Century Revival to the Present.* New York: Crossroad, 1987.

Jaffé, Aniela. *Aus Leben und Werkstatt von C. G. Jung.* Zurich: Rascher Verlag, 1968.

———. "C. G. Jung and National Socialism." In *From the Life and Work of C. G. Jung.* Translated by R. F. C. Hull and Murray Stein. Einsiedeln, Switzerland: Daimon Verlag, 1989. Also in *Jung's Last Years and Other Essays.* Dallas: Spring Publications, 1984.

Jung, C. G. "After the Catastrophe" (1945). *Collected Works,* vol. 10. R. F. C. Hull, trans. Princeton: Princeton University Press, 1970.

———. *Alchemical Studies. Collected Works,* vol. 13. R. F. C. Hull, trans. Princeton: Princeton University Press, 1967.
———. "Answers to Questions on Freud" (1953). *Collected Works,* vol. 18. R. F. C. Hull, trans. Princeton: Princeton University Press, 1976.
———. *Analytical Psychology.* Princeton: Princeton University Press, 1989.
———. "Answer to Job" (1952). *Collected Works,* vol. 11. R. F. C. Hull, trans. Princeton: Princeton University Press, 1969.
———. *The Archetypes and the Collective Unconscious. Collected Works,* vol. 9i. R. F. C. Hull, trans. Princeton: Princeton University Press, 1959.
———. *Briefe,* vol. 1, 1906–1945. Freiburg: Walter Verlag, 1972.
———. *C. G. Jung Letters.* Edited by Gerhard Adler and Aniela Jaffé. 2. vols. Princeton: Princeton University Press, 1973.
———. *C. G. Jung Speaking.* William McGuire, ed., R. F. C. Hull, trans. Princeton: Princeton University Press, 1977; London: Picador,1980.
———. *Civilization in Transition. Collected Works,* vol. 10. R. F. C. Hull, trans. Princeton: Princeton University Press, 1964.
———. *The Collected Works of C. G. Jung,* 20 vols. Bollingen Series XX. Princeton: Princeton University Press, 1953–1979.
———. "Commentary on *The Secret of the Golden Flower*" (1929). *Collected Works,* vol. 13. R. F. C. Hull, trans. Princeton: Princeton University Press, 1968.
———. *Contributions to Analytical Psychology.* New York: Harcourt, Brace, 1928.
———. "The Development of Personality" (1934). *Collected Works,* vol. 17. R. F. C. Hull, trans. Princeton: Princeton University Press, 1954.
———. "Epilogue to 'Essays on Contemporary Events.'" (1946). *Collected Works,* vol. 10, R. F. C. Hull, trans. Princeton: Princeton University Press, 1964.
———. *Essays on Contemporary Events: Reflections on Nazi Germany.* Princeton: Princeton University Press, 1989; London: Routledge, 1989.
———. "Gnostic Symbols of the Self" (1951). *Aion: Researches into the Phenomenology of the Self. Collected Works,* vol. 9ii. R. F. C. Hull, trans. Princeton: Princeton University Press, 1969.
———. "Memorandum for UNESCO" (1947/1948). Collected Works, vol. 18. R. F. C. Hull, trans. Princeton: Princeton University Press, 1975.

———. *Memories, Dreams, Reflections*. Edited by Aniela Jaffé and translated by Richard and Clara Winston. New York: Vintage Books, 1965.

———. *Modern Man in Search of a Soul,* W. S. Dell and C. F. Baynes, trans. New York: Harcourt, Brace & Co., 1933.

———. *Mysterium Coniunctionis. Collected Works*, vol. 14. R. F. C. Hull, trans. Princeton: Princeton University Press, 1955.

———. *Psychological Types. Collected Works*, vol. 6. R. F. C. Hull, trans. Princeton: Princeton University Press, 1971.

———. *Psychology and Alchemy* (1944). *Collected Works*, vol. 12. R. F. C. Hull, trans. Princeton: Princeton University Press, 1968.

———. *Psychology and Religion: West and East. Collected Works*, vol. 11. R. F. C. Hull, trans. Princeton: Princeton University Press, 1958.

———. "A Rejoinder to Dr. Bally." *Collected Works*, vol. 10. R. F. C. Hull, trans. Princeton: Princeton University Press, 1964.

———. "The Relations Between the Ego and the Unconscious" (1928). *Collected Works*, vol. 7. R. F. C. Hull, trans. Princeton: Princeton University Press, 1966.

———. "Religious Ideas in Alchemy" (1937). *Collected Works*, vol. 12. R. F. C. Hull, trans. Princeton: Princeton University Press, 1968.

———. "The Role of the Unconscious" (1918). *Collected Works*, vol. 10. R. F. C. Hull, trans. Princeton: Princeton University Press, 1964.

———. "The Shadow." *Collected Works*, vol. 9ii. R. F. C. Hull, trans. Princeton: Princeton University Press, 1951.

———. "Die Sprache des Unbewussten," *Kölnische Zeitung,* October 9, 1937

———. "The State of Psychotherapy Today" (1934). *Collected Works*, vol. 10. R. F. C. Hull, trans. Princeton: Princeton University Press, 1964.

———. *Two Essays in Analytical Psychology*. *Collected Works*, vol. 7. R. F. C. Hull, trans. Princeton: Princeton University Press, 1953.

———. "Vom Werden der Persönlichkeit." *Wirklichkeit der Seele.* Zurich: Rascher Verlag, 1934.

———. "Wotan" (1936). *Collected Works*, vol. 10. R. F. C. Hull, trans. Princeton: Princeton University Press, 1964.

Kirsch, James. "C. G. Jung and the Jews: The Real Story." *Journal of Psychology and Judaism* 6, no. 2 (Spring/Summer 1982.).

———. "Interview with David Serbin." *Psychological Perspectives*, Fall, 1985.

———. "Jung's Transference on Freud: The Jewish Element." *American Imago* 41, no. 1, 1984.

———. "Reconsidering Jung's So-Called Anti-Semitism." In Daniel M. Young, Estelle Weinreid, et al., eds., *The Arms of the Windmill: Essays in Analytical Psychology in Honor of Werner H. Engel.* Baltimore: John D. Lucas, 1983.

Kegley, Jacquelyn Anne, ed. *Paul Tillich on Creativity*. Lanham: University Press of America, 1989.

Keyserling, Herman. *Europe.* New York: Harcourt, Brace, 1928.

———. *The Recovery of Truth.* New York, Harper and Brothers, 1929.

Krauskopf, Alfred A. "Tiefenpsychologische Beiträge zur Rassenseelenforschung." *Rasse* 5 (1939): 362–368.

Kretschmer, Ernst. "Konstitution und Leistung," *Westfdlische Landeszeitung,* August 20, 1944; microcopy T78, roll 190, frames 1866–67, National Archives, Washington, DC.

Landau, Sidney I. *Chambers English Dictionary*. Cambridge, England: Cambridge University Press, 1988.

Le Bon, Gustave. *The Crowd: A Study of the Popular Mind*. Marietta, GA: Larlin Corporation, 1982.

Levy, Richard. *Anti-Semitism in the Modern World: An Anthology of Texts.* Lexington, MA: D. C. Heath & Co., 1990.

Lowenstein, R. M. *Christians and Jews: A Psychoanalytic Study.* New York: International Universities Press, 1952.

Maidenbaum, Aryeh and Stephen A. Martin, eds. *Lingering Shadows.* Boston: Shambhala, 1991.

Masson, Jeffrey Moussaieff. *Against Therapy*. New York: Atheneum, 1988; London: Collins, 1989.

McCully, Robert S. "Letters." *Quadrant* 20, no. 2, 1987.

McDougall, William. *Is America Safe for Democracy*? New York: Scribners and Sons, 1921.

William McGuire, ed. *The Freud/Jung Letters: The Correspondence Between Sigmund Freud and C. G. Jung*. R. F. C. Hull, trans. Princeton: Princeton University Press, 1974.

McLynn, F. *Carl Gustav Jung.* New York: St. Martin's Press, 1996.

Milner, Marion. "The Role of Illusion in Symbol Formation." *New Directions in Psychoanalysis.* M. Klein, P. Hermann, R. E. Money-Kyrle, eds. New York: Basic Books, 1957.

Morse, Arthur D. *While 6 Million Died: A Chronicle of American Apathy*. New York: Ace Publishing, 1968.

Mosse, George. *The Crisis of German Ideology.* New York: Grosset and Dunlop, 1964.
———. *Germans and Jews.* New York: Fertig, 1970.
Neumann, Erich. *Depth Psychology and a New Ethic,* Eugene Rolfe, trans. New York: G. P. Putnam's Sons, 1969; Boston: Shambhala Publications, 1990.
Noll, Richard. *Aryan Christ: The Secret Life of Carl Jung.* New York: Random House, 1997.
———. *The Jung Cult: Origins of a Charismatic Movement.* Princeton: Princeton University Press, 1994.
———. "The Rose, the Cross and the Analyst." *New York Times,* October 14, 1994.
The Oxford Dictionary of the Christian Church. London: Oxford University Press, 1974.
Parelhoff, A. D. "Dr. C. G. Jung—Nazi Collaborationist." *The Protestant* I (June/July 1946); II (August/September 1946); III (February/March 1947).
Patai, R. *The Jewish Alchemists.* Princeton, NJ: Princeton University Press, 1994.
Perera, Sylvia Brinton. *The Scapegoat Complex: Toward a Mythology of Shadow and Guilt.* Toronto: Inner City Books, 1986.
Petersen, Neal H., ed. *From Hitler's Doorstep: The Wartime Intelligence Reports of Allen Dulles 1942–1945.* University Park, Pennsylvania: Pennsylvania State University Press, 1996.
Poliakov, Leon. *The Aryan Myth.* New York: Barnes and Noble Books, 1996.
Proctor, Robert. *Racial Hygiene.* Cambridge: Harvard University Press, 1988.
Reich Education Ministry 2954. Zentrales Staatsarchiv, Potsdam.
Reich Education Ministry 2797. Zentrales Staatsarchiv, Potsdam.
Reuchlin, J. *On the Art of the Kabbalah.* M. Goodman & S. Goodman, trans. Lincoln: University of Nebraska Press, 1983.
Roazen, Paul. *Freud and His Followers.* New York: New York University Press, 1985.
Robinson. J. M., ed. *The Nag Hammadi Library* (3rd edition). San Francisco: Harper & Row, 1988.
Rohan, Prince Karl Anton. "Manifesto of the Transnational Intellectual Union." In *Der Geistige Problem Europas von Heute.* Verlag der Wila, 1922.
Rubenstein, Richard L. *After Auschwitz: Radical Theology and Contemporary Judaism.* Indianapolis: Bobbs-Merrill, 1966.

Rubenstein, Richard L. and John K. Roth. *Approaches to Auschwitz: The Holocaust and Its Legacy.* Atlanta: John Knox, 1987.

Rudolph, K. *Gnosis: The Nature and History of Gnosticism.* R. M. Wilson, trans. San Francisco: Harper, 1987. Original work published 1980.

Ruether, Rosemary. *Faith and Fratricide: The Theological Roots of Anti-Semitism.* New York: Seabury, 1974.

Samuels, Andrew. "Comment on 'Jung: A Racist' by Dalal." *British Journal of Psychotherapy* 4, no. 3 (1988).

———. "National Socialism, National Psychology, and Analytical Psychology." In Aryeh Maidenbaum and Stephen Martin, eds. *Lingering Shadows: Jungians, Freudians, and Anti-Semitism.* Boston: Shambhala, 1991.

Scheler, Max. *Man's Place in Nature.* Noonday Press, New York, 1971.

Schochet, J. "Mystical Concepts in Chassidism." In *Likutei Amarim-Tanya.* S. Zalman, ed. Brooklyn, NY: Kehot, 1981.

Scholem, Gershom. *Jewish Gnosticism, Merkabeh, Mysticism and Talmudic Tradition.* New York: Shocken, 1960.

———. *Major Trends in Jewish Mysticism.* New York: Shocken, 1961.

———. *Sabbatai Sevi: The Mystical Messiah.* Princeton: Princeton University Press, 1973.

———. *Kabballah.* Jerusalem: Keter, 1974.

———. *Origins of the Kabbalah.* R. J. Zwi Werblowski, trans. Princeton: Princeton University Press, 1987. Original work published 1962.

Segal, R. A. *The Gnostic Jung.* Princeton: Princeton University Press, 1992.

Sherry, Jay. "Jung, the Jews, and Hitler." *Spring,* 1986.

Shamdasani, Sonu. *Cult Fictions.* London and New York: Routledge, 1998.

Sklar, Dusty. *The Nazis and the Occult.* New York: Dorset Press, 1989.

Slochower, Harry. "Freud as Yaweh in Jung's *Answer to Job.*" *American Imago.* Spring 1981.

Sperling, H., and M. Simon. *The Zohar.* London: Soncino Press, 1931–1934.

Stein, Richard. "Jung's 'Mana Personality' and the Nazi Era." In Aryeh Maidenbaum and Stephen A. Martin, eds., *Lingering Shadows: Jungians, Freudians, and Anti-Semitism.* Boston: Shambhala, 1991.

Stern, Chaim. *Gates of Repentance: The New Union Prayerbook for the Days of Awe.* New York: Central Conference of American Rabbis, 1978.

Stern, Fritz. "The Burden of Success: Reflections on German Jewry." In *Dreams and Delusions.* New York: Knopf, 1987.

Stevens, M. D., Anthony. "Critical Notice." *The Journal of Analytical Psychology* 42, no. 4 (1997): 671–690.

Struve, Walter. *Elites Against Democracy.* Princeton: Princeton University Press, 1973.

Suler, B. "Alchemy." In *Encyclopedia Judaica,* vol. 2. Jerusalem: Keter, 1972.

Tishby, I., and F. Lachower. *The Wisdom of the Zohar: An Anthology of Texts, I, II, and III.* D. Goldstein, trans. Oxford, England: Oxford University Press, 1989.

Ulanov, Ann Belford. "The Ego as Spacemaker," unpublished paper, 1981.

———. *The Feminine in Jungian Psychology and Christian Theology.* Evanston: Northwestern University Press, 1971.

———. *Picturing God.* Cambridge: Cowley, 1986.

———. "When Is Repudiation Differentiation?" unpublished paper, 1987.

———. *The Wisdom of the Psyche.* Cambridge: Cowley, 1988.

van der Post, Laurens. *Jung and the Story of Our Time.* New York: Pantheon Books, 1975.

van Scheltema, Frederik Adama. "Mutter Erde und Vater Himmel in der germanischen Naturreligion." *Zentralblatt für Psychotherapie* 14 (1943): 257–277.

von Franz, Marie-Louise. *C. G. Jung: His Myth in Our Time.* New York: G. P. Putnam & Sons, 1975.

Webb, James, *The Occult Establishment.* Glasgow: Richard Drew Publishing, 1981.

Wiesel, Elie. *And the Sea Is Never Full: Memoirs, 1969.* New York: Alfred Knopf, 1999.

Whitmont, Edward C. *Return of the Goddess.* New York: Crossroad, 1982.

Wilson, R. M. "Jewish 'Gnosis' and Gnostic Origins: A Survey." *Hebrew Union College Annual* 45, 1974.

Wolff, Toni. *Structural Forms of the Feminine Psyche.* Privately printed for the Students' Association of the C. G. Jung Institute, Zurich, July, 1956.

Young-Eisendrath, Polly. "The Absence of Black Americans as Jungian Analysts." *Quadrant* 20, no. 2 (1987): 42.

Other Significant Works

Bakan, David. *Sigmund Freud and the Jewish Mystical Tradition*. Princeton: Van Nostrand, 1958.

Cocks, Geoffrey. "C. G. Jung and German Psychotherapy, 1933–1940: A Research Note." *Spring*, 1979.

Diamond, Stanley. "Jung contra Freud: What It Means to Be Funny." In Karin Barnaby and Pellegrino D'Acierno, eds., *C. G. Jung and the Humanities: Toward a Hermeneutics of Culture*. Princeton, N.J.: Princeton University Press, 1990, pp. 67–75.

Jones, Ernest. "The Psychology of the Jewish Question." *Miscellaneous Essays*, vol. 1. London: Hogarth, 1951.

Klein, Dennis B. Jewish *Origins of the Psychoanalytic Movement*. New York: Praeger, 1981.

Lowenstein, Rudolph M. *Christians and Jews: A Psychoanalytic Study*. New York: International Universities Press, 1952.

Robert, Marthe. *From Oedipus to Moses: Freud's Jewish Identity*. Ralph Manheim, trans. Garden City, N. J.: Anchor, 1976.

Wylie, Philip, and Frederic Wertham. "What about Dr. Jung?" *Saturday Review*, July 30, 1949.